90 0717666 7

Literacy Crises and Reading Policies

This widely researched critical study examines the issues underpinning current debates over 'falling literacy standards'. Rather than engaging in short-term debates about the efficacy of particular reading programmes, it argues that the 'problem' of how to teach reading needs to be re-conceptualised as part of a social phenomenon. The authors discuss how reading practices and the teaching of reading arise from social activity which is in turn shaped by historical, social and political contexts.

Literacy Crises and Reading Policies examines particular episodes where a 'great debate' has occurred over approaches to reading in England, and their links to similar debates in New Zealand and the USA. Examples of crises from different periods are discussed, leading to the argument that literacy crises have particular ideological, political underpinnings that have in turn influenced literacy curriculum policy documents and practices.

Rather than championing any one method of teaching reading, certain key questions are addressed. They include:

- Whose interests are being pursued under the guise of particular literacy policies and programmes?
- How do particular methods of reading come to dominate?
- To what extent do debates over reading commit protagonists to a narrow fixation on the 'one right method'?
- Are such debates exclusively a symptom of right-wing conservative reaction?

Any academic or student with an interest in literacy, in addition to politicians, policy-makers, teachers and parents will find this book a challenging and invaluable read.

Janet Soler is Senior Lecturer at the Open University, UK. **Roger Openshaw** is Professor at Massey University College of Education, New Zealand.

Literacy Crises and Reading Policies

Children still can't read!

Janet Soler and
Roger Openshaw

Routledge
Taylor & Francis Group

LONDON AND NEW YORK

First published 2006
by Routledge
2 Park Square, Milton Park, Abingdon, Oxon OX14 4RN

Simultaneously published in the USA and Canada
by Routledge
270 Madison Ave, New York, NY 10016

Routledge is an imprint of the Taylor & Francis Group

© 2006 Janet Soler and Roger Openshaw

Typeset in Garamond by Wearset Ltd, Boldon, Tyne and Wear
Printed and bound in Great Britain by MPG Books Ltd, Bodmin

British Library Cataloguing in Publication Data
A catalogue record for this book is available from the British
Library

Library of Congress Cataloging in Publication Data
Soler, Janet.
Literacy crises and reading policies : children still can't read! /
Janet Soler and Roger Openshaw.– 1st ed.
p. cm.
Includes bibliographical references and index.
1. Reading–Social aspects–Great Britain. 2. Education and
state–Great Britain. I. Openshaw, Roger. II Title.
LB1050.2.S66 2006
379.2'4'0941–dc22

                 2005018271

ISBN10: 0-415-33676-7
ISBN13: 978-0-415-33676-5

Contents

Acknowledgements

While researching and preparing the manuscript for this book we have had help from various colleagues and support staff. In particular we would like to acknowledge the secretarial staff at the Department of Social and Policy Studies, College of Education, Massey University and also staff at the New Zealand Parliamentary Library for their expertise and help beyond the call of duty. We would also like to thank staff for their help at Archives New Zealand, The British Newspaper Library and the Open University.

Part I

Are our standards slipping?

Exploring post-Second World War reading debates from a historical perspective

Chapter 1

Introduction

The teaching of reading is currently the subject of intense national and international interest. In this book we attempt to address broader questions about the origins and contexts of national literacy policy rather than engaging in debates about the efficacy of particular programmes. In particular we aim to investigate specific episodes where a 'Great Debate' has occurred over approaches to reading.[1] A powerful motivation for our study of the debates over reading standards and methods has arisen from our previous work in this area which has had a particular focus upon the role of the media in shaping educational policy. This has alerted us to the need to understand how public debates have shaped the specific contexts in which professionals currently engage in the teaching of literacy.

The central question we seek to address in this study is what role did public debates over reading play in the shaping of the National Literacy Strategy (NLS)? This is a crucial question not only for literacy educators but also for anyone interested in the processes which have driven educational policy in a specific direction over the past four decades. In England, the sixty-year period from 1945 to 2005 has seen a remarkable transition from an environment where the pedagogy and programmes related to the teaching of reading was essentially a matter for schools, teachers and local authorities, to one in which successive governments and their agencies progressively implemented a policy of extensive national assessment at all levels. This has led in the 1990s to the creation of the NLS, and the instigation of a Literacy Hour in which both content and pedagogy are prescribed in detail. In this book we argue that an understanding of the history of the increasingly intense public debates over reading standards reveals that these debates were a driving force in creating a sense of national crisis in the 1990s that was to ultimately lead to both measures. What this history particularly demonstrates is the central role that fears concerning declining English reading standards played in creating a climate where government intervention and national testing were viewed as both necessary and natural. Also highlighted is the key role that reading standards debates have played in the increasing politicisation of the literacy curriculum and education in general.

Aims, purposes and scope

A further reason for undertaking this study is our conviction that historical research has an important part to play in enabling educational professionals at all levels to make sense of contemporary professional contexts. In looking back we endorse the recent call for educational historians to link the past to the present thereby illuminating the taken for granted structures within which we teach.[2] Because literacy has been at the heart of mass education since its inception in the nineteenth century, our investigation of the debates over reading standards serves to further reveal the processes that underpin the contemporary contexts of schooling. In our own work with teachers and educators we have come to see the power that such understandings can give practitioners to critically debate, negotiate, make decisions and modify their own professional environment.

From a critical literacy perspective it can be argued that the 'problem' of how to teach reading needs to be re-conceptualised as part of a deeper social phenomenon. Reading controversies cannot be resolved by apparently neutral evidence from universally comparable skills competencies or abilities.[3] Critical literacy theorists have alerted us to the fact that we must examine the way in which different historical and socio-political contexts can give rise to specific ideological beliefs, the development of different reading programmes, national literacy policies and new ways of addressing the 'problem' of how to teach reading. Their work shows that reading practices and the teaching of reading arise from social activity, which is in turn shaped by historical, social and political contexts.[4]

In utilising a historical methodology which is informed by a critical literacy approach, we will draw upon but not necessarily replicate an emerging body of literature that goes beyond a relatively narrow focus upon the mechanics of teaching reading. Whilst valuable in itself, much of this work is highly theoretical, drawing upon limited specific examples. To date very few studies provide an in-depth examination of specific national contexts. Fewer still attempt to illuminate the particular political processes that provide an important key to understanding literacy debates.

Additionally, we have chosen to interweave parliamentary exchanges, newspaper reports and professional commentary in order to illustrate not simply the ebb and flow of literacy debates at particular junctures, but also to demonstrate the interactions between various influential individuals, reading researchers and professional lobbies, various interest groups, media commentators and political parties that contribute to the intensification of the debate in the public forum. As curriculum historians, working on debates over reading standards we came to view the dynamic processes that shaped these debates as best fitting Herbert Kliebard's conclusion that different interest groups, each representing a force for a different selection of knowledge and values from the surrounding culture, compete for dominance over the curriculum.[5] Through viewing the debates over reading standards and the micro-politics surrounding their visibility in the public arena, we found ourselves questioning the Left-versus-Right dualism implicit in educational policy accounts. Instead, our attention became increasingly drawn to the multi-faceted nature of the dynamics that drive curriculum policy, programmes and approaches. For us this raised critical questions about the complex processes that surround educational decision-making at the intersection of politics, schooling, standards and literacy.

In responding to these complex historical issues, we have chosen to follow chronologically the extended post-war debate over reading standards. In order to further our appreciation of the English experience, however, we have elected to include some comparative examples. This inclusion allows us to better illustrate, not only the shared nature of the ideals that underpin the development of different literacy programmes and national literacy curriculum policies, but also to appreciate the reasons for differences at the national level. A considerable body of literature argues that there has been a shift from a liberal humanist discourse in schooling towards a discourse of management.[6] Underpinning these arguments is a debate over the purposes of schooling, and questions about learning and teaching in the context of the post-modern, globalised nation state. In England, this debate has had a profound impact, moving schools away from earlier liberal humanist understandings and towards a technicist/rationalist notion of learning and a view of the individual as a subject to govern and/or be governed. This, in turn, has led to an emphasis on the politics of governance and surveillance.[7]

Critiques of the 1988 Education Reform Act have noted the central role that conforming to national standards and surveillance through national testing has played in changing the 'narratives of the pupil'. They have further argued that examining this process through a Foucauldian notion of 'moral technologies' highlights the way in which government policy is bringing about a shift in, and reorganisation of schooling through an emphasis upon testing and grading and the publication of league tables of school performance.[8]

In the decade following the introduction of the National Curriculum, the literacy curriculum and its associated pedagogies has been exposed to a normalising gaze, a surveillance that makes it possible to qualify, to classify and to punish.[9] Improving literacy standards became a central part of New Labour's educational thinking. It was also a key consideration in the development of the party's electoral platforms in 1997 and 2001 and subsequent educational policy initiatives such as NLS[10] that have proliferated during the New Labour administration.

Moreover, recent reviews of the literacy and numeracy strategies, introduced from the late 1990s onwards, have drawn attention to the implicit notions of governance and surveillance and the adoption of technicist, prescriptive, less flexible pedagogical approaches. There has also been a rejection of progressive, child-centred ideals in the key documents designed to present or implement these policy initiatives.[11]

Commentators have drawn particular attention to the technicist, assessment-orientated agenda embedded in the NLS that attempts to counter previously held progressive, child-centred professional ideals by reducing the individual child to an invisible 'normal' individual who is constructed around quantifiable norms. They also note the conflict with the rhetoric of previous documents such as the *Plowden Report*[12] with its emphasis upon teaching as an art, and the tendency in the NLS to regulate teacher behaviour whilst simultaneously tightening control over the profession as a whole through a prescriptive curriculum emphasising testing and grading.

Finally in this section of the introductory chapter, we wish to stress that, in highlighting the constructions of literacy that take place in reading debates and the associated development of particular reading programmes and strategies, we are not necessarily viewing reading practices as lacking cognitive and behavioural aspects. Neither are we denying their role in individual agency.[13] As we have already emphasised, we do not intend to enter the current debate as participants in 'a binary dispute over method (e.g., phonics vs. word recognition, skills vs. whole language, genre vs. process, liberal vs. conservative)'.[14] Instead, rather than championing any 'one best' method of teaching reading, we will directly address the central questions that Welch and Freebody identify as hinging on relativities of power.[15] These key literacy questions are essential for politicians, policy-makers, teachers and parents to consider. They include:

- Whose interests are being pursued under the guise of particular literacy policies and programmes?
- How do particular methods and models of reading come to dominate?
- What part do reading debates play in determining what kinds of literate practices get enshrined in policy, and for whom?
- To what extent do reading debates commit protagonists to a narrow, essentially unproductive 'either-or' fixation on the 'one right method'?
- Are such debates exclusively a symptom of right-wing conservative reaction to progressivism?[16]
- How can a better understanding of reading debates across time and international boundaries improve the teaching of reading in the future?

Have reading standards declined? Issues and problems

While the above questions address the political construction of literacy policy, curriculum and pedagogy through the controversies over the teaching of reading, they do not address the underlying issue raised in the debate and implied in the title of this book: 'Have reading standards declined?'

This is an entirely legitimate question for educators to expect historians studying the debates over reading to consider. It is, however, an extremely difficult question to definitively answer. One persistent difficulty for those conducting scientific studies into reading standards lies in ascertaining just what is meant by terms such as 'standards', 'literacy' and 'illiteracy'. Richard Aldrich points out that the terms 'standard' and 'standards' have had many different meanings that have changed over time.[17] Citing the 1997 White Paper, *Excellence in Schools*, as an example, he states that confusion occurs even in official documents. Sometimes 'standards' seem to imply the setting of an acceptable level against which all should be judged, but at others the term seems to relate more to the unacceptable levels of achievement of those failing to reach the expected standard.[18] Aldrich observes that standards, like examinations, curricula and education itself, have a complex history that has been contested by both contemporaries and by later historians. He goes on to contrast government policies since 1988 to improve the quality of education, that have been based on the concept of an expected standard of achievement for all children of a particular age, with the 1967 *Plowden Report*'s conclusion that it was not possible to describe a standard of attainment that should be reached by all or most children.[19]

When we turn to key terms in the reading standards debate such as 'literacy' and 'illiteracy', these definitional problems are further compounded. Sir Cyril Burt's early research on illiterate adults was one of the first to critique commonly accepted definitions of illiteracy, exemplified by the contemporary *Oxford English Dictionary* entry as, 'one ignorant of letters, unable to read' for giving a wrong impression of the problem.[20] According to Burt, tests now showed that nearly all those loosely described as unable to read could read something, even if this was, by itself, of little value. Burt's comments alert us to the fact that it has always been historically difficult to define and quantify illiteracy and hence to talk meaningfully about reading standards. Burt certainly felt that it was essential to arrive at more scientific definitions and to more widely utilise standardised tests.[21] He thus went on to suggest that:

(i) an illiterate may be defined as meaning one who in everyday life is able to make no practical use whatever of reading or writing, and (ii) a semi-literate as one who is able to make no effective use of these activities, that is, one who is debarred by his disability from using the ordinary machinery of a civilized country: (e.g., he will not be able to read with any understanding a short paragraph in a newspaper, or to write an intelligible letter home, or to comprehend simple printed instructions). In terms of standardized tests this may be taken to mean that an illiterate adult is one who has an average educational age for reading, spelling and composition of less than 6.0, and a semi-literate adult as one who has an average educational age of 6.0 to 8.0.[22]

Growing post-war public concern obliged government agencies to further define the terms 'literacy' and 'illiteracy' in order to address the issue of reading standards in England. Policy-makers continued to experience difficulties in clarifying and therefore measuring 'illiteracy'. Published in 1950, the HMSO pamphlet, *Reading Ability: Some Suggestions for Helping the Backward*, reported the findings of a committee of inquiry set up by the Minister of Education in September 1947 to consider the nature and extent of the illiteracy alleged to exist among school leavers. The Committee consisted of representatives appointed by the Ministry of Education, the Defence Departments, the Prison Commission and the Home Office.[23] It recognised that the word 'illiterate', which originally meant 'unlettered', had subsequently acquired so many shades of meaning that it had ceased to be of much use for exact thought. However, whilst the pamphlet conceded that there was an inevitable degree of arbitrariness in any definition, it nonetheless observed that a specific definition of the word 'illiteracy' was required for the Committee's purposes.[24] Aware of the large-scale disruption of schooling during the war years, the report based its definition of illiteracy on the attainments of 'average' children in 1938. Thus, an individual having a reading age of less than the 'average' seven-year-old in 1938, as measured by the Watts-Vernon Reading test, was assumed to be 'illiterate'. Those with reading ages of between seven and nine years were defined as 'semi-literate'.[25] However, elsewhere in the report, the term 'backward reader' was employed loosely and interchangeably. Thus it was asserted that, 'obviously, there will be some who simply from lack of ability, will be backward in reading, even to the point of illiteracy'.[26] This slippage in terminology illustrates the profound difficulty in defining and therefore assessing reading standards that was to complicate the debate for decades to come.

To be sure, the somewhat later Ministry of Education publication, *Standards of Reading* 1948–1956,[27] attempted to employ a finer-grained nomenclature than had its predecessor. Thus, it was claimed that:

> The pupils in the samples were classified as: 'Superior, Average+, Average−, Backward, Semi-literate, and Illiterate, the lower limits of these categories being taken as scores of 31, 23, 18, 9, 3, and 0 for the seniors and 20, 13, 9, 3 and 0 for the juniors, for whom the last two categories were combined.'[28]

The publication did concede, however, that terms such as 'backward' were, in fact, relative terms. What was important, therefore, was not the absolute proportion of 'backwardness', but the change in proportion as time went on. Nevertheless, from the later 1960s, as the debate became more intense, politicians and newspaper correspondents in particular tended to employ terms such as 'illiteracy' and 'standards' very loosely, making it difficult for subsequent curriculum historians to ascertain just what was being referred to.

Newspaper debates present a further difficulty, with allegations of declining standards from both the left- and right-wing press posing a particular problem for any curriculum historians. Aldrich reminds us that the belief that standards were better in the past has considerable nostalgic appeal, being frequently urged in the popular press. During 1975–1976, for instance, when concerns over literacy standards peaked, excerpts from the *Daily Mail* alleged that 'the brutal truth is that standards have fallen'. It was also suggested that 'most parents and many teachers believe that children are less literate and numerate than they were 20 years ago'. From the opposite end of the political spectrum, the *Daily Mirror* claimed that 'literacy in Britain is marching backwards'; the paper further alleging that 'general educational standards have slipped alarmingly in the past decade or so'. This type of allegation led Aldrich to conclude that:

> Educational standards may indeed, have fallen in the 1970s as in the 1990s, and in the 1980s as well, but due allowance must be made for the polemical style of many journalists, and for the well-attested fact that bad news sells more copies of newspapers (and of some books) than good.[29]

The inherent difficulties in reaching a definitive conclusion about 'falling standards' has been highlighted by recent research into national literacy standards across time. Greg Brooks, of the National Foundation for Educational Research (NFER), is one of the relatively few researchers to have extensively examined the evidence on whether reading standards in England as a whole have risen or fallen since the end of the Second World War.[30] Brooks contends that the evidence from the Watts-Vernon and National Survey 6 (NS6) tests, that constituted the only national monitoring survey information available for England and Wales over the 1948–1976 period, suggests that the average reading score rose slightly between 1948 and 1952. This, he maintains, is widely attributed to the recovery of the education system from the war years. Following this rise, average reading scores then remained essentially unchanged from 1952 to 1979.

Brooks goes on to observe that between 1979 and 1988 the Department of Education and Science's (DES) Assessment of Performance Unit (APU) Language Monitoring Project based at NFER carried out six surveys at eleven years (Year six) and at fifteen/sixteen (Year eleven). These surveys covered reading and writing in England, Wales and Northern Ireland. As far as reading is concerned, they detected a slight rise for both age groups between 1979 and 1983. There was also a further slight rise for eleven-year-olds between 1979 and 1983, but there was no overall change for the fifteen/sixteen year group.[31] The APU was subsequently abolished in the early 1990s, and since then no monitoring surveys funded by central government have taken place in England and Wales. Some monitoring surveys were, however, carried out that were not centrally funded, and in Years three and four, rather than in the traditional monitoring Years six and eleven. In 1991 a survey was also conducted by NFER.

The existing evidence leads Brooks to note a fall amongst English eight-year-olds between 1987 and 1991, but he also perceives that, between 1991 and 1995, there was a recovery that brought things back to 1987 levels, so that the 1995 score is in effect almost identical to that of 1987. This fall in the average score was 2.5 standardised points, equivalent to about six months of reading age. Hence, it constitutes an educationally and statistically significant decline. Brooks emphasises that this was 'one of the very few reliably recorded falls during the entire period covered by this article'.[32] His suggestion is that this fall might have been associated with the introduction of the National Curriculum that reduced the amount of time devoted to literacy in primary schools, coupled with the high numbers leaving teaching at that time. Brooks concludes that:

> The British educational system has been generally successful in maintaining the standard of achievement in literacy despite economic cycles, the rise in numbers having a first language other than English, the spread of other sources of information and entertainment, and the substantial broadening of the curriculum. The international evidence seems to show that the levels achieved by middling and high performers are high. But the international evidence and the results of surveys of adult literacy also show that there is a significant proportion of the population who have poor or very poor literacy skills; and that this pattern seems to have persisted for many decades.[33]

Assuming that Brooks' conclusion is accurate, we will need to explain the high degree of concern over literacy and the prolonged, often highly politicised controversy over reading standards during the post-war years in ways other than simply pointing to allegations of any sharp decline in standards nationally. Examining the politicised nature of the reading standards debate appears to be central to this task, given the way in which concerns over literacy standards in turn generates debates over the best method of teaching reading and calls for legislative action.

National Strategies: same vision – different options

Much of the research over literacy which surfaced in the 'Great debate'[34] and the more recent 'Reading wars'[35] was generated by concerns over literacy standards. The overriding and continual concern in these debates and the research they have generated has been the development and assessment of the most up-to-date and correct way of teaching. This in turn leads to gov-

ernmental and local authority decisions regarding the 'best' reading programme to officially uphold and financially support. It could also be argued
that recent legislative activity arising from reading standards debates in
America has opened up the potential for these research findings to be dis-
torted or exaggerated in legislative advocacy campaigns seeking to justify
the adoption of prescriptive top-down solutions to this issue.[36]

In the United Kingdom, international comparisons, national assessment
evidence and results from literacy initiatives have been used in a successful
legislative advocacy campaign to justify the development of the NLS. *The
Preliminary Report of the Task Force* and subsequent explanations of the
research base for its report cited international and local data as being influential in the development of 'best practices' in the NLS. They also referred
to New Zealand research and 'initiatives' and general practices found in
New Zealand schools – a further reason for our interest in comparisons with
that country. The United Kingdom Literacy Task Force drew upon this
research base to help justify its use of a 'framework' to structure and
sequence the pedagogic activities and specify the content that was to be
taught during the 'Literacy Hour'.[37]

The New Zealand Literacy Taskforce drew upon a similar research base
of assessment evidence and 'best practice in the teaching of reading'. It was
also guided by a similar goal to that given to the English Literacy Task
Force.[38] Despite the use of this research base and the similarity between
English and New Zealand government goals in addressing 'literacy standards', the New Zealand Literacy Task Force did not recommend the adoption of a National Literacy Hour. Thus, whilst both England and New
Zealand developed national literacy strategies in the late 1990s, differing
allegiances and political contexts led to the implementation of distinctive
approaches.

The international nature of the literature dealing with reading wars provides another important justification for comparing and contrasting outcomes across national boundaries. In examining the reading standards debate
across time, in different national contexts, we seek to better understand the
complex and sometimes contradictory ways in which reading debates and
national politics surrounding the literacy curriculum give rise to selective
notions of literacy. Accordingly, we will argue that reading debates have
particular ideological, political underpinnings that have, in turn, influenced
literacy curriculum policy documents, programmes and practices.

Structure and organisation

This book is divided into three Parts. Part 1, 'Are our standards slipping?
Exploring post-Second World War Reading debates from a historical
perspective', raises and explores the general theoretical and practical issues
and problems that confront historians seeking to investigate public debates

over literacy. This introductory chapter has mapped out the theoretical approaches and methodologies that underpin this study. The chapter also makes a plea for a more complex and dynamic account of the political struggles surrounding public debates of reading standards. It also examines the difficulty in determining historically the various claims of 'declining reading standards' which initiated and sustained these struggles over time. Chapter 2 argues that, despite periodic concerns over reading standards, the early post-war period did not witness any major change in literacy policy. Together, therefore, these initial chapters set the historical context for the chapters which follow in Parts 2 and 3.

Part 2 examines the politicisation and escalation of literacy education in England from the late 1960s to the early 1990s. In this section we examine the ways in which public debates over reading standards in this period sowed the seeds for the National Literacy Strategy in the 1990s. Chapter 3 examines the growth of public and parliamentary concern focusing on the initial Black Papers which led to the release of the *Bullock Report* in 1975. Whilst the *Bullock Report* can be seen as a balanced and liberal document which attempted to reconcile opposing points of view in relation to teaching of reading, we would argue that this report also opened up the possibilities for the limitation of teacher autonomy and the external monitoring of standards. In Chapter 4, we examine the further intensification of the reading debates and especially their contribution to the ongoing development of centralisation and accountability in the later 1970s and early 1980s. This specific concern over reading standards during this period can also be seen to have given impetus to more general debates over educational standards and the development of the National Curriculum in the late 1980s. The final chapter in Part 2 reflects upon the renewal of concern over the reading standards and the teaching of reading in the early 1990s. This period saw the culmination of the longstanding debate over reading standards and previous political responses. Accordingly, the chapter focuses upon the key role played by influential individuals and the press, politicians and pressure groups that led to a political climate which supported the development of the NLS.

Part 3 of this book, 'Recent policy developments: Antipodean synergies', widens the analysis through comparative case studies of policies and programmes in England and New Zealand. In this final section, we argue that there are similarities between national contexts but also significant differences related to national and local contexts. In Chapter 6 we explore the complexities and contradictions in the recent development of nationally-based Literacy Strategies. Finally in Chapter 7 we build upon these understandings through an exploration of the political contexts which hindered adoption of Reading Recovery in England, despite its official recognition in New Zealand and elsewhere.

Chapter 2

Re-emerging debates over methods and standards, 1945–1965

In England, concerns over literacy were being expressed by reading researchers, government officials and the media well before the 1960s. Concerns over literacy standards in this period were underpinned by a growing conviction, beginning in the 1940s and extending through the 1960s, that there was a connection between democratic progress in 'modern' societies and a literate population. Connected to this was a view that 'scientific' approaches to the teaching of reading would promote reading skills. Writing in 1959, Joyce Morris claimed that:

> The ability to read has become an essential part of life in all but the very primitive societies. Consequently, lack of this skill has created social problems demanding the attention of legislators and other reformers whose opinions have often required support from the results of scientific studies.[1]

In particular, key questions were being raised in this era concerning the attainment of both beginning readers and young adults. The years 1945–1960 also witnessed an emerging (or rather more accurately, re-emerging) professional debate over the best method to teach beginning readers. There were, however, significant differences between these early post-war literacy concerns and the intense, sustained debate that was to characterise the period from the late 1960s on. In the earlier era, neither reading failure nor methodology became the subject of a sustained campaign that might have made them issues for urgent government action. Moreover, the long-standing tradition of localism in curriculum was not yet to be directly challenged by irresistible calls for a national literacy strategy at the expense of curtailing the freedom of schools and LEAs. This chapter therefore attempts not merely to outline instances of reading controversy during the period 1945–1965, but to suggest some reasons for its failure to impact more profoundly on policy-making at the national level.

Professional consensus over teaching reading

The early post-war period was to witness the gradual re-emergence of debates over the best methods for teaching beginning readers. Chall has described how, from about 1930 until the mid-1950s, a broad consensus existed amongst the reading establishment concerning the teaching of beginning readers.[2] As a result of this consensus, most teacher textbooks and reading programmes tended to share a number of assumptions about readers and text. There was general acceptance that the teaching of reading should be expanded to include not only word recognition, but also comprehension, appreciation and textual relevance to the learner. After 'sight' recognition of about fifty words, children were to proceed to the 'meaningful' study of whole words. Instruction in phonics was still to occur, but only in conjunction with other strategies such as context clues. Isolated drill in phonics was to be avoided, with some programmes emphasising that children should use phonics only when other strategies had failed. In addition, a general acceptance of the concept of 'reading readiness' allowed for pupils to be introduced to reading only after they had demonstrated their readiness to do so.[3]

Chall was mainly referring to the United States in her survey of reading, however, in England, reading programmes also tended to share some broadly common assumptions. During the inter-war period, the comprehensive *Beacon Reading Scheme* was introduced into England from the United States.[4] Education in England had also witnessed the growing influence of Piagetian concepts of readiness during the 1950s. This development was facilitated by an increasing emphasis on promoting methods of teaching reading based on modern 'scientific' research. In England, the Ministry of Education pamphlet, *Reading Ability*,[5] echoed conventional wisdom in maintaining that reading readiness depended on a certain stage of maturity that was in turn dependant on home conditions, social environment, emotional stability and innate ability.[6] As a 1959 NFER study by J.M. Morris was to reveal, many head teachers appear to have agreed with these conclusions. Her research revealed that forty-five out of sixty head teachers of Kent primary schools surveyed believed in the concept of reading readiness, even though they may not have understood precisely what the term meant. Whilst it is more difficult to accurately assess attitudes among classroom teachers, Peter Cunningham has demonstrated how the key tenets of educational progressivism, already well established in primary schools prior to the Second World War, were effectively disseminated, post-war. A number of new factors aided dissemination in this period. These included the changing nature of professional training, the work of professional organisations and new developments in school architecture.[7]

Public and official concern over literacy

Professional consensus not withstanding, factors such as the lingering impact of wartime disruptions to schooling, the early post-war debate over the organisation of secondary education and the emerging concern over juvenile delinquency, coupled with the onset of the Cold War, stimulated public, media, governmental and professional interest over literacy standards in England. School leavers were a particular source of worry both to Defence officials, who complained about the low educational standards of those entering the armed forces, and to those who focused on rising post-war crime statistics. An article by Sir Cyril Burt, published in the *British Journal of Educational Psychology* in 1945, estimated that 1 per cent of sixteen-year-olds and 1.5 to 2 per cent of twenty-to-twenty-five-year-olds were illiterate, with 10 per cent and 15 to 20 per cent respectively being semi-literate.[8] An article by Dr W.D. Wall, a colleague of Professor F.D. Schonell, on the incidence of illiteracy and semi-literacy in the army, appeared in the same issue of *BJEP*.[9] In February 1946, the *Times Educational Supplement* published an article by Schonell dealing with the problem of post-war illiteracy.[10] Schonell observed that recent school surveys revealed that there was 'still an astonishing amount of illiteracy and semi-literacy amongst pupils leaving school at the age of 14', for which he blamed the education system rather than individual teachers. The solution lay with the establishment of small, special classes for slow-learners, along with the provision by educational authorities of courses for teachers on the latest diagnostic and remedial reading materials for dealing with backwardness in reading. Decreased illiteracy amongst both children and adults in England and Wales, Schonell concluded:

> would mean less unhappiness, less delinquency, less crime, and less neurosis; and, with an estimated total of three million illiterates and semi-literates, the improvement in personal and social efficiency would be a major gain to the nation.[11]

Both the dangers of illiteracy and the gains of literacy were to become common themes in reading standards debates during the early post-war years. The growth of public and professional concerns over the extent and nature of illiteracy provoked an official response. In September 1947, Labour's Minister of Education set up a committee consisting of representatives from the Defence Departments, the Prison Commission and the Home Office, as well as from the Ministry of Education. The Committee's terms of reference were 'To consider the nature and extent of the illiteracy alleged to exist among school leavers and young people and, if necessary, to make recommendations'. In the course of their inquiry, the Committee administered a new reading test developed by Dr A.F. Watts and Professor P.E. Vernon to two sample groups of children aged eleven and fifteen, drawn from across England and Wales. The test contained thirty-five questions, with a time limit of ten minutes. For each question, pupils had to choose the correct answer from five given words, with the questions becoming progressively more difficult. The results appeared in the Ministry of Education pamphlet, *Reading Ability: Some Suggestions for Helping the Backward*. Acknowledging the growing concern over the amount of illiteracy among young people as reflected in recent investigations and public statements, the preface to the pamphlet posed the question: 'Is illiteracy increasing in this country?'[12] Whilst it was pointed out that illiteracy was not an exact term, and that reading ability had not been measured by any standard scale, it was nevertheless conceded that during the 1939–1945 period, reading standards had fallen by twelve months for children of eleven years, and by one-and-three-quarter years for pupils of fifteen years.[13]

Public concern over reading standards continued to be expressed during the early post-war years, especially after the Conservatives under Winston Churchill were returned to power in October 1951. In February 1953, just prior to the conclusion of the Korean Conflict, *The Times* published an article entitled, 'Illiterates and backward readers. Conditions in England since the War'. Written by the educational correspondent to *The Times*, the article sought to defend the efforts of post-war schools to improve the teaching of reading, notwithstanding the difficulties they faced. The correspondent observed that: 'ever since the War Office began, some few years ago, to publish statistics about the illiterate and semi-literate men being received into the Army, the wildest exaggerations have been circulated and, unhappily, believed by many people'. The figures were 'wildly bandied about by authorities', who took little account of the problems caused by wartime dislocation.[14]

Public concern over illiteracy and reading standards also prompted a number of local authorities to investigate the extent of the problems amongst school children in their areas. A 1948 investigation by Hammond involving Brighton children indicated that the actual number who were 'seriously retarded' was considerably higher than the pre-war estimate, and that these children tended to 'lag more and more behind'. Concern about a possible decline in reading standards also prompted two studies by Birch, in Burton-on-Trent, in 1949 and 1950. In 1953, the Middlesbrough Head Teachers' Association surveyed 2,236 children in the final stages of their primary school careers. Whilst this study suggested that schools were to some extent recovering from wartime staffing problems, it also revealed a significant difference between the sexes, in favour of girls. During the early 1950s, further research was carried out by the Leeds Education Committee (1953), the Monmouth Education Committee (1954) and in Swansea (1954), all of which indicated that improvements in standards had occurred during the early post-war years.[15]

Despite these findings, public and press concern over reading standards remained relatively high. In particular, the statistics of illiteracy and semi-literacy revealed in *Reading Abilities* and the social consequences of allowing the problem to continue, along with the particular difficulties of English language pronunciation and spelling, were sharply revealed in the extended and relatively non-partisan debate that followed the second reading in the Commons of a Private Member's Bill sponsored by the Labour member for Loughborough, Dr Mont Follick, in February 1953. This bill, termed the Simplified Spelling Bill, aimed to simplify spelling in the English language in order to ease the task of learning to read through compelling those responsible for the production of school readers to utilise a phonetic alphabet. Seconding the bill, the Conservative member for Bath, I.J. (later Sir James) Pitman, acknowledged the considerable problem of backward reading revealed in *Reading Ability*. He pointed out that 'Some 400,000–500,000 children beg[an] their schooling every year and some 120,000 to 150,000 [were] destined to come out of school unable to read properly'. Pitman, however, rejected a parliamentary interjector's claims that teaching methods might be at fault, instead stressing the difficulty posed by the un-phonetic and inconsistent structure of the English language. The result, he argued, was a high degree of shame, boredom and absenteeism caused by reading failure, which eventually contributed to 'juvenile delinquency and crime and great social embarrassment'.[16]

It is noteworthy that both support for, and opposition to, the bill, cut across existing political party divisions. Ralph Morley, the Labour member for Southampton, Itchen, for instance, generally supported the bill, but queried whether spelling and illiteracy in England were as bad as newspapers had suggested. Morley conceded, however, that, in addition to being a chief cause of juvenile delinquency, reading failure had further consequences for the individual and nation:

> The boy who leaves school unable to read is handicapped in his job. He can undertake only repetitive work. He has very little chance of promotion. His inability to read becomes known to his workmates and he is made the butt of their ridicule. Because he cannot read he is debarred from a great mass of information. It would seem to me difficult for him to fulfil properly his duties as a citizen. How can he vote intelligently if he has not read the leading articles in the newspapers?[17]

Those critical of the bill were equally revealing both of future disagreements over the causes of poor reading and of the remedies required. Dr H.M. King, Morley's Southampton Labour colleague and a past-president of the National Union of Teachers, felt a serious defect of the bill was that, for the first time in our history, 'it asks the Minister of Education to seek by

Statutory Instrument, to impose a method of teaching on the schools of this country'. King also observed that the bill had gained considerable support due to the 'alarming statistics' revealed in *Reading Ability*. This pamphlet, he pointed out, however, was based on a study of children in 1948 when the impact of war on schooling had been considerable. Moreover, the tests upon which its conclusions were based measured only one kind of reading ability.[18] James Johnson, the Labour member for Rugby, also questioned the rigidity of the definitions presented in *Reading Ability*, pointing out that if the debate did little else, it would at least underline the point that backwardness was not synonymous with literacy.[19] The Conservative member for Totnes, Brigadier Ralph Raynor, however, anticipated the anti-progressivist theme that was to become evident in future debates over reading standards when he suggested that:

> We should go back to some of those simple methods of teaching the three Rs that our little village schools with their small asphalt playgrounds used to make such a success of in the past, and we should move away from the fancy method of the de lux establishment we now look for in the way of a school, with its psychiatrist on the board of advisors.[20]

The Simplified Spelling Bill was eventually referred to a standing committee, but was subsequently withdrawn.[21] Neither it nor indeed further attempts by Pitman and others to legislate for a simplified spelling alphabet were to be successful.[22] Guy Eden, writing in the popular magazine, *Punch*, arguably summed up contemporary public opinion when he wrote: 'The commonz torked ov nu speling al dai – but it is cleer that the idea haz a long wai to go befor it catches on.'[23] Nevertheless, the increasing sense of urgency amongst those who sought to improve reading standards and to eliminate illiteracy was to be sustained in the early post-war years by the increasingly popular view that the backward reader now represented a significant danger to the rapid progress of post-war society. To the generation that had fought Hitler, the costs of illiteracy were not merely to be measured in terms of further educational opportunities and employment. This was illustrated during the debate on the Address immediately following the Queen's Speech in November 1954, when questions were raised regarding the influence of American crime and horror comics on young minds. King pointed out that:

> Learning to read is difficult. British and American educationalists face the problem of the backward reader, a problem made even more difficult by the irrationality of our spelling. It is among those who find it hard to learn to read that crime comics circulate most, and their very circulation makes it harder to teach such children to read.[24]

For King, as for many other parliamentarians on both sides of the House, the attractions of comics, films and television, especially when compared to the difficulties involved in learning to read, posed a grave social problem for the future of civilisation:

> It may be that television, the film and the comic strip will win in the long run and that mankind, which is just on the march towards literacy, may be allowed to slip back into a state in which there are more illiterates than literates. This conjures up for those who believe in social democracy, a more fearsome picture even than the horror comic itself, with comic strip election addresses and Frankenstein or Fascist legislation, and legislators.[25]

One result of this concern was to be the introduction of the Children and Young Person's (Harmful Publications) Bill early in 1955.

Further factors in the growth of concern

By the mid-1950s further factors were fuelling concern over reading. Alarmed at the spread of progressivism in post-war state schools, opponents sought more effective means of combating progressivist influence, both in the curriculum and over teaching methods. In his analysis of post-war Tory education policy, Christopher Knight employs the term 'Conservative Educator' (CE), in an educational rather than a political sense. This distinction is necessary, Knight argues, because whilst many CEs were Conservative Party members, some had earlier associations with Labour. Some CEs were also themselves practising teachers, in the state or independent school sectors.[26]

Knight also indicates the potential of debates over curriculum matters to become politicised, especially once Opposition parties recognised the election potential of raising questions regarding academic standards. This development was, however, relatively slow to occur. Knight observes that David (Lord) Eccles arrived at the Ministry of Education in 1954, becoming the first Conservative Minister to acknowledge the growing public concern with the content of education.[27] The genesis of CEs arrived with an alliance of nine Conservative MPs elected in 1950, who jointly produced the pamphlet, *One Nation – A Tory Approach to Social Problems*. The essay on education in this publication was written by CE, Angus Maude. Maude believed that the modern insistence on 'humanising' teaching methods should not become an excuse for abandoning the traditional disciplines of learning. He conceded, however, that curriculum change should come about organically, rather than being forced by the state. Thus, educational standards could be effectively preserved by the best schools outside the system, because these provided a yardstick and set the tone for competition over university scholarships.[28]

In the latter half of the 1950s, a further catalyst for public and media concern over reading attainment and the methods employed to teach the subject came with the publication in 1955 of Rudolf Flesch's controversial book, *Why Johnny Can't Read*. Chall has described how this book 'took the nation by storm', staying on the best-seller lists for over thirty weeks, and being serialised in many American newspapers, even though the Flesch approach was almost unanimously rejected by reviewers in educational periodicals:[29]

> Flesch challenged – strongly, clearly, and polemically – the prevailing views on beginning reading instruction, which emphasized teaching children by a sight method. He advocated a return to a phonic approach . . . as the best – no, the only – method to use in beginning instruction. He found support for this view in his interpretation of the existing reading research, particularly the research comparing sight and phonic methods. (Oddly enough, this same body of research formed the basis for the prevailing methods, and proponents of those methods used it to defend themselves.)[30]

In England, the growing United States controversy over the best method of teaching beginning readers was also to have an impact.[31] Whilst the overall influence of Flesch's book was less apparent than in the United States, the renewed methods debate within the professional literature did spill over into the public arena. In 1956, J.C. Daniels and Hunter Diack from the Nottingham Institute of Education, published *Progress in Reading*.[32] Daniels and Diack argued that their research on the teaching of reading in English schools clearly demonstrated that children taught by the phonic word method were better at recognising words in both single-word and sentence tests. At the same time they largely rejected the criticism that phonics teaching produced fluency without understanding. These conclusions attracted considerable interest. A report of the book's findings appeared in the *Times Educational Supplement* in November 1956, and reviews appeared in the *Schoolmaster*, *Education Today* and in the *BJEP*.[33] A sequel to *Progress in Reading* was subsequently published in 1960.[34]

Ongoing public and professional concern over reading was also a factor behind the setting up of NFER. Although NFER research work began in September 1953, it is significant that the first NFER publication to appear was a study of reading research.[35] Its author, J.M. Morris, pointed out that debate amongst English researchers over reading methods had begun to intensify greatly during the latter half of the 1950s.[36] Vera Southgate, a researcher from the School of Education, University of Manchester, during the early 1960s, was to subsequently confirm this view. Southgate cautioned, however, that the majority of reading teachers in England employed a combination of methods in what was sometimes termed 'an eclectic' approach to reading. Nonetheless, she conceded that with the sharpening debate in the professional literature now evident, 'Teachers who have read certain recently published research reports on new approaches to the teaching of reading to beginners may have assumed that the selection of an approach is the most important factor affecting children's progress'.[37] Southgate felt the problem for teachers was further compounded due to the fact that, both in classroom practice and in the growing volume of research literature on reading instruction, 'method' was used in a narrow sense to represent two kinds of emphasis in beginning reading instruction – 'global' methods, commonly referred to as 'look and say', and 'phonic methods'.

It is possible that the intensification of the reading debate amongst professionals, coupled with the increasing association of reading research with scientific method, served to increase the gap between home and school, parent and teacher, during this period. Writing in 1963, for instance, A.E. Sanderson claimed that:

> Parents today appear to play a lesser part in teaching their children to read than was formerly the case. This trend was probably initiated when 'look and say' and similar methods came into general use. Whilst some schools attempt very successfully to explain the new methods to parents and secure their active co-operation, most merely discourage parents from helping with the teaching of reading on the grounds that only the 'new' methods are to be used. Readiness ideas have probably maintained this split between parents and teacher – since it has been assumed that only the teacher could know when a child was ready. Clashes between the opinions of parents and teachers on this matter, are not uncommon particularly when the parents are intelligent, articulate and ambitious.[38]

Certainly, as Morris has demonstrated, the early 1960s witnessed a number of events that were to strengthen considerably existing links between the teaching of reading and the research community. These included the formation of the United Kingdom Council of the International Reading Association (later renamed the United Kingdom Reading Association (UKRA)) in 1961; the setting up of a British affiliate of the American National Council for the Teaching of English (NATE), in 1962, along with the establishment of the Association for Programmed Learning which subsequently encouraged the development of programmed reading materials; the reconstitution of the Central Advisory Council for Education in 1963 which was to report on reading standards, methods, materials and reading problems generally; the creation of the Schools Council in 1964; the initiation of a ten-year programme of research into the teaching of English as a second language to immigrant children; and the 1964 establishment of an experimental television unit to develop programmes to motivate backward readers.[39]

Within the English context, the growing global debate over the teaching of reading became inexorably fused with the developing national debate over the spread of progressive education ideals in the endowed schools. Morris observed that the official explanation of the 1950 Ministry publication – that schools had not yet recovered from the effects of war – was not accepted by educators who were critical of progressive education itself.[40] It was in order to address these concerns that the Ministry published its second pamphlet, *Standards of Reading*, in 1957. This pamphlet sought to directly compare the results of the 1948 survey, and to calibrate these results with those obtained from earlier pre-war tests. To this end, HMI had been instructed to utilise the same tests in 1952 and 1956 as it had in 1948. The Foreword to the pamphlet conceded that there was still some leeway to be made up since pre-war times.[41] Between 1948 and 1956, however, it was asserted that there had been 'on the whole an improvement in the ability of school children to read with understanding'. It was claimed that improvement was most marked in primary schools, where eleven-year-old pupils were about nine months more advanced than their 1948 counterparts.[42] At secondary school level, the increase amongst fifteen-year-olds was about five months. The publication could thus claim that:

> The new picture is encouraging. The success achieved over the past eight years is plain to see, and I hope this survey will be read and appreciated from this point of view, especially by our critics.[43]

Morris, however, was not entirely convinced by the claim. She argued that progress in reading attainment since 1948 had not been as satisfactory as expected. She also pointed to the fact that there had been no significant change in the proportions of fifteen-year-olds who could be classed as 'backward readers', 'semiliterate' or 'illiterate'.

The general debate over progressive methods in turn stimulated further research and debate into the question of informal versus formal methods of teaching reading.[44]

The limits to crisis

Given the impetus of the American reading debate, the continuing levels of concern over literacy standards, and the renewed controversy within the reading establishment over the most appropriate methods to teach beginning readers, it is important to consider some possible reasons why professional and press concern over reading did not become the national issue it became in the United States just a few years earlier. There were probably two key factors involved here.

The first factor was the relative freedom that English schools and LEAs continued to enjoy, particularly in respect to curriculum matters. Given that English teachers have now experienced nearly a decade of the centrally imposed NLS and the Literacy Hour, it is important to emphasise that, at this juncture, state schools retained considerable freedom of choice regarding their adoption of reading programmes and teaching methodologies. In fact, such a degree of freedom was indeed remarkable to various Commonwealth visitors who came to examine the curricula and teaching methods throughout the country. One such visitor was New Zealand infant teacher, Miss E.M. Harper who, after twelve months in England visiting nursery schools and infant schools in Birmingham, Leicester and London, submitted a report to Dr C.E. Beeby, the New Zealand Director of Education. Prior to leaving, Harper had been furnished with a letter of introduction from Terence McCombs, the New Zealand Minister of Education, with the condition that, on her return she would let the New Zealand Department of Education have the benefit of her recommendations. Harper's seven-page handwritten report, 'Nursery and Infant Schools in England', clearly illustrates the great variance in approaches and standards across the country during 1949–1950, due to both the exercise of local control and the uneven impact of war. She observed that Leicester was much better off than London, where overcrowding, shortages of accommodation, substantial waiting lists, together with chronic shortages of even basic equipment such as blackboards and paper, resulted in the majority of Infant schools being drab and dismal, with many still war-damaged.[45] Turning to the teaching of reading, Harper revealingly commented that:

> the Head Teacher has much freedom. Children in different schools under the one educational authority were using different types of reading books, which must cause difficulty to the child transferring to another school. The standard of reading in the schools I saw was not so high as in the schools in which I have taught in New Zealand, nor is the reading as wide. Extra reading books varied owing to the shortage of supplies available.[46]

The second key factor in limiting the impact of reading concern was that neither of the two major political parties in the United Kingdom was prepared to make the curriculum in general, and reading in particular, into a national issue at this juncture. Given the commitment to local control, references to curriculum issues in the House of Commons were relatively rare in the 1950s. Reading was to provide no real exception. In March 1955, Brigadier Raynor asked the Minister of Education, Sir David Eccles, whether his Department could undertake an education case history of every National Service entrant found unable to write his name and address on a form. In response, Eccles promised to arrange with the Secretary of State for War to investigate a sample of such cases.[47] In May 1957, the Conservative member for Bath, I.J. Pitman, asked the Minister of Education, Sir Edward Boyle, what plans he had for investigating the degree of reading failure in schools at the age of fifteen and whether the tests of reading ability to be employed would include comprehension to afford a 'true scientific comparison' with the earlier 1948 survey.[48] In April 1958, Sir Frank Markham, the Conservative member for Buckinghamshire, asked the Minister of Education whether he could supply the figures for illiteracy in England at all ages up to school-leaving age, and how these figures compared with those of 1938.[49] In both cases, the inquirers were referred to the Ministry of Education pamphlet, *Standards of Reading*.

Political parties tended to steer shy of curriculum matters, even where there seemed to be a case for intervention. Knight observes that, as early as 1961, the Conservative Minister of Education, Sir David Eccles, was beginning to express a personal concern regarding the view that teachers were simply neutral educators. In contrast, he believed that the curriculum and those who taught it should embrace sound moral principles that would provide spirituality and strengthen the bulwark against Communism. Eccles was also reflecting a general societal concern over increasing permissiveness amongst young people, reflected in such phenomena as juvenile delinquency.[50] The so-called '61 Society' can be seen to reflect the early linking of educational-right and educational centre-right, but at the same time Knight emphasises that these initial groupings of CEs occurred in isolation. Only when the Conservatives were in opposition from 1964–1970 did clear links develop between the opinions of CEs, committees, party lobbies and policymakers that were to provide an effective framework for a more sustained attack on curriculum autonomy focused primarily on literacy issues.

Whilst political parties tended to eschew any plans for interfering directly with the preserves of local authorities, however, the threat of eventual curriculum intervention was nonetheless clearly present at this time. Thus McCulloch, Helsby and Knight make reference to the House of Commons debate of March 1960 on the recently published *Crowther Report, 15 to 18*, where Eccles made a comment that attracted little attention at the time but later came to symbolise an entire era. Eccles said that the report's findings on sixth forms were 'an irresistible invitation for a sally into the secret garden of the curriculum'. He went on to say that he regretted that so many education debates were devoted entirely to bricks, mortar and system organisation, and rarely discussed what was taught in the curriculum. Although he quickly added that 'Parliament would never attempt to dictate the curriculum', McCulloch *et al.* argue that Eccles' statement was highly significant for two main reasons. First, it evoked the general orthodoxy of the period from the Second World War until the 1970s, that teachers should be virtually autonomous in the curriculum domain and that the curriculum was a matter neither for public debate nor state involvement. Second, however, it contained a predictive message that this would not always be the case, thus anticipating the very different orthodoxy of the 1980s and 1990s.[51] As we shall see, the debate over reading and literacy standards was to be crucial in making this orthodoxy a reality.

Part 2

The politicisation and escalation of literary education in England

Chapter 3

Reading debates and the *Bullock Report*, 1968–1975

This chapter examines the origins of a major English literacy crisis, beginning in the mid-to-late 1960s, and concluding with the publication of the *Bullock Report* in February 1975. It is the first of three chapters that seek to examine the increasing politicisation of literacy education that, in turn, was to sow the seeds for the NLS from the mid-1990s.[1] Collectively, these three chapters also explore the tensions and pressures that arose when concerns over 'literacy standards' and 'basic skills' merged with a renewed attack on child-centred progressive ideals. The narrative woven through these chapters indicates the ways in which the emerging debate contributed to the eventual development of skills-based, centralised, assessment-driven policies in literacy curriculum policy. In doing this we hope to arrive at a finer-grained understanding of a period which Ken Jones has characterised as a time that witnessed 'a rebirth of radical, non-consensual Conservatism in education'.[2]

Prelude to the crisis

During the early-to-mid-1960s, questions over reading standards continued to be raised sporadically, both in the press and in the House of Commons. In June 1963, for instance, the headmaster of Rugby school, Dr W. Hamilton, claimed during a speech at the school's annual prize giving that he found it 'hard to resist the conclusion that the general standard of literacy in the schools of this country may be even lower than I feared'.[3] As we have seen, such concerns about literacy standards from various quarters were hardly new to English education. Parliamentary questions during this period, however, tended to be either requests for further information, or an appeal for more resources to tackle specific aspects of literacy, rather than a direct attack on government attitudes towards reading standards. In March 1962, the Minister of Education, Sir David Eccles, faced parliamentary questions from the Opposition Labour Party regarding the number of primary schools providing remedial classes for backward readers. The Minister was urged to take more active steps to increase the number of remedial classes, and to encourage the utilisation of ex-quota, part-time, married women teachers for this purpose. Whilst the Minister's response to this invitation was relatively positive, he emphasised the difficulty of obtaining precise statistical information from district to district.[4] Likewise, a similar question in July called upon the Minister to take more active measures to ensure that local authorities provided such classes.[5]

In March 1964 the Labour member for Sunderland, F.T. Willey, urged Eccles' successor, Sir Edward Boyle, to issue a public statement on reading standards in primary schools. Boyle simply responded as had his predecessor, citing the conclusion of the Ministry's 1957 pamphlet, *Standards of Reading*, to the effect that the reading standard of eleven-year-olds had increased by nine months over the 1948–1956 period.[6] In June of the same year the Conservative member for Bath, Sir I.J. Pitman, asked the Minister to re-publish the figures of reading ability for fifteen-year-olds in the same form, as they were supplied in *Standards of Reading*. He also referred Pitman to the survey commissioned by the Central Advisory Council under the Chair of Lady Plowden.[7]

The shaping of a new literacy crisis

Whilst it would be premature to claim that a major national crisis over reading standards was evident early in the decade, the 1960s as a whole were to see many of the elements of future debates over reading begin to coalesce. There was to be, for instance, an early foreshadowing of the highly politi-cised concern over dyslexia that was later to both broaden and sharpen the reading standards debate. This occurred as early as February 1962, when the Conservative member for Galloway, H.J. Brewis, first raised the issue of 'dyslexia' in the House by inquiring 'what special facilities [were] available for the teaching of children suffering from dyslexia or word blindness. The Minister's relatively low-key response, however, emphasised that opinions differed as to the nature of dyslexia, claimed that a medical officer was cur-rently engaged in examining several hundred children 'said to be suffering from it', and reassured the questioner that remedial teaching for backward readers was already arranged in many districts.[8]

The 1960s also witnessed the culmination of a growing political concern over national reading standards in England. The previous chapter has exam-ined the upsurge of interest in literacy research and development in England that occurred during the late 1950s and early 1960s. In part, this stemmed from the growing international interest in combating illiteracy. In 1957, the ambitious *World Illiteracy at Mid-Century*, the first systematic attempt to document illiteracy in every country in the world, was published. By the late 1950s, illiteracy was seen as a problem of major international dimen-sions.[9] An influential report, entitled *World Campaign for Universal Literacy*, was presented to the United Nations in 1963. In 1964, the Third Commonwealth Education Conference for the first time discussed the issue of adult illiteracy, and its conclusions were appended to the conference report.[10] What has been described as a revolutionary decade in terms of global commitment culminated in 1965 with the UNESCO-organised Teheran conference, where 'a solemn and urgent appeal' was made for the global eradication of illiteracy.[11]

In England, the London press in the summer of 1966 carried reports of a voluntary movement aimed at combating adult semi-literacy throughout the country, then believed to be high as 20 per cent.[12] The 1960s also witnessed renewed interest in the possibilities of spelling reform as a means of making the teaching of reading easier. In March 1962, Eccles was strongly urged to devote careful attention to current experiments at the University of London into the teaching of spelling by means of a reformed alphabet.[13] In April 1967, however, there was a much more intense and extended parliamentary discussion regarding the future of the initial teaching alphabet (ITA). Whilst the ITA discussion largely confirmed the earlier pattern of support for further research without any firm commitment to action, the comments of those who spoke were once again to be revealing. These comments indicated both a growing concern over literacy standards and a feeling that more should be done to improve the teaching of reading in schools, particularly amongst new teachers. Introducing the ITA debate, R.P. Hornby, the Conservative member for Tonbridge, observed that the House now took considerable interest in ITA because everyone recognised the immense importance for a child in learning to read. Those who did fall behind were almost certain to join the ranks of the unskilled and lose many opportunities. Thus:

> There [was] no room for complacency about our achievements in teaching our children to read. It is estimated that 14 per cent of school leavers leave school at the age of 15 as backward readers – that is to say, not having gone beyond the age of 11 in their reading ability. To take a rather gloomy social picture, United States statistics show that 90 per cent of all those who are convicted of indictable offences come from the ranks of the backward readers. I make these points merely to stress that learning to read and the skills that we apply to that task are of immense importance to every individual child and to the country as a whole.[14]

In agreeing with the account of ITA research to date, Labour's Minister of State for the Department of Education and Science, Mrs Shirley Williams, stressed the general improvement in the standards of schools and teachers demonstrated in *Standards of Reading 1948–56*, and subsequently repeated in the *Plowden Report* that had led to 'the remarkable increase in reading attainment in terms of age levels as between 1948 and about 15 years later'.

This level of official response, however, was soon to be deemed insufficient. By the late 1960s, the heightened concern over the social consequences of illiteracy was rapidly fusing with renewed attacks on progressive education, with significant implications for literacy policy in the future. During the ITA discussion, Hornby had been at pains to point out that 'one needs to go out of one's way to say that educational methods are the province of the teacher and no one else...'[15] The extension of the literacy debate to include the controversy over progressivism, however, served to stimulate political party interest and, hence, further politicisation. In his analysis of post-war Tory education policy development, Knight highlights the activities of what he terms the 'preservationists'. This was an increasingly influential grouping of conservative educators that came to include such key figures as Dr Rhodes Boyson, Anthony Dyson, Gilbert Longden and Professor Brian Cox. A number of this group had been Labour Party members or supporters during the early 1960s, who had subsequently become increasingly disenchanted with what they regarded as the disastrous impact of progressivist philosophies in both primary and secondary education. Preservationists argued against egalitarian, child-centred ideals that they believed threatened academic standards. Instead, they promoted a vision of high culture through academic excellence, and respect for traditional subject-discipline based knowledge.[16]

The growing political party debate over progressivism that emerged from the late 1960s was further sharpened by the publication of the *Plowden Report* in early 1967. Released under a newly elected Labour government, the report was 'warmly welcomed by Secretary of State, Anthony Crosland'.[17] Opposition Conservatives, however, were to be increasingly galvanised by 'preservationist' arguments. Indications of a growing Conservative Party interest in curriculum matters in general and in literacy standards in particular was foreshadowed in May 1967, when it was reported that a survey of literacy standards in London primary schools was to be made by the Inner-London Authority under a new Conservative leadership.[18]

In 1968, freelance journalist Nicholas Smart, inspired by a series of *Daily Express* articles on the impact of the cuts in educational expenditure penned by Bruce Kemble, edited a *Daily Mirror* sponsored book, provocatively entitled, *Crisis in the Classroom*.[19] Contributors to the book included Christopher Chataway, Chairman of the Inner-London Education Authority, Tyrell Burgess, Rhodes Boyson and Keith Gardner, a leading literacy expert. Gardner's chapter, 'State of reading', opened with what the author saw as 'one sign of the failure of modern education': a group of young army recruits working, not on weaponry or signal systems, but on learning to read at an army training centre. In his chapter, Gardner was particularly sceptical of the tendency to use national survey figures to demonstrate that reading standards had improved, post-war. In contrast, his own study of trends in early reading standards in junior schools in one local area revealed a steadily deteriorating standard of literacy to the extent that, by 1967, 40 per cent of first-year primary pupils had not even made a start in learning to read. The causes, argued Gardner, lay both in the failure of colleges of education to instruct their entrants in how to teach reading, and in the fact that the teaching of reading in schools now lacked method and system due to the prevailing conviction that reading was something to be acquired rather than taught. The result, concluded Gardner, was that equality of educational opportunity as promised under the 1944 Education Act was a myth. Whilst most socially favoured children would attain a degree of literacy despite current educational practice, the majority of under-privileged children would never really become literate.[20]

In highlighting the unequal impact of alleged shortcomings in literacy teaching across social classes, Gardner was reflecting the broad appeal of *Crisis in the Classroom* to Labour as well as Conservative politicians. Thus, in December 1968, M.C.J. Barnes, the Labour member for Bentford and Chiswick, asked the Secretary of State for Education and Science, the Right Hon. E.W. Short, if he would take steps to set up a national centre for reading research. When he was informed that this was not necessary, Barnes retorted that the recent publication of *Crisis in the Classroom* underlined the need for improving primary school literacy. He went on to suggest that many technical advances in the teaching of reading were not passed on because no body existed to perform the task. Short's attempt to counter this with the argument that the four-yearly surveys of reading conducted since 1948 revealed steadily rising standards was immediately seized upon by the Tory educational preservationist, Gilbert Longden, then the Conservative member for Herts.[21] Longden, a prominent defender of educational excellence, posed the counter: 'Does not all this recent research reveal that because trainee teachers in colleges of education are not being taught to teach a child to read, the standard of literacy in our schools is abysmally low and getting lower?' In response the Secretary claimed that 'the quality of teaching in the primary and infant schools ha[d] improved out of all recognition over the last two decades'. By this juncture, however, such a response served only to shift the issue back to the wider question mark that increasingly loomed over progressive education.[22]

Extending the literacy debate

The period 1969–1976 was to witness a steep rise in concern over both literacy standards and progressive education in both the national press and in the House of Commons. A major catalyst for the debate was undoubtedly the publication of the first of the so-called Black Papers, edited by Brian Cox and Anthony Dyson, in March 1969.[23] The degree of national urgency invoked in this document was underscored by the fact that the volume was prefaced with an open letter to members in both Houses of Parliament.[24] That there was widespread press interest in facilitating the debate over literacy standards during this period is evident in the way that the letter drew upon both conservative and liberal commentary to argue that many educational experts had become increasingly unhappy about progressive educational trends such as 'free play', 'comprehensive schemes', the abolition of streaming and the increasing practice in primary schools whereby 'some teachers were taking to an extreme the belief that children must not be told anything, but must find out for themselves'.[25] On the inside cover of the document the editors reproduced a quote from Reginald Maudling in *The Times* questioning the erosion of traditional discipline and standards both in education and the wider society.[26] Stephen Ball, citing Raymond Williams, argues that the basis of this type of critique is within the tradition of 'old humanism' which 'contains both a defence of the elitist, liberal curriculum and an attack on the de-stabilizing effects of progressivism'.[27]

In the House of Commons, Conservative attacks on the Government's alleged failure to deal with falling literacy standards and its support for a progressivism they believed to be running rampant in schools became much more forceful following the publication of the first Black Paper. In July 1969, D.G. Smith, the member for Warwick and Leamington, asked Short if he was satisfied with the primary school reading and writing standards, challenging him to make a statement.[28] In January 1970, Longden quizzed the Secretary of State for Education and Science regarding how many students had left school unable to read, what criteria inspectors used to measure reading ability and whether he was satisfied that colleges of education taught students how to teach reading. In reply, Short emphasised that the teaching of reading formed 'an important part of the college of education curriculum which is under constant surveillance', adding that he knew that colleges were giving 'increasing attention to this subject'.[29] The growing acceptability of government monitoring of literacy standards that was to be a feature of the next decade was thus already clearly foreshadowed.

The national press both reflected and amplified the widening debate over reading standards. A September 1969 article by *The Times'* educational correspondent, Brian MacArthur, specifically linked the wider debate over progressivism that had been raised by Cox and Dyson to declining literacy standards. The article spoke of a new controversy that had erupted over standards of literacy in some English schools. MacArthur revealed that 'informed critics', led by Dr John Downing and Dr Joyce Morris, had earlier in the year written unpublished letters to *The Times* in response to Sir Alex Clegg's public defence of the modern primary school. The critics had allegedly claimed that, in the most recent survey conducted in 1964, about 20% of all eleven-year-olds read less well than the average child of nine, whilst almost half had a reading ability at less than an average eight-year-old. MacArthur, however, felt that this to be a somewhat thin criticism which ignored the fact that the standard of the average eight-year-old was continually rising.[30]

The critics referred to in McArthur's article also claimed that all post-war

English schools had really achieved was to regain lost ground, with any improvements due to general improvements in health, social environment and the spread of television. Once again, however, it should be stressed that MacArthur took a relatively critical view of such claims, pointing out that all reading surveys since 1950 had been administered by Gilbert Peaker, a former member of HMI, now retired. According to MacArthur, Peaker still maintained that there had been a steady rise in literacy standards since systematic measurements began. MacArthur also stressed that Peaker's position was fully supported by the view of HMI that standards were indeed rising, leading the correspondent to conclude that 'sober facts seem, therefore, to refute the allegations that are now in the air'. Literacy concerns, moreover, tended to focus specifically on Inner-London schools, where Asian immigration was high. Thus, in November 1969, *The Times* reported that the Inner-London Education Authority (ILEA) had asked the Department of Education and Science (DES) for a full inquiry into teacher training, following the release of a survey revealing that, although the proportion of poor readers in London junior schools was twice the national average, and included nearly 17 per cent immigrant children, only one in eight junior teachers had specific training in reading teaching.[31]

The stance taken in these articles was consistent with MacArthur's view in other publications during this period, in suggesting that the progressive achievements of the 1960s defined education 'as an area of definite achievement whatever the general failures of the period'.[32] Interestingly, in the late 1960s, *The Times'* press coverage of preservationist anti-progressive arguments centred on the demise of the grammar school which was viewed as a 'progressive collapse' by the authors of the Black Paper, *Fight for Education*.[33] The MacArthur articles, however, did not link literacy standards to a preservationist view attacking progressivism, nor did they support the view that literacy standards were declining.

Renewed attack on progressivism

The 1970s were to witness dramatic developments, both in the nature of parliamentary debate over literacy, and in the reporting of reading by major newspapers such as *The Times* and the *Times Educational Supplement*. A key reason for this radical shift in debate clearly lay in the successful lobbying by preservationists of the Conservative Party central organisation, which in turn gradually absorbed the philosophy into official Party thinking.[34] Margaret Thatcher was appointed Shadow Secretary of State for Education and Science in June 1970, shortly before the Conservative election victory. Knight argues that the actual incorporation of 'Black Paper' thinking into Party thinking and policy dates from her speech to the Annual Conference of the Association of Education Committees (AEC) at Scarborough, 28 October 1970, when she warned delegates: 'We must avoid becoming preoccupied with systems and structures to the detriment of the actual content of educa-tion.'[35]

The continuing literacy debate in the House of Commons, together with reporting of literacy issues in the *TES* and *The Times* during these years, tend to confirm Knight's analysis. With the Tories in power and Thatcher now installed as Secretary of State for Education and Science, plans proceeded to initiate an inquiry into the teaching of reading in schools. Like the Conserv-atives before them, however, the Labour Opposition also sought to put school literacy shortcomings, and the role of the government in ensuring adequate standards, under a critical spotlight. In July 1970, the Labour member for Birmingham, Ladywood, Mrs Doris Fisher, asked the Secretary if she would extend the methods involved in the teaching of reading to include teaching college students intending to teach in junior schools. Parliamentary Under Secretary, William van Straubenzee, responded that the teaching of reading was already included in the curriculum; an answer that differed but little from that of his Labour predecessors.[36]

Further queries regarding the standard of instruction in teaching colleges, particularly in regard to literacy, were raised in November 1970. The Labour member for Rother Valley, Peter Hardy, pressed the Secretary of State for further information regarding the number of teaching college lec-turers with less than five years' teaching experience, pointing out that experienced teachers were very concerned that those responsible for profes-sional subjects possess adequate and relevant teaching experience.[37] Hardy then went on to ask what proportion of college students received no instruc-tion in the teaching of reading. However, van Staubenzee replied that a survey completed earlier that year revealed that all students in the colleges sampled had received some instruction in teaching reading. He was then pressed by Hardy to issue an assurance that adequate instruction was given to all college students since it was 'obvious that the vast majority of teachers sooner or later in their careers [were] involved in classroom teaching and need[ed] to know a good deal about this important subject'.[38]

On a number of occasions when questions were asked about literacy standards, members were referred to the forthcoming inquiry into the teach-ing of reading. In May 1971, Thatcher responded to a question from the Labour member for Wolverhampton, North-East, Mrs Renee Short, on the levels of illiteracy among secondary school leavers. Thatcher observed that 'illiteracy' could not be exactly defined. She emphasised that the improve-ment in standards of literacy since 1948 had been described in the Depart-ment's pamphlet, *Progress of Reading*, and predicted that the results of the latest NFER survey would be available later in the year.[39]

Labour also increased the pressure on the new government to deal more effectively with the dyslexia issue, which was then assuming increasing prominence. In November 1970, the Labour member for Stoke-on-Trent, Jack Ashley, asked Thatcher if she would take steps to direct LEAs to provide information on the provisions made for the education of deaf, blind and autistic children, as well as those suffering from 'acute dyslexia'. Thatcher responded that whilst she had already requested such information concerning deaf and blind children, she was not convinced that similar action was required for children who had difficulties in learning to read, as this problem had many causes. Ashley went on to claim that the dyslexia problem was seriously underestimated, but in her response Thatcher maintained that the difficulties of reading extended to a much wider group than Ashley had in mind.[40] The existence of a growing public lobby on behalf of dyslexic children stimulated parliamentary debate on the issue that was to intensify a sense of crisis concerning reading standards, with Labour arguing that dyslexia was a specific problem demanding further research, and the Conservatives claiming that the term was a catch-all for reading problems that the schools were failing to address. Nevertheless, Conservative members too were soon to join in the increasing national concern over dyslexia. Thus, in July 1971, the Conservative member for Bedford, Trevor Skeet, asked whether there were any special schools in Bedfordshire for dealing with dyslexic children, what provision was made where such schools did not exist and whether grants for dyslexic children were now available.[41]

An indication of the extent to which attitudes towards the monitoring of literacy standards, and the government's role in maintaining standards were changing, were not long in coming. In February 1972, an NFER report on reading was released. This report, co-authored by K.B. Start and B.K. Wells, presented the results of a national survey on reading comprehension undertaken in 1970/1971 at the request of the DES.[42] In order to maintain a degree of continuity with previous surveys conducted in 1948, 1952, 1955, 1956, 1960, 1961 and 1964, both the twenty-three-year old Watts Vernon Test (VW) and the sixteen-year-old National Survey Form 6 (NS6) were employed with two different age groups. The conclusion to the report began by emphasising the uncertainty surrounding the results obtained. This included the high proportion of randomly selected schools that chose not to participate, the high degree of absenteeism amongst fifteen-year-old early school leavers and the 'aging' language employed by both reading tests.[43] Nevertheless, the report claimed that there was a high probability that the reading comprehension standard of juniors had declined somewhat since 1964 as measured by the VW test, and that according to the combined results of both tests, the mean scores of both juniors and seniors had undergone no significant rise or fall since the early 1960s.[44]

In attempting to address some possible reasons as to why reading standards had not continued to rise, the report turned to the key question of what reading instruction children now received. Here, it was concluded that less formalised teaching methods would not necessarily imply that less time was devoted to reading, though the report did cite the opinion of the 1971 president of the UK Reading Association, Vera Southgate, that there had been a declining interest in reading, especially in 'progressive' infant classes. The report emphasised, however, that a multiplicity of methods, curricula and content was a striking feature of the British curriculum scene.[45] In the end, the report left the debate over literacy still unresolved in its conclusion that 'reading standards today are no better than they were a decade ago and we have no hard experimental evidence from which we can explain why the post-war improvement has apparently ceased'.[46]

The somewhat ambiguous tones of the NFER survey did little to halt the political reaction that subsequently followed. An editorial in the *TES* reported an address by Thatcher to the National Union of Teachers in April 1972, in which she referred to the very large public expenditure on education over the previous decade, Thatcher was quoted as having observed that the NFER report published earlier that year indicated that school literacy standards had not increased since the mid-1960s and, in case of juniors, could well have declined. Perhaps with her May 1971 response to Short in mind, Thatcher emphasised that this was the first time they had not improved since regular testing began in 1938. The *TES* editorial went on to commend Thatcher for having sensibly appointed a small expert committee (the Bullock Committee) to inquire into teaching of reading in schools. The editorial noted that there was an increase in demand amongst teachers for courses in teaching reading, and drew attention to the low proportion of new teachers with initial training in the field. Significantly, and in direct contrast to the earlier McArthur article on literacy, the editorial concluded by linking current reading problems to the ongoing debate over progressivism:

> If there have been defects in the initial training of teachers which have contributed to the lack of improvement in reading standards, they are probably associated with a general attitude in the primary schools which places less emphasis than there used to be placed on the acquisition by children of particular skills. The failure to put emphasis where it is due is not a necessary concomitant of the methods which have had such a liberating effect on the primary schools. But it is evidently a danger.[47]

In the House, Thatcher now came under pressure from both sides to announce the membership of the inquiry committee. In May 1972, she was able to announce that Sir Alan Bullock, the Vice-Chancellor of Oxford University, had agreed to serve as chairman.[48] Despite continued questioning over literacy standards, however, she was no more able than had been her predecessors to supply the House with any reliable estimate of the numbers of children unable to read at any level of the education system, as 'The Department [did] not collect information which would enable it to make such estimates'.[49]

Meanwhile, on a wider political front, the November 1972 appointment of the preservationist-minded Norman St John-Stevas as Parliamentary

Under-Secretary of State for Education, and the subsequent Tory election defeat of March 1974, were events that further galvanised the Conservative Party into moving the education debate away from the kind of institution children attended, and towards the kind of education they actually received.[50] This was to further impact on the literacy standards debate because an influential body of political opinion with direct access to the media was now actively seeking to relate concern over the teaching of reading to the wider controversy over progressive teaching methods and the alleged decline in academic standards.

The heightening of this debate can be linked to wider social events of a period that helped to stimulate renewed anxieties over school literacy. The oil price rises of the early 1970s had accentuated England's long-term economic decline, leading to widespread youth unemployment.[51] Brian Simon alludes to the polarisation of English society across a whole range of educational, social and economic issues during the first half of the 1970s. Simon further contends that a number of significant incidents contributed to the coming of the so-called Great Debate over education. These included the so-called 'Summer's Outrage' of 1973; the culmination of a period of confrontational politics between local authorities, parents and central government.[52] Newly trained teachers entered a tight job market with no guarantees of finding a position.[53] In the schools, teachers threatened industrial action over pay and conditions, a situation only partially addressed by the *Houghton Report* released in December 1974.[54] The so-called Tyndale Affair brought the long-standing debate over progressivism to a head. The attention of the nation centred on a small ILEA primary school where teachers set out to operate 'what some interpret[ed] as an extreme version of the Plowden committee's philosophy of "child-centred"' education.[55] In October 1975, the ILEA determined on a full public inquiry.

In turn, the increasingly polarised controversy over educational progressivism galvanised political interest in the deliberations of the Bullock Committee. From late December 1974, pressure steadily increased for publication of the definitive report. In the *TES*, coverage of the literacy standards debate from late 1974 onwards demonstrates both a growing tendency amongst commentators to politicise educational controversy and an increasing readiness to link literacy debates to the wider debate over progressivism. In December 1974, there appeared an article by *TES* correspondent Tom Howarth, a former Head of St Paul's School and a preservationist supporter of both Cox and Dyson. Prior to 1968, Howarth had written a series of letters to *The Times* expressing grave concern over slipping literacy standards.[56] Now, he revealed that he had been sent a recent cutting from a Sunday newspaper quoting a primary school head as having said that it did not matter when a child learned to read properly, as long as he did so before he left school. In this head's school, there were 'no teachers and no taught' and the children were left to 'gyrate freely from one activity to another'. Yet the head's response to those concerned about reading progress was to say: 'You stick a book in a child's hand and if he has difficulty, then this is associated with failure. How can you bear to inflict this on a child of seven?' Howarth's blunt rejoinder was: 'Surely the answer is to apply your professional skills in such a way that he jolly well does not fail. As for being associated with failure, there is more likely to be a good deal more of that on the way if you can only just learn to read before you finally leave school.'[57] Howarth went on to complain that:

> Concurrently with this, there appears a Schools Council survey of children's reading interests to show that 29 per cent of 12-year olds read no books and that, worse still, nor do 36 per cent of 14-year olds. In general, the situation appears to be much worse than it was 35 years ago when the last full-scale survey was carried out. We can blame the television or find ourselves any other excuse we like, but if I were a parent with a child at the school described above, I should be decidedly alarmed, whether the child was an advanced or a backward reader. I confess to lingering doubts about the efficacy and probity of the voucher system, but this newspaper report has gone a long way to resolve them. For, after all, what can a parent do if he finds his child involved in a school, operated according to a theory which he might well regard as bordering on the insane?[58]

In January 1975, *The Times* carried a report by its educational correspondent, Tim Devlin, suggesting that Britain's leading professional bodies were likely to call for measures to improve literacy in schools, due to the inability of even A-level students to express themselves or to write clearly. Devlin added that, during the previous week, the Associated Examining Board, one of the country's largest examiners, had claimed that last summer's results showed a marked deterioration in spelling and punctuation among candidates sitting for two main English GCE O-level exams.[59]

Shift to literacy skills and government intervention

Meanwhile, on 18 February 1975, the Bullock Committee had finally presented its report. Despite the controversy over progressivism that had been raging, the report itself found 'no evidence of a large body of teachers committed to the rejection of basic skills', and argued that it was facile 'to assume that all manner of weaknesses can be ascribed simply to the wholesale spread of a permissive philosophy'.[60] The Committee also asserted that improvements in the teaching of reading would come, not from the acceptance of simplistic statements about methods, but rather was dependent on first defining what was meant by reading.[61]

The *Bullock Report* represented a concerted attempt to reconcile the opposing claims of structure and flexibility in teaching reading.[62] It did not produce evidence to support the view that there had been a decline in literacy standards due to what it claimed were 'unsatisfactory tests and a lack of definition on literacy, which made it difficult to judge'. The report also noted that: 'There appears to be little substance in the generalizations that large numbers of schools are promoting creativity at the expense of basic skills.'[63] The day after it had been published, an editorial in the *Guardian* expressed the conviction that it 'should end the sterile debate that has been rumbling on since the start of the decade, and allow everybody to explore the means of improving literacy to which Bullock has pointed'.[64] Despite its measured tones, however, the *Bullock Report* manifestly failed to silence the debate over literacy. Rather, the debate was to shift decisively from a general attack on progressivism to a preoccupation with literacy skills through promoting the notion of 'functional literacy' and the view that 'standards are not satisfying present day requirements'.[65]

Moreover, contemporary press commentary was often sharply divided regarding exactly what the *Bullock Report* had concluded regarding reading standards, with the various education correspondents of the major dailies tending to select the sections of the report that best suited their respective politics. *Daily Mail* education correspondent Max Wilkinson observed that the report found evidence indicating a decline in standards amongst seven- and eleven-year-olds over the preceding decade. Standards did not satisfy present-day requirements and thus failed parents 'particularly amongst those in slum areas and among children of semi-skilled and unskilled workers'. This was linked to concerns over progressivism, with the report's criticism of some young teachers who had misunderstood modern 'permissive' principles to the extent that they believed that they should never directly teach children.[66]

In the same issue, Wilkinson's article was supported by a further story citing the views of Bullock Committee member Stuart Froome, an ex-junior-school headmaster with forty-six years' teaching experience. Froome was quoted as saying that, in spite of long battles in the Committee, the final report had been dominated by progressive educators who dared not admit how low standards had actually sunk because 'that would be to say the methods employed for the past 30 years were wrong'.[67] The following day Wilkinson cited the opinion of Lord Blake, provost of Queen's College, Oxford, that the last twenty years had seen a fall in students' reading and writing fluency that reflected the connection between progressive teaching methods and the decline in educational standards. According to Wilkinson, Blake's views could be interpreted as being in direct disagreement with the *Bullock Report*'s conclusion that it was difficult to be certain of evidence pointing to any fall or that modern school methods were to blame.[68]

In contrast to the *Daily Mail*, the *Guardian* tended to highlight the positive conclusions of the *Bullock Report* together with testimony from selected reading experts and teachers. On the day the Report was to be published, the *Guardian* education section edited by Maureen O'Connor reported *Guardian* correspondent Anna Sproule's conversations with four reading experts: an infant teacher, a primary head, a local authority adviser and Betty Root, of Reading University's Centre for the Teaching of Reading. These commentators emphasised the need to motivate beginning readers, the need for a mixture of methods to teach reading, the importance of the teacher having a love of books and the key role played by high standards of professional practice.[69] In the same article a section by correspondent Michael Pollard asserted that if reading was to be taught more effectively, then teachers required better training and more in-service courses to update their skills – requirements that were being endangered by the current economic situation. He also stressed the importance of local teachers feeling themselves to be in a sufficiently strong position to be able to argue on the basis of their own experience. Pollard cited the fears of both Root and Alan Lawson, the warden of St Albans Teachers' Centre, that the Report would make teachers feel even more insecure. He then went on to observe that:

> Teachers of reading have tremendous enthusiasm – so much that it carries over into their own time – but theirs is a craft, not an academic study. It remains to be seen whether the essential difference will have been grasped.[70]

Some commentators, however, have also identified a strong theme in the *Bullock Report* that foreshadows the gradual limitation of teacher autonomy and the external monitoring of standards from this point on. The first of its 333 recommendations was that 'a system of monitoring' be introduced to both assess a wider range of attainments than had been attempted in the past and allow new criteria to be established for the definition of literacy.[71] Steps were to be taken to develop the language ability of preschool, nursery and infants, including improved staffing rations and more teacher aides, whilst schools were urged to devise systematic policies for the development of reading competence.[72] In her contemporary review of the report, Anne Corbett notes that 'Undoubtedly, one of the most important significant themes in Bullock was the necessary limitation of teacher autonomy: there should be an agreed and systematic policy for each school, and standards should be externally monitored' by a national research organisation. This system would employ 'new instruments, to assess a wider range of attainments than had been attempted in the past to enable the monitoring of standards of children between eleven and seventeen in order to provide an ongoing estimate of literacy standards'.[73]

It can therefore be argued that the controversy over literacy standards during the late 1960s and early 1970s, together with the resulting *Bullock*

Report, should be regarded as a policy turning point leading to earlier traditions of teacher autonomy in curriculum becoming progressively eroded through increasing government intervention in the curriculum. Here, we should once again recall Gary McCulloch's citation of a germane House of Commons debate in March 1960, in which the Minister of Education, Sir David Eccles, made comments on the school curriculum that both symbolised the consensus of the 1945–1970 era, that teachers should retain autonomy over curriculum matters, but also delivered a predictive message that this would not always be the case in the future.[74]

In the context of this prediction it is highly significant that, directly after the appearance of the *Bullock Report*, politicians on both sides of the House called for centralised testing and monitoring of reading standards. On 26 February, eight days after the report had been released, C.R. Freud, the Labour member for the Isle of Ely, asked the Secretary of State for Education and Science whether he would seek an improved formula for testing all aspects of reading ability in place of the Watts-Vernon and National Survey Form 6 Reading Tests. Freud also inquired of the Secretary whether he accepted the *Bullock Report*'s recommendation that 1977 be a target date for the introduction of a new system to monitor reading and writing ability.[75] The following month saw Opposition Conservatives resume their attack, with Boyson and Fookes demanding that the Government take immediate steps to improve the training of teachers whilst encouraging infant schools to return to the teaching of literacy as its primary purpose. Joining the debate, St John-Stevas asked the Government to give priority to a monitoring system and go even further, to introduce national standards of reading, writing and mathematics so that the achievements and shortcomings of individual schools could be readily known.[76]

Thus, our historical examination of the developing debate over literacy standards in England suggests that Eccles' prediction was being clearly foreshadowed by the latter half of the 1960s and had become a distinct possibility by the mid-1970s. Moreover, the widening of the debate during this period also illustrates how educational and political themes tended to coalesce to the point where, by the early 1970s, a specific debate over literacy standards had become inexorably merged with a growing controversy over teacher accountability and curriculum control that would have a signal impact on English education over the next three decades.

Chapter 4

Post-*Bullock* reactions to a literacy crisis, 1975–1983

During the early 1970s, the publishing of the Black Papers had made a major contribution to a public perception of a crisis in education, and initiated a backlash against progressive teaching methods which united disparate groups, interests and cross-political affiliations. In early 1975, the Black Paper movement re-emerged in conjunction with the Conservative Party's own *Fight for Education* campaign[1] and an extensive newspaper coverage of issues associated with 'reading standards' in both the national broadsheets and tabloids.[2] By the mid-1970s, the 'Great Debate' and the accompanying media coverage were highlighting arguments against progressivism and the need to address falling literacy standards so that the fourth Black Paper 'was able to claim with satisfaction a wide realization that "education had not delivered the goods ... there was now a case that had to be answered"'.[3] This coverage, as we have seen in the previous chapter, ensured growing support for the need to measure educational standards, and the increasing claims by various groups that schools were failing to produce a literate workforce.

Re-emergence of the Black Papers

The release of the first Black Papers had involved a range of groups, ranging from academics and primary teachers to probation officers. Rhodes Boyson, the co-editor of the Black Paper, 1975 was a Conservative politician and MP for Brent North who had formerly been a headmaster in a secondary modern school and was serving as the chairman for the National Council for Educational Standards in 1974 when he published his book, *Crisis in Education.* In his opening statement in the first chapter of *Crisis in Education*, Boyson argued that 'The first of the three R's was and always will be reading' and that the radio and television would never replace 'the written word'. Initially he presented a preservationist stance, arguing that his concerns over reading standards were motivated by a concern over participation in democracy and the need to produce a cultured individual, because 'a person who cannot read is severely limited in his private, personal and leisure life' and 'In so many ways a person who cannot read cannot fully enjoy the freedoms available to others in our society'.[4]

However, as his arguments developed, there was an increasing emphasis upon the technical skills of reading and measurement of reading standards. He argued that there were three crises in literacy which result from falling standards where 'bright children are functioning below their mental age' and that 'adult literacy in 1970 is lower than in 1914 or even 1870'. Thus, while Boyson adhered to preservationist arguments, his predominant concern that standards have fallen led him to conclude with a technocratic solution which stressed 'basic literacy, numeracy' and skills as, without these, 'no cultural superstructure can be built'.[5]

While Boyson was clearly aligned to the Conservative Party, The Black Papers, 1975, like the earlier Black Papers, drew contributors from a mix of educationalists, writers, journalists and academics. As in the earlier papers, the authors came from a range of educational and political backgrounds with some ardently claiming to come from the left while others were conservative politicians. Iris Murdoch, a recognised writer and academic, clearly labelled herself as a 'socialist' in her paper; Brian Cox had worked as an academic since 1954 and was a former Labour Party supporter; Hans Jurgen Eysenck, another prominent academic, had left his native Germany in the 1930s where he had been anti-fascist, refused to join the Hitler Youth and fled the Nazi regime.[6]

The 'Black Paper Basics', listed in ten points on the first page of the document, indicate that they were drawn together by their critique of the impact of progressive reforms in education and calls for standards to promote freedom of speech, academic standards and 'open debate', and to guard against the ill effects of illiteracy and 'social engineering'.[7] There are similarities with earlier Black Papers in the contributors and attacks on progressivism and arguments for preservationist arguments for upholding a liberal curriculum and humanistic values. However, this later Black Paper highlights the increasingly central role that the issue of declining reading standards played in shaping the debate, as the critique shifted from an emphasis upon a cultural crisis, to increased demands that reading skills need to be addressed.

In the introductory 'Letter to MPs and Parents' it is noted that the Black Paper movement had been motivated by a 'justification by faith and not by works' and a false sense of achieving advances in reading standards in the Plowden era 'which were really invalid'.[8] Boyson's experience of chairing the National Council for Educational Standards is evident in the detailed account and use of surveys to support the claim that literacy standards were declining. For example, the Wells and Horton surveys of reading standards of eleven- and fifteen-year-olds are cited as indicating that literacy is declining so that 'Half the adult illiterates are below the age of 25'. There is also an increased call for politicisation and an enhanced sense of crisis in these later Black Papers, with calls to 'increase' the strength of the National Council for Educational Standards by regular bulletins and meetings so that we shall channel the great interest of parents to demand reform if all else fails.[9] Early chapters by Stuart Froome, an ex-member of the Bullock Committee, and George Weber, Executive Director, Council for Basic Education, also focused upon the decline of reading standards. Boyson's own chapter on vouchers together with Cox's chapter on examinations, and its arguments for national continuous assessment, foreshadowed themes that would come to dominate the curriculum developments in the 1980s.

In the House of Commons, R.A. McCrindle, the Conservative member for Brentwood and Ongar, asked Reginald Prentice, Labour's Secretary of State for Education and Science, what his policy was towards the proposals the Black Paper contained. When Prentice replied that he had found the document neither helpful nor constructive, McCrindle pointed out that given one of its contributors was herself a committed socialist, this was an indication that comprehensive education did not necessarily work in the best interests of the working-class child. Continuing the Opposition attack, Boyson asked:

> Is the Minister aware that the Black Paper was the sixth best selling paperback in the country, something which has never occurred to an educational document before? Whatever the Minister says, does not that show the degree of public discontent? Does he agree that, since practically all newspapers and periodicals reviewed and talked about the Black Paper at length and are still doing so, there is massive discontent? For a Government who talk about participation, might a participatory discussion and analysis of what the Black Paper says be to the advantage of the Government and the children of this country?[10]

Labour members too, were expressing concern over literacy standards. L. Carter-Jones, the Labour member for Eccles, for instance, asked how many LEAs had furnished information on the results of screening of children for reading ability at the end of their first stay at school, what tests were employed in the screening and what percentage were found to be still in need of remedial assistance. The official response drew a distinction between the screening of individual children for reading ability carried out by LEAs, for which there was no information available, and the national monitoring of standards.[11] Labour members also articulated a growing national concern over both the incidence of adult illiteracy and the allegedly poor reading skills of many secondary school leavers.

These issues had strong links to the growing press coverage of the standards debate initiated by the Black Paper editors earlier in 1975. Brian Cox was reported as arguing that the arguments against progressive education in the Black Papers have 'alerted parents to declining standards in schools'. He called for teachers to reassert their authority and return to 'formal reading instruction', and to turn away from child-centred methods in order to 'allow teachers to reassert their authority'.[12] Boyson repeated these arguments to stress his argument for the state to enforce better standards and was quoted as stating 'what matters in education are the standards achieved and not the years of attendance'.[13] Letters to the Editor and articles in the *Daily Telegraph* picked up these concerns with readers linking the concern over the 'lowering of school standards' into concerns over the failure of the comprehensive school system.[14]

Increasing politicisation of the reading standards debate

The increasingly politicised and alarmist nature of the reading standards debate was appropriately noted in the *TES*. The front page lead article on 31 October 1975 was evocatively entitled 'Broomsticks and bednobs and witch hunts galore'. The article lamented that 'this edition of the *TES* abounds in public inquiries and tribunals, in rancorous dissension among professional colleagues and in allegations of witch-hunts on the one hand and under-bedded reds on the other'.[15] It noted that the Tyndale inquiry had opened; that a dispute at Fircroft College had swapped allegations of paternalism with counter-allegations of radical militancy; that in Kent the LEA was sorting out a case of a teacher at odds with colleagues; whilst at South Bank Polytechnic, a dispute between staff and administrators represented yet another quarrel between the Association of Teachers in Technical Institutions and the Association of Polytechnic Tutors. The article somewhat wistfully concluded that:

> It almost seems as if it is no longer possible for good men and women to agree to disagree amicably; before anyone knows what has happened, the issues have grown out of all recognition, parties have formed behind one proposition or another, allegations of bad faith and professional malpractice are being tossed around with reckless abandon, and a case has been made out for the inevitable committee of inquiry, the appointment of which, in itself, is seen as victory for one or other party to the dispute. So the witches emerge from their covens and the reds creep out from their beds, exploiting a whole range of tensions which pre-exist their Halloween. And the long-suffering majority – who lack both the comforting simplified certainties of the authors of the *Rape of Reason*, and the ideological artillery of the new left – take refuge in the time-honoured public inquiry.[16]

Moreover, the debate, as reported in the *TES*, was clearly and inexorably shifting towards an emphasis upon reading and reading skills, rather than simply reflecting a concern over the cultured literate individual as embodied in the original preservationist stance. On 31 October, a report on a demand for immediate government action to improve reading standards in schools made at the National Council of Women's Annual Conference at Buxton, Derbyshire, by Sheila Penny, Chair of the Council's Education Committee, was largely concerned with implementing the recommendations of the Bullock Committee.[17] Less than a month later, however, the *TES* reported on the exchanges in the House during a recent education debate between the Labour Government's Secretary of State for Education, Fred Mulley, the Opposition Tory spokesman on education, Norman St John-Stevas, and the Conservative member for Plymouth, Drake, Janet Fookes. When Mulley touched briefly on the Government's promise to provide more money for sixteen-to-nineteen-year-old students, Fookes alleged that a friend serving on an LEA had told her that in his area FE colleges were holding remedial classes in English so that students could follow the courses. Fookes went on to claim that 'Education colleges had been too concerned with the philosophy of education and not enough with the practical craft of teaching'.[18]

This exchange between Mulley, St John-Stevas and Fookes furnishes further evidence that the literacy debate was becoming ever more narrowly focused on the teaching of reading skills rather than on any maintenance of cultural heritage through the promotion of academic standards. This trend was reflected in a drawn-out controversy in the *TES* correspondence column concerning the ILEA survey on secondary school literacy. On 7 November 1975, a *TES* article focused on a recent report to the school's subcommittee by Dr Eric Briault, the education officer for the ILEA, claiming that, contrary to the considerable amount of bad publicity centring on allegedly low reading standards in Inner-London secondary schools, poor readers had made remarkably good progress since leaving primary school. Braiult pointed out that, in 1973, the average reading standards of 26,000 inner-city children in one year group rose to ninety-eight on the EH2 reading comprehension test, only three points below the national average, whereas the same children whilst at primary school two years previously, in 1971, had averaged only 94.2.[19]

These claims, however, were soon to be publicly challenged. On 21 November, a letter appeared in the *TES* correspondence section written by G.E. Bookbinder, an educational psychologist with the City of Salford Education Department. Referring to the *TES* article of 7 November, Bookbinder expressed surprise that the report had been accepted at face value by the subcommittee, especially given that the results obtained were at great variance with estimates of teachers concerned. Bookbinder claimed that by uncritically accepting the results of the EH2 test, the subcommittee was implying that it had little confidence in the ability of ILEA secondary teachers to distinguish between average and poor readers. He also alleged that he and his colleagues had administered a similar NFER reading test, the EH1 reading vocabulary test, to 1,000 Salford fifteen-year-olds in 1973, getting unexpectedly high results. Bookbinder concluded, however, that the subsequent use of Holborn and other tests showed that EH1 overestimated the reading ability of most pupils. This had led them to reject it as a valid measure of reading attainment.[20]

Bookbinder's stance received support from a further report in the same *TES* issue. This report cited the view of Robert Vigars, leader of the Conservative Opposition on the ILEA. Vigars likewise criticised the claims of the ILEA literacy survey that poor readers made 'remarkably good progress' since being at secondary school. Some gains, he argued, were bound to occur anyway, but the fact that those tested were still three points below the national average was hardly a matter for congratulation.[21]

The matter was very far from being laid to rest, however. Some three weeks later, a letter to the editor of the *TES* from Harvey Hinds, Chairman of the ILEA Schools Subcommittee, appeared in print. This letter claimed that members had, in fact, decisively rejected Vigars' views by forty-one votes to seven. Hinds also emphasised that the survey in question showed that the reading standards of the year group entering secondary school had improved, and that secondary schools had been particularly successful in reducing the proportion of poor readers from 18.4 per cent to 13.2 per cent.[22] Moreover, two letters in this *TES* issue responded directly to the original letter by Bookbinder. In the first letter, Shipman, the ILEA Director of Research and Statistics, directly challenged Bookbinder's criticism of the subcommittee. Shipman asserted that the subcommittee was never faced with any choice between the academic views of educational theorists and the commonsense views of classroom teachers, as alleged by Bookbinder, because the results of a test programme administered outside the school could not be directly compared with assessments from teachers within a school. The second letter, by R. Sumner and P. Davies, of the NFER, conceded that the ILEA literacy report had drawn attention to the 'discrepancy' between test classification as 'poor reader' (a standard score of eighty or less), and teacher's estimates of the need for remedial help. Like Shipman, however, the NFER researchers warned that Bookbinder's comparison of EH1 scores in Salford with those from the Holborn Reading Scale was actually misleading, because the latter test had been first published in 1948 and was taken out of print in 1974.[23]

The following year was to see further politicisation of the reading standards debate, centring particularly on concerns over reading skills, and on critiques of child-centred approaches. It was in this climate that Labour moved inexorably towards the introduction of regular monitoring of standards. In April 1976, James Callaghan succeeded Harold Wilson as Labour Prime Minister. The new leader faced increasing pressure from within his own party for decisive action over education. The release of a report from a University of Lancaster research team headed by Neville Bennett was given considerable media coverage, with its claim that 'formal' methods of teaching were more effective than the informal type advocated in the *Plowden Report*.[24] In June, Gwilym Roberts, the Labour member for Cunnock, asked the Secretary of State for Education and Science if he would initiate an inquiry into the advantages and disadvantages of traditional and non-traditional teaching approaches.[25] Roberts undoubtedly spoke for many on both sides of the House when he claimed that those committed to comprehensive education had nevertheless become seriously worried about the detrimental impact of modern teaching methods on numeracy and literacy, particularly amongst working-class students.

Earlier that same day, however, Labour had already clearly signalled new measures for monitoring literacy standards. Hugh Jenkins, the Labour member for Putney, asked what proportion of children of parents in the professions were unable to read as compared to the children of unskilled workers, and what action was being taken to increase reading ability among children whose parents were in the lower socio-economic groups.[26] In response, Margaret Jackson revealed that the DES's Assessment of Performance Unit was 'looking at ways to provide a new national monitoring system, as suggested by the *Bullock Report*, so that the extent of this problem [could] be reviewed regularly'.[27]

Apparent confirmation of the need for such a system was not long in coming. In July 1976, the eagerly awaited *Aud Report* on the Tyndale affair appeared. Following this, teachers, schools and local authorities faced a powerful 'accountability' movement from both major political parties.[28] The whole Tyndale episode has been seen as having invoked complex issues such as the relationship between learning and the deliberate structuring of a child's activities; the links between progressivism, militant teachers and the radical Left; and the looming question of accountability in education.[29] In turn, traditional local autonomy over the curriculum, including the teaching of reading, was to be sharply called into question. The stage was thus set for direct government intervention in both the curriculum as a whole, and in literacy policy.

The impetus for government intervention was aided by an intensive attack on 'do-as-you-please teaching' and 'crumbling standards' launched by the *Daily Mail* during this period. Max Wilkinson, writing as the *Mail's* education correspondent, initially highlighted the standards issue with a whole-page article which compared educational standards in Germany with those in comprehensive schools in Britain. In this article, he argued: 'Too late we are finding that do-as-you-please teaching methods, contempt for exams and the doctrinaire pursuit of equality can lead into dangerous blind alleys'.[30]

This article was followed five days later by another article by Max Wilkinson in the *Daily Mail*. This two-page article had a large headline which took up a third of the front page. It announced that the government had hushed up a 'sensational report that suggests that educational standards in British schools have slipped drastically since the late 1960s'. The article claimed that a study which used intelligence tests to compare the GCSE results of two groups of students, one in 1968 and one in 1973, had shown that 'the average intelligence of those getting GCSE passes in 1973 was lower in all subjects', so that the conclusion was that standards had fallen in all subjects.[31] This claim was backed by the secretary of the Conservative Education Committee who argued that it supported claims from 'parents and employers and the universities' that there had been an exorable decline in the quality of standards confronting university lecturers and an 'appalling state of affairs in basic maths, English and Foreign languages' as the 'schools had lost the emphasis on old fashioned skills'. At the end of the article, it was noted, however, that a spokesman for the National Union of Teachers had pointed out that 'By every objective test, standards have improved enormously. It is the height of irresponsibility to draw exaggerated conclusions from selected quotations from an unpublished report.'[32] The release of the Tyndale Report resulted in a series of similar articles in the *Daily Mail* and *Daily Mirror* throughout July.[33] These articles argued that the Tyndale Report clearly indicated that the blame for 'crumbling standards' and 'mediocre pupils' rested firmly on progressive education.[34]

Clyde Chitty describes how the widespread debate in education prompted the Prime Minister to plan a significant speech on educational standards. In preparation for the forthcoming Callaghan speech, leading members of the Labour Government gave evidence, leading to the appearance of the so-called '*Yellow Book*', a confidential DES report on key issues which included the teaching of the 3Rs, and the place of formal assessment. Chitty, however, argues that edited extracts from the *Yellow Book* were deliberately leaked to the *TES* to 'prepare the educational world for the shock of the Callaghan speech' which endorsed viewpoints hitherto promoted by the Conservatives.[35]

The 15 October lead article in the *TES* supports this contention with its account of a widening literacy debate across party lines leading to Labour taking up many Tory arguments for improving reading skills, combating progressivism and increasing government control over education. The article described how the leaked DES report to the Prime Minister had suggested that the Department should have a greater say in deciding the curriculum of the nation's schools, and that this had in turn triggered angry protests from teachers' organisations.[36] A further article in the same *TES* issue alleged that the leaked report had been written in response to a request from the Prime Minister for a memo covering a number of current problems in education, including the teaching of the 3Rs in primary schools.[37] The *TES* article cited the report as having acknowledged concerns expressed in the press, and in response had posed questions such as: 'What has gone wrong?' and 'How is it to be put right?' The article further claimed that although the child-centred approaches advocated by Plowden were adopted in only a minority of schools, its general influence was widespread to the extent that:

> while primary teachers in general still recognize[d] the importance of formal skills, some ha[d] allowed performance in them to suffer as a result of the uncritical application of informal methods; and the time [was] almost certainly ripe for a corrective shift of emphasis.[38]

A week later, *TES* carried the full text of Callaghan's speech on education at a foundation-stone laying ceremony at Ruskin College. This landmark event provided a clear public announcement that the Labour Government had now taken up the debate over literacy standards. After praising the adult residential college with its strong trade union connections, and alluding to the success of the recent adult literacy campaign, the Prime Minister expressed concern that new recruits for industry sometimes did not have the basic tools to do the job. Whilst Callaghan did not lay the blame solely on schools, he did refer to 'the unease felt by parents and teachers about the new informal methods of teaching which seem[ed] to produce excellent results when they [were] in well-qualified hands but [were] much more dubious in their effects when they [were] not'. Callaghan also emphasised that his remarks were not meant to be 'a clarion call to Black Paper prejudices', nor a demand for a basic curriculum (although he was inclined to think that there should be one), but rather that it would be advantageous if these concerns were aired, 'shortcomings righted or fears put to rest'.[39]

Although the Prime Minister's speech incorporated Tory views on the perceived literacy crisis in the early 1970s, the emphasis was on the need for improving literacy skills for the workforce rather than a targeted attack upon progressive educational methods through an uncritical endorsement of the Black Papers. *TES* commentary on the speech both supported Callaghan's call for raising literacy standards but critiqued what it regarded as a blatant 'popularist' appeal by the Prime Minister. The *TES* argued that the much-heralded speech was anticlimatic. It dodged the question of whether the Prime Minister really thought standards were rising or falling; whistled up 'weasel words to exploit popular prejudices', and sought to divert popular indignation from his own management of the economy, to teachers' management of curriculum. However, the *TES* went on to state:

> There it is, however – a major speech by a Prime Minister to serve notice on the schools that they are accountable to the public, and can reasonably be expected to give an account of their stewardship. But he also set out – less brutally, perhaps, than he originally intended – to cut the teachers down to size, and assert some bluff, plain man attitudes to primary school teaching methods, basic standards of achievement, and education for industry and technology.[40]

Other newspaper commentaries also highlighted the raising of standards and a need to improve the 3Rs as key aspects of the Prime Minister's speech. *The Daily Mail* headed its report of the Prime Minister's speech with '3Rs must come first, says Jim',[41] while the front-page report in the *Daily Telegraph* quoted Callaghan as declaring that 'We cannot be satisfied with maintaining existing standards let alone observe any decline' and that he 'personally favoured a "basic curriculum" although he did not intend to become enmeshed in such problems'.[42]

Mindful of the Prime Minister's speech, and under intense pressure in the House, Labour's Secretary of State for Education and Science, Shirley Williams, promised to promote further debate on schools, curricula and standards, 'to which all concerned with the education service [could] contribute'.[43] In response to repeated questioning, Williams revealed that:

> during the next three or four months I intend to discuss the school curriculum and the maintenance of educational standards with organizations representing teachers, their employers, industry and the TUC. These discussions will be followed early next year by wider consultation on specific proposals. The Government's policy on curricula and standards in schools will be announced as soon as possible thereafter.[44]

Williams denied, however, any intention to seek new legislation to control or alter school curricula, pointing out that, in the case of reading, the *Bullock Report* had already inquired into precisely this matter.[45] She also firmly rejected Opposition proposals for introducing legislation that would prevent anyone from leaving school without a mastery of basic literacy or numeracy, on the grounds that such legislation was impracticable.[46]

Further confirmation of the extent to which the standards issue had become politicised came when the final issue of the *TES* for 1976 again shifted from an endorsement of literacy basics, to a more critical stance on the politics of educational debate. Reviewing the key educational events of 1976, the lead article conceded that Williams had succeeded in putting education back into the news, but it also argued that she was 'doing this in a way which divert[ed] attention from resources and organisation (where the Government is vulnerable) to aims and curriculum content, where everybody has a view and is dying to express it, and where the scapegoats are more likely to be the teachers than the Government'. The paper went on to argue that this was a 'populist trick as old as democracy', but there was no reason 'why the professionals should accept the myth that they stole the curriculum: in truth, the teachers were left carrying the can for the public curriculum because the politicians and the public were only too happy to turn it over to them'.[47]

In July 1977, the Government presented its long-awaited Green Paper on education. Entitled *Education in Schools*, this forty-five-page document with a joint foreword by Williams and the Secretary of State for Wales, John Morris, assessed the present state of schools in England and Wales and made recommendations for their future development.[48] Introducing the Green Paper in the House of Commons, Williams emphasised that whilst the Government rejected any idea of a centralised curriculum, it nevertheless invited all those with responsibility for schools to consider whether pupil aspirations and national needs were being adequately met. The Green Paper also raised, once again, the whole question of school accountability, along with the need for a comprehensive system of assessment for both schools and pupils. Whilst the movement of HMI towards quantitative analyses of school performance was acknowledged, reference was also made to the needs of local authorities to identify problems in school performance and to take remedial reaction. The development of diagnostic tests and greater consistency of practice in their use was to be encouraged, whilst further consideration was to be given to the concept of a leaving certificate for all pupils. At the same time, the Green Paper warned that 'league tables' based on standardised tests used in isolation could be misleading, and it firmly rejected the view that universal national testing of basic literacy and numeracy was desirable.[49] Nevertheless, the Green Paper conceded that 'In some schools the curriculum has been overloaded, so that the basic skills of literacy and numeracy, the building blocks of education, have been neglected'.[50] It also warned that while child-centred approaches had become widespread and frequently beneficial, this had:

> ...proved to be a trap for some less able or experienced teachers who applied the freer methods uncritically or failed to recognize that they require careful planning of the opportunities offered to children and systematic monitoring of the progress of individuals. While the majority of primary teachers, whatever approach they use, recognize the importance of performance in basic skills such as reading, spelling and arithmetic, some have failed to achieve satisfactory results in them. In some classes, or even some schools, the use of the child-centred approach has deteriorated into lack of order and application.[51]

The mixed 'carrot-and-stick' tone of the Green Paper served an overtly political purpose. Whilst the Opposition attacked the Green Paper as having not gone sufficiently far, particularly in the matter of parental choice, Labour was able to counter such criticism by arguing that the measures it was foreshadowing 'emphasized the importance which the Government attach to basic literacy and numeracy'.[52]

Moreover, further monitoring measures were soon to follow. In November 1977, DES circular 14/77 was sent out, asking LEAs to report on their arrangements for promoting English and mathematics within the school curriculum. In addition, the Assessment of Performance Unit (APU), originally set up in 1975 to undertake the systematic collection of objective information about specific aspects of the performance of pupils in schools nationally, had conducted its first surveys of subject performance in 1978, with plans well advanced for mathematics and English language surveys in 1979.[53] In September 1978, the DES published *Progress in Education*, which reported on recent initiatives undertaken by the DES and the Government.[54] The document reflected four broad themes that had been seen to dominate recent debate and policy in education: extending educational opportunity and participation, improving the quality of education, managing the system in the face of declining roll numbers and providing educational support for the Government's industrial strategy.[55] It was claimed that HMI had 'undertaken two of the most searching reviews ever conducted of primary and secondary education on the ground'. The DES was to publish a survey of primary education later in the year that would include the latest in a series of NFER surveys designed to assess reading standards in the primary schools.[56] A preliminary examination, however, had suggested that reading performance had steadily improved since 1955.[57]

It is, therefore, somewhat ironic that when the Conservatives came to power under Margaret Thatcher in May 1979, the new Government was able to cite these measures, enacted under their Labour predecessors, in defence of their own literacy policy. That the debate over declining literacy standards was always highly politicised was further underlined by the response to an early parliamentary question regarding which LEAs made assessments of reading. In reply, Boyson was able to state that replies from 14/77 showed that results from reading tests administered to a national sample of eleven-year-olds was consistent with a rising trend in standards between 1955 and 1976–1977.[58] Such an answer was, as we have previously seen, almost identical to those given by his many predecessors. In debates over reading standards, party politics were to be, henceforth, a major ingredient in shaping and defining debate.

The Thatcher years

In May 1979, the Conservatives swept into power under Margaret Thatcher. Mark Carlisle became Secretary of State for Education and Science, with Boyson as one of the two Ministry Under-Secretaries. Asked by a colleague to make a statement on the new Government's progress towards implementing its policy of national standards of literacy and numeracy in schools, Boyson reiterated that the Government's aim was to promote the highest possible standards of achievement in these key areas. This was to be reflected in both the proposals for a curriculum framework at secondary level, and the monitoring programme of the Department's Assessment of Performance Unit (APU).[59]

While there was little coverage of reading and literacy issues in the tabloid press in the early 1980s compared to the extensive coverage during the mid-1970s, discussions of falling standards and the links to progressive education continued to appear periodically in the *TES*. Claims that standards were falling were being more actively refuted by educationalists and researchers during this period. Evidence that the latest recruitment tests given by employers was failing to substantiate a fall in standards was also cited on the front page of the *TES* as placing claims of falling standards in doubt.[60] The authors of the ORACLE report, Maurice Galton and Brian Simon, argued that their research, a systematic and prolonged investigation of both pupils and teachers engaged in classroom activities, supported a recent HMI primary survey which had found that there was a 'heavy concentration on basic skills'. Galton and Simon argued that the ORACLE project 'gives no support what ever to the generalized charges leveled at schools'.[61]

Yet, despite these counter-attacks on the claims that standards were falling, the Education Group at the Centre for Contemporary Cultural Studies in Birmingham, writing in the *TES* in mid-1981, saw education in the 1980s as a 'grotesque inversion' of a previous utopian vision that left the 'economanics' firmly installed in power with 'educationalists, teachers and egalitarians in the wilderness'. In their view the 'depopulated ventriloquism of the mass media' had redefined political citizenship and democratic participation into the 'mean and self regarding doctrine of "parental choice"'.[62] They argued that there had been a 'rightwing change' instigated by the Black Papers who had been 'hand-in-hand' with the tabloid press in the 1970s.[63]

Galton and Simon and other writers in the *TES* during 1980 and 1981 drew attention to the links between the rise of these concerns over standards and the preceding debates surrounding the Black Papers, Callaghan's speech, the *Yellow Book*, and the Tyndale episode which had contributed to the 'Great Debate' of the 1970s. Max Morris and John Kirkham and an unnamed 'LEA advisor' argued that the 1970s had been a decade of criticism of schools in the public arena from a diverse range of non-educational groups 'such as politicians, the captains of industry and commerce, the press, social workers, and policy and any one else who cared to pitch in'. It was noted that there had been a shift from a liberal to a skills-based, centralised curriculum in the previous decade and the writers predicted that this would usher in a decade of curriculum revision during the 1980s. The LEA advisor, in particular, argued that the most significant document (with hindsight, seen to be the 1977 Green Paper) 'looked suspiciously like a collection of skills' and reflected the need to be justified in economic terms despite phrases which espoused the individual experiences of the child.[64]

These three commentators also argued that the key change arising from the debates over standards during the 1970s would be 'curriculum reassessment' and 'revision', which they predicted 'will be clearly made a major item on the educational agenda for the next decade, *irrespective of resources*'. They also argued that the revision of the curriculum would be a major item on the agenda of both parties and that 'the consequent pressures on schools [would] be strong, as the curriculum restructuring [would] be accompanied by cuts designed to reduce educational provision permanently to a level far below previous expectations'.[65]

The Conservative Government, as they had indicated in their election manifesto, were committed to more national assessment. This was seen to be directly linked to the public concern 'about standards in the past 10 years' which had 'led to a significant increase in the amount of testing done by LEAs', most of whom were involved in 'testing of one sort or another'.[66] Early in 1980, Lady Young, the junior Education Minister responsible for schools, was reported as wanting an 'early warning system to catch the children who now turn up in secondary school remedial reading groups'. She was supported in this aim by the Department of Education and Sciences Assessment of Performance Unit who had gone on record as stating that 'The APU will set national standards in reading, writing and arithmetic monitored by tests worked out with teachers and applied locally by education authorities'.[67]

LEAs were invited to consider implementing an educational voucher scheme (later abandoned) to permit parents a greater degree of choice in selecting an appropriate school for their children. At the same time, the government proposals for 1980–1981 included an overall reduction in educational expenditure of some 3.5 per cent. It was this apparent anomaly in its policy regarding educational standards that brought the Government under immediate fire. The emphasis of subsequent debates throughout the 1980s largely centred on the impact of static or dwindling educational funding, and government attempts to counter Opposition attacks.

In contrast to the last years of the Labour Government, literacy during the Thatcher years became an issue largely in the context of the funding and resourcing of schools. In April 1980, a Government White Paper announced that the Government's plans for the next five years were to decrease the teaching force by 67,000 teachers and to cut £820 million from the education budget. It was predicted that this would result in spending targets that were up to 10 per cent less than envisaged by the previous Labour Government. It was also noted that the areas that would be badly affected were to be the under-fives and adult education.[68] Following this announcement came reports that the teaching cuts were directly affecting part-time women teachers which posed a direct threat to a drive to raise literacy standards, as many of these part-time teachers were employed to support individuals who needed to develop basic skills.[69] Adult literacy programmes were also suffering under these cutbacks; the cut in budgets had resulted in local councils being unable to pay for adult literacy programmes from their budgets.[70]

From the beginning of the first Conservative term in office, the Labour Opposition focused on the detrimental impact educational cuts would have on existing standards of literacy and numeracy. Thus, the Labour member for West Stirlingshire, P.A. Canavan, argued that if the Government was seriously intent on improving educational standards in these crucial areas, then why was more money not being provided to reduce class sizes in state schools rather than giving £60 million of public money to a minority of parents who wished to send their children to selective, fee-paying schools? Neil Kinnock then pointed out that, as the educational cuts resulted in a £4.5 million cut in capitation on books, the equivalent in real terms of a 26 per cent cut in expenditure on school books, it was not credible for the Secretary to claim that educational standards were not being undermined.[71]

In response to targeted attacks in parliament, the Government increasingly emphasised the role of systematic monitoring in maintaining literacy and numeracy standards. Reacting to a question from a colleague regarding what arrangements were being made for testing the reading progress of primary school pupils, Boyson claimed that 'Carefully constructed and well administered tests [could] play a useful part in the assessment of children's development at different stages of their education'. In addition to the testing programmes administered by local authorities, APU monitoring surveys would measure pupils' levels of performance in language and mathematics on a national scale at the end of the primary stage of education and again at fifteen.[72]

In particular, the Government envisaged the APU playing a key role in both promoting the development of methods of assessment, and in monitoring school performance, through the contracting out of services. Queried as to the unit's function, Boyson pointed out that:

> The assessment of performance unit promotes the development of methods of assessing and monitoring the achievement of children at school, and seeks to identify the incidence of under-achievement. The unit itself consists of five full-time and five part-time staff. It commissions universities and research bodies to undertake the development of test materials and the administration of surveys on its behalf.[73]

In early 1981, however, an HMI report entitled, was released that cast considerable doubt on the Government's strategies for raising standards in basic literacy and numeracy. This report claimed that standards of achievement in basic subjects were being jeopardised by larger classes, less individualised attention, and fewer teachers, whilst those with remedial needs suffered additional difficulties. As a result of these claims, Carlisle in particular came under intense attack from the Opposition. Kinnock demanded an immediate response when he asked: 'If the standards of provision and performance are not directly related, why has the Secretary of State got something to hide about the publication of information on the impact of cuts on standards in schools which is already available to him from Her Majesty's Inspectorate?'[74]

Less than two months later, Kinnock forced a vigorous debate on the issue of educational standards, moving:

That this House, recognizing the direct relationship between the maintenance and enhancement of educational standards and an appropriate investment of resources and the fundamental importance of this investment in the struggle for national economic recovery notes with grave concern the Report by Her Majesty's Inspectorate on 'The effects on the educational service in England of Local Authority Expenditure Policies – Financial Year 1980–81 – and calls upon Her Majesty's Government to undertake positive action to safeguard standards of provision, opportunity and performance in education.[75]

The subsequent debate proved to be both long and bitter. Whilst the motion was eventually lost, the Opposition was able to further embarrass the Government by referring to a document published in the *TES* of 30 January 1981 entitled, 'Manifesto for change'. This document castigated the reduction in teachers as self-defeating and had been signed by a number of distinguished people, including the father of the 1944 Act, Lord Butler, and the sitting Conservative member for Ealing North, Harry Greenway.[76]

The Government, moreover, was now obliged to defend school literacy standards rather than attack them. This necessitated the Government falling back on the very HMI reports upon which its members had previously cast doubt whilst in opposition. Thus, in response to a question on levels of literacy in Scotland, the Secretary of State for Scotland, A.M. Fletcher, asserted:

The foundations of literacy must of course be laid in school and I am satisfied that this is being done. Her Majesty's Inspectors' report on the education of pupils with learning difficulties, published in 1978, showed that very few primary or secondary pupils experienced learning difficulties because of inadequate basic literacy skills. The report by Her Majesty's Inspectors on learning and teaching in primary 4 and primary 7, published in August 1980, showed that high standards in basic literacy were being maintained in primary schools.[77]

The HMI report on *The Effects of Local Authority Expenditure on the Education Services in England 1981* showed an apparent marginal deterioration in educational standards. An editorial in the *TES*, on 9 March 1981, noted that 'HMIs have once again reported that the standard of provision is getting more uneven' and that the message of the report was that 'cuts in resources are leading to declining standards of education' as 'it is not possible to maintain standards, let alone improve them without increasing the resources per child as pupil numbers fall'.[78] The editorial warned Keith Joseph, who was Carlisle's immediate successor, that it was now time to act upon the message from Her Majesty's Inspectors.

HMI surveys were also used during this period by the teaching profession to defend their teaching methods. Len Marsh, the chairman of the National

Association for Primary Education to rebut Rhodes Boyson's continuing allegations that informal teaching methods had 'wasted time and money' leaving 'children less disciplined and weaker in the 3Rs'. Marsh argued that the HMI surveys gave 'the lie to this "crude generalization" as they showed the dangers that lay in over-caution and in over-traditional teaching'.[79]

This situation resulted in Sir Keith Joseph facing questions in parliament regarding his Government's apparent ambivalence over standards of literacy and numeracy. When the Labour member for Holborne and St Pancras South, F.G. Dobson, asked him whether he proposed to provide additional resources to counter the threat to the maintenance of literacy and numeracy standards identified by the HMI report of March 1982, Sir Keith replied that the existing grant provided for 1982–1983 was sufficient to maintain adequate standards. Dobson, however, responded to this by drawing a stark contrast between the recent Conservative pledges to improve educational standards, and its subsequent disregard for adverse HMI reports as well as the recommendations of an all-party Select Committee since they had assumed office.[80]

One Government strategy to counter allegations of falling standards due to dwindling resources was to draw upon a growing body of literature on school effectiveness that appeared to contradict arguments based on social class. Thus, when asked if he would institute a survey of educational stand-ards in city schools in relation to the nature of their catchment areas, Boyson expressed considerable gratitude at having Professor Michael Rutter's book, *Fifteen Thousand Hours*, drawn to his attention by a parliamentary colleague, as this showed that 'between matched schools, the poorest 25 per cent of children in academic ability were doing better than the top 25 per cent in a neighbouring school'. Furthermore Rutter's book, claimed Boyson, made it clear that 'with the same resources and teaching formula, the difference in achievement between schools with the same intake is tremendous, according to the commitment to the school of the head teacher and the staff and their agreement on the methods to be used'.[81]

A further Government strategy, and one which the Conservatives had pursued whilst in Opposition, was to re-focus teacher training methods away from theoretical considerations, towards classroom competence and practical experience. In March 1983, the Government introduced a White Paper setting out Government policy to improve teaching quality in English and Welsh schools through the more efficient use of existing resources. Introducing the White Paper, Sir Keith pointed out that initial training courses would now be funded on the basis of 'explicit criteria'. Newly trained teachers would, in addition to being expected to have greater know-ledge and expertise in the subjects they were to teach, would require more practical experience and would have to provide satisfactory evidence of class-room competence, whilst training institutions would have to demonstrate that their staff possessed recent successful experience of classroom teaching.

Bert Lodge, reporting in the *TES*, noted that the White Paper's proposals on teacher training had struck an 'especially familiar chord', but despite this there were 'doubts that progress would be made with raising the quality of the teaching force without the injection of more funds to release teachers from the class room'. Lodge noted that Sir Keith had ruled out the possibility of extra money to implement the plans.[82]

In 1983, all reports by HMI were published and these included assessments of reading for individual schools. This in turn led to a greater scrutiny, 'new worries', moves towards 'serious curriculum planning' and drives for national assessment as the reports 'allowed armchair tourists to explore the highways and byways of education system in astonishing detail, reading about staffing, teaching and resources' across the educational sector.[83] As the reports began to be published, and also became available free of charge from the Department of Education and Science, they were interpreted as calling for better curriculum planning, and higher expectations, as well as more changes for children to learn through experience and discussion. Individual schools were commented upon in relation to the English and literacy curriculum, but this was alongside comments on other areas of the curriculum, so that the emphasis became increasingly upon the need for planning and depth across the curriculum.[84]

By mid-1983, Sir Keith had developed another strategy to control the debate over standards and to any deflect criticism arising from the increased ability to pin-point the assessment procedures and difficulties faced by funding cuts. The *TES* reported that he would now 'unusually devote some attention to the primary school curriculum' and the ways in which parents could contribute. He also stressed the importance of centralisation and local government relationships.[85] This was followed by an announcement that the primary schools in the Inner-London Education Authority would be scrutinised by an HMI-led inquiry which would examine curriculum organisation to examine under-achievement of working-class children in the capital. The *TES* linked this inquiry to Sir Keith's statements that 'he was growing more concerned about improving standards in primary schools to ensure they had high expectations and stretched children to their full abilities'.[86]

At the 1983 Labour Local Government Conference it was announced that there was a strong probability that the Labour Party's next manifesto would introduce national standards for education and other social services.[87] The governing Conservative Party began to expand the HMI 'in line with the Government's view that numbers should be brought up to strength "as a matter of urgency" in order to secure higher standards'.[88] This drive for accountability also extended to school records and psychologists' reports, which had previously been confidential, being opened up to allow inspection by parents and guardians.[89]

Over the rest of the 1980s there was no real peaking of concern over literacy in parliament and the press. There were, however, periodic Opposition attacks on the Government over its apparently contradictory policy of claiming to be primarily concerned with maintaining high standards of literacy and numeracy, whilst at the same time keeping a tight control on educational funding. The increasing move towards the systemisation and centralisation and of assessment and standards in the early 1980s gradually moved the debate over literacy standards to a focus upon educational standards in general, as both major parties began to focus more specifically upon national standards. A specific focus on literacy and reading standards would emerge again after the establishment of the National Curriculum in the early 1990s.

However, while it may have appeared that there was a uniform move towards centralisation and control of the curriculum, there were tensions and struggles as competing power groups with conflicting ideologies struggled for control. Writing at the end of 1983, Denis Lawton noted that the apparent unity of purpose within the education authorities concealed growing tensions as politicians, bureaucrats and HMIs sought to impose their differing ideologies:

> it is a mistake to think of the DES as a monolith single-mindedly tightening its grip on the school curriculum. Although the trend towards centralized policies continued, the department's apparent unity of purpose concealed growing tensions as politicians, bureaucrats and HMIs sought to impose their differing ideologies ... For example, on curriculum we might differentiate between the politico's addition to standards; the DES (officials') concern for core and options the HMI desire for a common curriculum ... On the Assessment of Performances Unit, the politicians' view might be something like a return to 'payment by results'. The DES would be concerned with monitoring the schools and the general questions of efficiency; whereas the HMI would see the APU as a means of improving the curriculum. I am suggesting the central authority should be treated as a 'tension system' rather than a unified consensual group.[90]

Conclusion

Michael Apple has recently argued that the work of Kliebard, whose insights have helped to inspire this book, demonstrates how the history of curriculum debates has 'consistently involved major conflicts and alliances among groups with competing visions of "legitimate" knowledge, what counts as "good" teaching and learning and what is a "just society"'.[91] It is these ongoing struggles and allegiances which can be seen to constantly shape the terrain of curriculum policy and practice. The public debate over literacy and 'falling standards' during the 1970s and early 1980s clearly illustrates the process of struggle and alliance between what educational historians have termed internal 'clientist' groups within the education authorities formed by the 1944 Education Act, and external pressure groups.[92]

This period also illustrates how the dynamics and interactions between and within groups with differing visions of literacy education can change wider political dynamics and influence views of how the curriculum should be taught, assessed and utilised to produce a just society. It also highlights the role that these views play in the formation of wider allegiances, shifts in power blocks and the possibility of new alliances and power blocks which came to change the overall aims of education from the 1970s through to the early 1980s.

The 1970s began with a dominant concern amongst external pressure groups who held preservationist views. These views advocated 'higher standards' in terms of preservationist and traditional views of what it is to be literate. This viewpoint was initially held by a disparate group who ranged from conservative dissidents such as Rhodes Boyson to socialist-affiliated authors and academics such as Iris Murdoch. Their ability to make a popularist appeal through published texts and the press enabled them to influence public opinion and trigger a perceived crisis in literacy standards. Ironically the very success of their allegiance led to an emphasis on social efficiency and instrumental approaches, rather than a humanist-based perservationist vision of the literacy curriculum. The very success of the public campaign and strong alliances between the various pressure groups ensured political coherence amongst the two main political parties, which resulted in a consensus that enabled a skills-based approach, which focused upon technique rather than culturally derived values. Along with and supporting this approach came measurement, accountability, standardisation and central management to detract and allay the fears of a continuing literacy crisis and 'falling literacy standards'.

The perceived literacy crisis of the 1970s was, therefore, a key element in shifting power away from traditional educational bureaucracies to a neo-liberal and neo-conservative stress on consumer choice and 'market forces' in public education. It has been noted that the post-war period can be described as a period where policy was 'effectively determined between the unions and the Local Education authorities with the third, passive party being the Department of Education and Science'. The public crisis over literacy standards had helped to ensure that this process would be overturned as it demonstrated the power of outside pressure groups to impact upon the curriculum and the school system. The stage was set for a restructuring of the curriculum and the intrusion of outside pressure groups into educational policy-making and the processes that would lead to the National Curriculum and testing becoming embodied in the 1988 Education Act.

Chapter 5

The renewed reading standards debate of the early 1990s

This chapter examines the renewed debate over reading standards in the Commons and in the national press during the early-to-mid-1990s. In it we argue that this debate not only facilitated a commonsense consensus that literacy standards were low, but also a belief that progressivist pedagogy had unduly impacted upon schools and their underlying purpose. The debate was, therefore, an important catalyst in the emergence of a new dominant narrative in the literacy curriculum and pedagogy that came to replace earlier child-centred ideals. Thus, this period was to witness the final overturning of the earlier child-centred vision of primary teachers, which focused upon the individual child, learning through play, child development and readiness for learning, and its replacement by a technicist narrative. This narrative stressed basic skills of literacy and numeracy controlled by market mechanisms. As we shall see, the media debate which developed in the early 1990s helped to ensure that this narrative would become imbedded in the subsequent New Labour directive to the Literacy Task Force that a national literacy strategy be developed, aimed at 'substantially raising standards of literacy in primary schools in England over a five to ten year period'.[1]

In this chapter, then, we will argue that the public debates over 'falling reading standards' in the early 1990s contributed to the forming of a particular context and set of constraints that continued the process that Ball[2] has identified as being implicit in the implementation of the National Curriculum. Widespread public acceptance of the view that standards were falling and that drastic steps needed to be taken to replace the use of 'progressive' methods with a formal, skills-based focus upon the basics in literacy helped continue the process by which teachers were 'reduced to agents of policies which are decided elsewhere'.[3]

Initiating the narrative: the public outcry over 'The biggest drop in literacy standards for 40 years'

The beginning of the 1990s was to be marked by a further literacy crisis that was to demand a much more comprehensive and far-reaching range of governmental responses. This time, the focus was to shift towards the methods of reading instruction and the quality of courses in the teaching of reading during Initial Teacher Training (ITT) rather than centring largely on the impact of educational funding cuts on literacy standards. In June 1990, a group of educational psychologists released data based on reading tests on seven-year-olds in nine LEAs that appeared to indicate a significant decline in reading standards since 1985.[4] One of them, Martin Turner, an educational psychologist at the London Borough of Croydon, was to become a pivotal figure in the subsequent reading debate.

The allegations by the psychologists gained immediate nationwide press coverage, and this was followed by a widespread public outcry over 'falling literacy standards'. Press reports largely tended to support the view that there had been a dramatic decline in reading standards. In turn, the press appears to have been utilised by politicians to convey an impression of swift, effective action in order to meet the crisis. In June 1990, the *TES* carried a front-page story reporting that Turner had found that tests among seven-year-olds had shown 'the biggest drop in reading standards for more than 40 years'. It was further revealed that 'secret data collected by a cross-section of nine local education authorities' had indicated that 'average reading scores fell from 100 in 1985 to 96.80 in 1989.[5] A further *TES* article reported the Education Secretary, John MacGregor, as expressing his concern over the methods of teaching reading and the economic implications of falling reading standards.[6]

Some newspaper reports even appeared to give credence to the view that LEAs were deliberately suppressing information and data. In the event, this had the effect of giving renewed support to the Government's plans to introduce national tests at the ages of seven, eleven, fourteen and sixteen. Thus, even in the normally Left-Liberal-leaning *Guardian*, it was maintained that data released by Turner and the other psychologists in the reports showed that parents had a right to know how their children were progressing.[7] This article also lent support to a growing conviction that teachers' behaviour should be more carefully monitored through the introduction of national testing. It was pointed out that without national tests it was not possible to provide genuine comparative results, as some LEAs had not carried out any testing of seven-year-olds. Even those that had done so used different methods, making comparisons difficult. Whilst it was conceded that tests were being used at a greater rate than ever before, they were not coordinated. Neither were most external tests linked to the normal work of teachers.[8]

The initial media attention was followed by Turner's publication of a report entitled *Sponsored Reading Failure: an Object Lesson* (1990) which aimed to justify the earlier claims.[9] This report, based on reading test results from nine LEAs 'assembled voluntarily by concerned professionals', argued that reading standards had suffered a serious decline across the southern half of England and perhaps throughout Britain by the early 1990s.[10] The reason, Turner claimed, lay in the introduction of a whole language/real book 'new methods' based approach to teaching reading. Its main instigators were 'two North American gurus who, for purposes of glory like to appear severally, but who to weather obloquy might prefer to be lumped together: Frank Smith and Kenneth Goodman'.[11] The approach was anti-formal reading instruction, anti-phonics teaching, anti-dyslexia, anti-testing and anti-formalism. Its child-centred philosophy 'produces strikingly opposite effects: working-class children are disproportionately disadvantaged by middle-class romanticism'.[12] The political conditions of local government, without accountability, had 'sponsored' this adoption and this needed to be addressed. The solutions, argued Turner, lay in a plurality of curricula and syllabi, competing 'in a free market in which the prize [was] excellence'. Whilst Turner believed that the National Curriculum should not be mandatory, he nevertheless advocated a clear national framework for assessment, including 'independent testing at 7 and 11 in "toolkit" areas only: writing (to include reading) and number skills'.

It could be argued that the extent of political concern which followed the publication of Turner's report was provoked, not only by his claims of wide-spread reading failure, but also by his willingness to make direct links with other contemporary educational issues such as the longstanding debate over progressivism, current concerns over dyslexia, continuing social class inequalities and the need for national testing and assessment. Certainly, doubts regarding the efficacy of the data presented did not prevent Turner's claims being 'taken seriously in the Tory Party'. A revamp and reshuffle of junior ministers in the weeks following his revelations was linked to 'the current panic about schools'.[13] The Education Secretary also announced that inspectors visiting primary schools in the following months would focus upon the teaching of reading.[14] In September, two months after the revelations were published, the Education Secretary ordered new investigations into reading standards in primary schools. The inspectorate and the School Examinations and Assessment Council were to report to him on the assessment of standards by December. A meeting was also arranged between the Education Secretary and Turner to discuss the evidence published in Turner's *Sponsored Reading Failures*, the Independent Primary and Secondary Education Trust. Turner had already met with the Labour education team and Jack Straw, Labour's educational spokesman, had been reported as stating there were serious grounds for concern.[15]

Turner's allegations, that particular methods dominated the teaching of reading to the detriment of standards, was also reflected in questions raised in the House of Commons. On 10 July 1990, the Secretary of State for Wales, Sir Wyn Roberts, was asked how prevalent the 'look-and-say technique' of teaching reading was in Welsh schools. He replied that the technique was used in many schools, but that teachers were eclectic in their teaching, selecting the method that best suited the needs of individual children. It was, he claimed, 'unusual to find schools exclusively committed to one method of teaching children to read'.[16] The following day, however, Straw asked the Secretary of State for Education and Science to place a note in the library of the House summarising the main evidence and conclusions of the psychologists.

Straw also asked the Secretary what conclusions HMI had come to regarding the claims. The Secretary's initial response was simply to claim that the information available provided an insufficient basis to support firm conclusions that reading standards had significantly fallen.[17] However, with public concern growing,[18] the Opposition continued to press the government to unveil a comprehensive strategy for dealing with the crisis. Asked yet again on 25 July 1990 what action he intended to take to establish facts about reading standards among seven-year-olds, McGregor was obliged to admit that inquiries to LEAs from his Department revealed that local authorities did not have consistent policies of testing reading skills. Consequently he still could neither substantiate nor disprove claims of a fall in national standards. McGregor, however, did indicate that the National Curriculum would remedy the current lack of information about reading skills. National Curriculum assessment arrangements provided for the reading skills of all pupils to be annually assessed against 'clearly defined statutory criteria at the ages of seven, 11, 14 and 16', with the first national assessment of seven-year-olds scheduled for 1991. In the meantime, the Secretary announced two measures. HMI was invited to focus on the teaching of reading in their autumn primary school inspections next term, and to report back to him. The Secretary also asked the School Examinations and Assessment Council (SEAC) to examine the evidence held by LEAs.[19]

The narrative develops: towards a regulation and assessment regime

Both major political parties appear to have been thoroughly aware of the opportunities the renewed reading debate presented to market themselves as strong supporters of educational standards through regular monitoring procedures. By early 1991, Kenneth Clarke was overtly using the concern over reading standards that had been generated by Turner's report to support national testing. He argued that 'it was deplorable that reading standards were unsatisfactory in one of five primary schools'. He reminded parents that they needed to 'find out about their children's reading standards, and to participate in helping improve them'.[20]

Fairly early on in the debate, commentators recognised that the psychologists' revelations also offered the Opposition Labour Party an opportunity to find a 'fundamental issue which would strike at the heart of the electorate. The issue of 'educational standards' could provide 'the killer punch against the Tories and help Labour regain power', as it was 'more punchy than constitutional reform and would steal the Tories' threadbare clothes from off their backs'.[21] This potential for the debate over reading standards and teaching methods to embarrass the ruling Conservative Party was fully exploited by Straw, who claimed that 'the findings are an indictment of the government's record and that it was a national scandal that one child in five was not receiving adequate reading lessons'. Straw also called for national testing, arguing that the Conservative Government:

> has wasted many years after quite scandalously abandoning the system of national monitoring of reading standards in 1988. What we need to have is regular and consistent monitoring of standards, so that when there are problems ministers know about them.[22]

The reports called for by the Secretary in the initial stages of the renewed reading standards debate were finally published by the DES in early 1991.[23] The Education, Science and Arts Committee (ESAC), a multi-party body appointed in December 1987 under SO No. 130 to examine the expenditure, administration and policy of several public bodies including the DES, was also invited to undertake a Select Committee investigation into the issues raised by the psychologists and the two published reports. The degree of urgency and the potential for political embarrassment the growing controversy represented was underpinned by the realisation on both sides of the House that the credibility of the Government's entire policy towards literacy was now at stake. This was aptly summed up when the Labour member for St Helens North, John Evans, rose to ask: 'Will the Secretary of State confirm that, after nearly 12 years of Tory government cuts in the education service, our children's reading standards are, not surprisingly, declining?'

The Select Committee was thus under considerable political pressure to produce solutions. In February 1991, the Committee took oral evidence from Martin Turner, the Secretary of State for Education and Science, Kenneth Clarke, and two 'independent' reading experts (Betty Root and Professor Asher Cashdan), as well as from HMI, SESAC and NFER.[24] In addition, a number of written submissions from interested bodies were received, including the British Psychological Society, the Dyslexia Educational Trust, the British Dyslexia Association, the National Association of Head Teachers, the National Union of Teachers and several universities.

Even as the Committee deliberated, the debate continued to widen. By April 1991, direct links were once again being made between progressive educational methods and the perceived decline in reading standards. This link was given media coverage after the screening of a BBC2 documentary, the visit to England of whole language/real books advocate, Frank Smith, and a widely reported condemnation of 'fashionable' trends in the nation's classrooms by Prince Charles. The BBC documentary had featured a primary school which was reported as being 'criticised by Her Majesty's Inspectors' for 'spending too much time establishing "caring relationships" while failing to teach pupils to read and write properly'.[25] This school, Culloden Primary School, situated in London's East End, was now to become the focus of the unfolding debate over reading standards. During March and April 1991, Culloden school was the subject of a blistering series of articles by *Mail on Sunday* education correspondent, Liz Lightfoot. Lightfoot's initial article, evocatively entitled 'Losing the battle at Culloden', argued that, although the documentary had represented the school as a 'triumph of modern education', visiting psychologist Martin Turner had applied the NFER-designed Suffolk Reading Test to discover that 'three-quarters of the seven year olds performed so badly at reading they got no score at all'.[26] A second Lightfoot article on 10 March reported that the Education Secretary, Kenneth Clarke, had set up an inquiry into standards at Culloden immediately following the release of the initial *Mail on Sunday* article.[27] On 21 April, a third article by Lightfoot claimed that she had subsequently been verbally harassed by teachers who had accused her of fabricating evidence and of being 'Right-wing'.[28]

In fact, the demonisation of opponents as political extremists rapidly became a feature of the new crisis. Frank Smith was reported by John O'Leary, writing in *The Times*, as occupying 'a place in the demonology of child development once reserved for Dr Spock', and was reportedly accused of 'triggering a national decline in reading standards with so-called "real books" theory of learning'. He was also described as having 'been dubbed the Billy Graham of the reading world, a guru of the left and a crank'. O'Leary also noted that Tim Eggar, the Education Minister, had now taken sides against the whole language/real book approach and attacked these beliefs. Eggar was quoted as stating that Mr Smith had a long way to go to prove his case. The Education Minister also felt that the real books campaign was a serious attack on standards in schools.[29]

Two days later, Prince Charles attacked progressive educators in a speech at Stratford-upon-Avon. Reporting the speech, *Guardian* reporter Clare commented:

> Are we all so frightened and cowed by the shadowy 'experts' that we can no longer 'screw our courage to the sticking place' and defiantly insist that they are talking unwitting nonsense?'. The Prince of Wales's own reply to the rhetorical question he posed in his Stratford-upon-Avon speech was a resounding 'No'. He said it was time to call the bluff of the so-called experts – the trendy educationalists who had become increasingly out of

touch with the feelings of ordinary people. But who are they? Where do they lurk? How do they exert their malign influence? And with what consequences?[30]

On 23 April, G.E. Riddick, the Conservative member for Colne Valley, rose in the House of Commons to ask the Secretary what plans he had to reform the training of teachers in reading methods. In response to the Secretary's announcement that the Council for the Accreditation of Teacher Education had been asked to conduct an inquiry into how students were trained to teach reading, Riddick inquired whether he agreed that:

the Prince of Wales was speaking for millions of parents when he voiced frustration at those educationalists whose experiments in the teaching of reading have done so much to fail millions of pupils? Will he ensure that the inquiry that he has just announced is not subverted by those same educationalists in his Department, local authorities and Her Majesty's inspectorate?[31]

Labour, however, were not to be outdone. The member for Oxford, Andrew D. Smith, launched a fierce attack on the Conservative Government for failing to adequately monitor reading standards during its term of office:

Will the Minister apologise to the people of this country for the Government's neglect of the teaching of reading in the past 12 years and for their abandonment, in 1988, of the national monitoring of reading standards? Does he accept that the Secretary of State and his predecessors have approved every teacher training course into which they are now launching an inquiry? Is that not a classic case of political buck-passing? Will the Minister and the Government accept responsibility where standards are inadequate and make way for a Labour Government who will put reading standards first?[32]

In response, the Hon. A.N.W. Soames, Conservative member for Crawley, attempted to swing the blame for falling reading standards squarely back on the schools, asking what implications could be drawn for the training of teachers from the recent *Mail on Sunday* articles about the failure of teachers to teach reading properly at Culloden school.[33]

In submitting its report in May 1991, however, the Select Committee emphasised that the scope of the inquiry had been restricted to the HMI and NFER reports. Moreover, wider issues such as the teaching and learning of reading, and the specific problem of dyslexia, were also left unresolved in the report, until a further inquiry could be set up.[34] The first part of the report was concerned with the issue of whether reading standards had, in fact, fallen. Indications of some decline in test scores amongst the 26 LEAs surveyed in the NFER study were viewed as inconclusive due to both the unrepresentative nature of the LEA samples, and the lack of uniformity in the testing and recording of results. The report thus concluded that the claim that reading standards had fallen in recent years had not been proved beyond reasonable doubt.[35]

The second part of the report examined the issue of how standards might be raised. It cited the HMI report's conclusion that in 'about 20 per cent of the schools ... the work in reading was judged to be poor and required urgent attention', but tempered this by adding that the broad position appeared to have changed little since the 1978 HMI National Primary Survey. Nevertheless, the Committee recommended that more time be spent in ITT on the teaching of reading, especially in learning the theoretical aspects of language and literacy.[36] Turning to teaching methods, the Committee noted Turner's claim that the apparent decline in reading standards could be attributed to the growth of 'real books' methods of teaching reading and the abandonment of the systematic teaching of phonics, but rejected it on the evidence from the HMI survey that found only 5 per cent of teachers described their approach as 'real books'. The HMI report, however, found a clear link between higher standards and systematic phonics teaching, although it was acknowledged that the questions of how to teach phonics, and with what frequency, were still controversial matters, requiring further research. Accordingly, the Select Committee Report recommended that 'the various methods of teaching phonics should be evaluated in order to establish the most effective way of using phonics in the teaching of reading'.[37]

The report concluded, however, that:

> It is important to keep a sense of proportion. Professor Cashdan told us that 'we have not got a crisis and we do not need a magic solution. What we need is for teachers to be well trained, to be well supported, to be well resourced and for the educational service and teachers to have the status they deserve'. We wholeheartedly agree. A great deal of excellent work is being done in our primary schools by competent and dedicated teachers and head-teachers, whose skills and achievements ought to be more fully recognized, both by other branches of the teaching profession and by society as a whole; and their work is significantly reinforced by active involvement of parents in reading schemes and other forms of support. If we can bring all primary schools up to the same high standards achieved by the best, we will be giving our children the appropriate teaching and resources to meet their current needs, and providing a firm foundation for their subsequent education.[38]

Given the high degree of public and professional interest in the reading standards issue, however, the release of the report was bound to have considerable political ramifications. The *Independent*, whilst noting that the

Committee had largely dismissed Turner's claims that current methods of reading instruction were at fault, nevertheless supported the need for the national testing of seven-year-olds, on the grounds that this would provide the 'first solid basis for judging standards'.[39] As it transpired, the National Standard Assessment Tasks (SATS) tests for seven-year-olds were administered for the first time in May 1991, despite the problems created by complaints that the tests were 'complicated', 'time wasting' and 'unfair'.[40]

By mid-July 1991, therefore, the preceding public outcry over falling standards had resulted in the establishment and acceptance of national testing in primary schools along with an overt political commitment to raising standards on the part of both major political parties. The teachers of seven-year-olds had administered their first national standard assessment tasks, enabling the press to comment for the first time on what they saw as clear evidence of the achievement level for seven-year-olds on a national scale.[41] The Prime Minister was calling for 'greater accountability from schools'[42] and the Labour Party had a formal commitment to initiating a standards council.[43]

The release of the results from the national assessment testing of seven-year-olds also hastened the demise of the inspectorate. In October, Her Majesty's Inspectors were given the news that 'more than half of them' would become redundant due to a decision which had been 'taken by the Prime Minister and the Downing Street policy unit and rushed through Cabinet. The decision had been taken so quickly that Whitehall accounts reported the Queen as having asked, 'What have they done wrong?'[44] Judith Judd, writing in the *Independent*, argued that they were being penalised for failing to support the right-wing agenda of protecting 'traditional standards'. The Inspectorate, she argued, had 'sold out to the progressives' and had become 'slaves to fashionable educational theory and shamefully soft on underachieving schools'.[45]

During this period, the debate over phonics versus real books/whole language continued to feature strongly both in House of Commons exchanges and in the press. In June, A.F. Bennett, the Labour member for Denton and Reddish, asked Clarke when he would be responding to the Select Committee Report. Bennett was particularly curious as to whether the Minister had considered the problem of organising lessons so that teachers could listen to each individual read, one after the other, arguing that this function would prove particularly difficult whilst teachers were also carrying out testing on seven-year olds. In response, Clarke emphasised that they could not give up arrangements in which each pupil read to the teacher in order to ensure the maintenance of reading standards.[46] In July, there was a further extended debate in the House over schooling. During the debate the Opposition argued that only Labour enjoyed the confidence of the public, because it was the only party that had clearly articulated policies for improving standards across the entire system. Fatchett observed that Labour would 'improve education performance school by school, local authority by local authority, through its powerful, independent, much-acclaimed and non-political education standards commission'.[47] In response, Boyson reiterated his long-standing view that it was the fact that intellectual 'trendies' within the inspectorate and teacher training colleges had forced the discovery methods of learning on teachers that had largely been responsible for the decline in educational standards they were now witnessing. Of reading, Boyson observed that 'At the same time there was a move to the "look and say" method and "real books" and away from phonics, which is the method by which most children learn to read'. Of teachers, he argued that 10 per cent could teach by any method if they were left alone; 10 per cent could not and should therefore be dismissed; but the remaining 80 per cent required the phonics method.[48]

In the press, some commentators, such as Roger Beard, at the time a senior lecturer in Primary Education at the University of Leeds, advocated caution and a 'mixed-method' approach which utilised phonics to help children with 'reading fluency and the need to decode unfamiliar words – on which the meaning of the texts often disproportionately depends'.[49] The release of the results of national testing of seven-year-olds in November 1991, however, led to a renewed press condemnation of teaching methods. The results were interpreted as showing that '28 per cent of our children cannot read'. This led to yet another attack on the *Plowden Report* in the right-wing press. The apparent decline in reading standards was contrasted with the success of reading in other countries such as France, Germany and Japan. The *Daily Telegraph* renewed its general condemnation of primary teaching methods and once again launched into a derisory rhetoric against progressive ideals:

> The issue goes far wider than reading. The results of these national tests should finally remove the widespread delusion that whatever else is wrong with our education service, our primary schools are the best in the world. It is simply untrue. The fact is that the hare-brained, sentimental concept of child-centred teaching is the principal source of the problems in secondary schools later on. Cosy, 'caring', well equipped classrooms are no proof that anything at all of educational value is being achieved.[50]

In November 1991, Clarke announced to the House that he had written to the Chairman of the Select Committee setting out the Government's response to the Select Committee Report. He hailed the report as 'an important timely contribution to the current debate on reading standards in schools'. Its conclusion that a fall in standards had not been proved beyond a reasonable doubt was, Clarke felt, no reason for complacency because it had highlighted the inadequacies of present data and supported the need for a 'reliable and consistent basis for the measurement of pupil's attainments', such as was to be provided by the National Curriculum with its associated testing regime. Once more the Secretary reiterated his Government's policy that pupil progress was hence to be measured at seven, eleven, fourteen and sixteen, and the results would be available to teachers, parents and the public to enable comparisons to be made between sexes, schools and LEAs.[51]

The Government's response took the form of a DES memorandum later to be appended to the Select Committee Report, outlining the Government's position on the various issues raised in the report. In response to the claim that a decline in reading standards had not been proven, the Government took the view that it was nevertheless a matter of serious concern that HMI had found 20 per cent of primary schools to have poor reading standards. Accordingly, the Government argued that it was taking action to promote higher reading standards through the National Curriculum which established clear national targets for reading attainments at each successive level. In addition, National Curriculum assessment arrangements were designed both to measure pupil progress in reading and to report findings to parents.[52] In response to the report's recommendation that more time be given in ITT to the teaching of reading, the Government noted that in April the Council for the Accreditation of Teacher Education had been asked to initiate an inquiry into the preparation of teachers to teach reading.[53] Turning to the recommendation regarding the teaching of phonics, the Government endorsed the HMI position that exclusive reliance on any single method of teaching reading hindered progress. It also stopped short of recommending any particular method, and went on to endorse the long-standing position of successive governments in its conclusion that:

> It is not for the Government to dictate teaching methods. They are for schools to settle in the light of the best evidence available of good practice. Nevertheless the Government will consider whether further research work is required on the most successful ways of combining a range of teaching methods, including phonics.[54]

Nevertheless, the ramifications of the debate over reading standards initiated by Turner were to be much more far-reaching than this conclusion was to suggest. The league table results for the achievement levels of seven-year-olds were released in December and were heralded by a leading article in the *Guardian* as 'a small piece of history' which, for the first time, would give 'clear evidence of the achievement levels of seven-year-olds on a national scale' and provide 'education authority members [and parents] with the comparative information they need to monitor the progress of their local school systems – and demand improvements where necessary'.

The *Guardian* clearly supported national testing and a system which would 'identify areas which are under-performing'.[55] Judith Judd in the

Independent, however, was more cautious, pointing out that, while reading standards could be improved, the 'test results show no evidence that standards are declining', as there were no previous tests of seven-year-olds to compare them with. She also cautioned that the league tables could not account for social and economic differences. They were, therefore, of little use to parents, as few could choose where to live. Moreover, the tables gave little information about local differences. Judd concluded that the 'most "shocking revelation" was that ministers are in the grip of league table mania'.[56]

'The political wind', however, as Judd and Wilby had pointed out in an earlier article in the *Independent*, was now firmly behind national testing in primary schools and the anti-progressive lobby.[57] It was announced that the testing of seven-year-olds would continue, and that it would be no longer 'hijacked' by liberal educationalists who had 'insisted on assessing children through more expensive classroom experiments rather than cheaper, more efficient sit-down tests'. The Prime Minister pledged that next year's tests would be 'simpler' pencil and paper tests that would concentrate on the '3Rs' and that the emphasis 'should be shifted towards a straight forward exam that could be taken by the whole class at the same time'.[58]

The publishing of league table results and their perceived support for 'falling reading standards' served to provide further support for an anti-progressive stance and the subsequent setting up of a government inquiry into 'primary school teaching methods'. Kenneth Clarke announced the inquiry in early December:

> Mr Clarke was careful to moderate his words announcing the inquiry last week but his language could not disguise his preference for over-turning teaching methods that have prevailed for 30 years – group and mixed ability teaching, topic work, encouraging children to find out things for themselves. Privately ministers admit that they cannot directly dictate teaching methods. But they can influence, partly by designing tests that require more formal approaches. And official inquiries can be highly influential.[59]

The narrative extends: challenging 'progressive' education and regulating through national testing

The new inquiry into primary education resulted in a report on primary school teaching methods which was published in late January 1992. This report was widely commented upon in the press and links were drawn between its conclusions and the public debate and political responses which had led to the inquiry. The Education Secretary was said to have appointed 'Three Wise Men' to produce the report: Robin Alexander, of Leeds University; Jim Rose, the Chief Primary Inspector in the Schools Inspectorate; and Chris Woodhead, the Chief Executive of the National Curriculum council.[60]

In *The Times*, the report was seen to support Turner's contention that there had been a drop in reading standards in the late 1980s and early 1990s. The *Daily Telegraph* also traced the origins of the report and its findings to the publication of Turner's claims of dramatically declining reading standards:

> The alarm bells began ringing two years ago when Martin Turner, an educational psychologist, produced evidence of a sharp decline in the reading standards of seven year olds. Then came the publication last summer of a five-year study of what actually goes on in progressive classrooms. Not a lot as it turned out: on average, pupils were wasting 40 per cent of each school day and not achieving very much in the rest. But it was the results of last year's tests for seven year olds that firmly shattered the primary school myth. One child in four could not read; the same proportion could barely count.[61]

According to the *Daily Telegraph*, 'Kenneth Clarke's three-man inquiry into primary education' was a 'response to widely felt concern over: the dismal showing in last summer's tests of seven year olds in maths and English'; the dramatic decline in reading standards; and 'doubts that current primary school methods are effective'.[62]

While most newspapers broadly agreed on the narrative relating to the genesis of the newly emerged attack on progressivism and support for national assessment, there was also an apparently paradoxical move to interpreting the report as having condemned the establishment of the National Curriculum and its associated move toward national testing, for not having sufficiently reported the move toward teaching the 'basics'. The report was thus cited as noting that 'the requirements of the National Curriculum and its attendant tests have led to reduced teaching time, especially in the basics'.[63]

David Tytler, writing in *The Times*, stressed Clarke's reliance on 'public pressure to reform primary teaching'. He noted that the evidence in the report on primary school teaching methods commissioned by Clarke had been carefully prepared and that the 'Three Wise Men' used 'the voice of reason' to explain 'what must be done if standards are to be raised'. Clarke was seen as relying on public pressure 'to force teachers to change their ways' as he believed that 'the Report would give them the self-confidence to express common sense views'.[64]

Professor Alexander was quoted as summing up the judgement of the 'three wise men' as 'arguing for a return to common sense'.[65] It was felt that this gave a stronger impetus to the report's implicit criticism of progressive-based primary education:

> The evidence in the report on primary school teaching methods commissioned by Kenneth Clarke had been painstakingly prepared so that

every claim is supported. The language used by the 'three wise men' appointed by the education secretary to write the report is moderate, so that when there is criticism of the 'highly questionable dogmas' adopted by some primary schools for the past 20 years it is all the more telling.[66]

The report also endorsed a change to traditional teaching methods and cautioned against too much diversity in teaching methods.[67] It recommended that the 'the best of all practices' should be incorporated into primary teaching and that this was to include 'specialist teachers to teach specialist subjects' and the promotion of 'whole class teaching where possible'.[68] While they did not advocate streaming, they did recommend that groups of children should be taught according to their ability, as the very able and the less able were seen to have suffered through primary schools concentrating on aiming their teaching at children in the middle ability grouping.[69]

The report was also seen to run counter to learner-centred ideals in the emphasis it placed on the role of the teacher and a subject-based curriculum, and argued for specialist teachers.[70] Primary teachers were to be encouraged to use more whole-class teaching 'rather than acting as facilitators moving between groups of children working semi-independently'.[71] While the report sanctioned whole-class teaching, it was interpreted as being against the use of topic work as this approach was considered not to be sharply focused enough, leading to superficial learning and teaching. The report also critiqued primary school assessment practices as being 'largely intuitive' and 'idiosyncratic' and giving very little real insight into students' abilities.[72]

Summary

The events described in this chapter once again reinforce the fact that answering the question, 'Have literacy standards declined?', is extremely difficult. Certainly, those seeking to discredit the revelations Turner and his colleagues provided have pointed out that their conclusions were based upon 'a fairly small number of children chosen only from those authorities which showed a decline', yet the media reports and statements made by Turner and the other LEA representatives misleadingly implied that the claim was 'based upon a large and representative sample'.[73] Other education researchers also expressed doubts regarding Turner's findings and conclusions, both at the time and subsequently. Researchers were reported as arguing that there was no scientific evidence that standards were falling and warned 'that single, small surveys, which have yet to come under public scrutiny, provide no firm basis for general conclusions'.[74]

In January 1991, the inspectorate and the NFER published separate reports on reading standards. The inspectorate argued that there had been little change in primary school standards over 12 years.[75] The inspectorate reported the views of head teachers who noted the impact of the National

Curriculum which was seen to encroach on the priority formerly given to reading. They also noted the impact of staff turn over, class sizes, lack of funding for books and reduction in the specialist support services for slower learners and bilingual children.[76] The NFER did find a decline in standards, but argued that, as the 'tests reflected a narrow and outdated view of reading, the data was meaningless'.[77] The Select Committee Report likewise found little evidence for a widespread decline.

The real issue for the purposes of this book, however, is not whether Turner's claims can be proved or disproved, but rather that the debate over reading standards he re-initiated was to have profound consequences for the future. The two years following the outcry over falling reading standards, that began in early 1990 with the publicity accorded the claims made by Turner and others, provided the impetus that led to a new dominant narrative in primary education. Whether justified or not, a general consensus developed that reading standards in England had drastically fallen. In turn, this led to the acceptance of the need for national testing in order to monitor reading standards. The commonly accepted assumption that standards were falling also fuelled attacks on the progressive ideals which had previously dominated primary pedagogy.

The *Report on Primary School Methods* which was widely debated in the press at the beginning of 1992 highlighted the increasing focus upon regulating primary pedagogy and the construction of a 'normal pupil', defined by quantifiable norms through national assessment. The stress upon attainment with its associated requirements that teachers' diagnosing ability was to be accompanied by whole class skills-based teaching of the basics in particular subject areas. The *Daily Telegraph* neatly summed up this narrative shift away from libratory child-centred progressivism to a more authoritarian, technicist, teacher-centred focus upon ability and basic skills:

> The immediate value of the Wise Men's report is that it exposes the chief components of the post-Plowden ideology: the topic work that leads to fragmentary and superficial teaching; the persistent belief that pupils should never be told things, only asked questions; the obsessive fear that anything might be deemed elitist, leading to the aims of the most able being neglected; and the conviction that teachers should offer nothing but praise, never pointing out when a pupil is wrong. Such are the child-centred dogmas which, the report urges, teachers must abandon in favour of subject-based instruction, in purposeful and orderly classrooms – grouped by ability where appropriate – in above all, the children can concentrate on the work in hand.[78]

The *Report on Primary School Methods* can therefore be seen to represent a discursive shift away from the progressive vision of literacy teaching as an 'art', which envisaged teachers working 'intuitively' and being 'sensitive' to the 'imaginative needs of their children'.[79] This ideal was largely replaced with a vision of literacy teaching as 'best practice' through regulation, performance and technical skill in the 'basics'. This discursive shift would ensure that it would be the latter vision which would become the dominant discourse underpinning the development of subsequent literacy policies and pedagogical initiatives such as the NLS. It is to these that we now turn our attention.

Part 3

Recent policy developments

Antipodean synergies

Chapter 6

The advent of national literacy strategies

Contexts for the development of the English National Literacy Strategy

The English National Literacy Strategy has been introduced against a background of an increase in external control being exercised over the curriculum and teaching styles. During the late 1980s and 1990s, England revised the National Curriculum first introduced in the 1988 Education Reform Act. This Act introduced a prescriptive and detailed curriculum with statutory national testing in the primary school at ages seven and eleven. It also initiated an inspection system which was controlled by the Office for Standards in Education (OFSTED). This situation is similar to developments in New Zealand curriculum policy,[1] though to date there is no mandatory primary school testing there.

There was, however, a further and crucial difference between the English and New Zealand contexts. In England, the mid-1990s also brought claims by policy-makers that there was a need to increase the effectiveness of teaching through separate subject teaching, the encouragement of subject specialism and the adoption of ability and whole-class teaching.[2] These claims have not been nearly so influential amongst New Zealand politicians and policy-makers.

Nevertheless, in New Zealand there has also been a public debate over how to increase the effectiveness of literacy teaching.[3] Public discussion around this issue has involved teachers, teacher educators, academics and the mass media as well as policy-makers. In contrast to England, however, much of the debate has focused upon the utilisation of the whole language or phonics methods of teaching reading, rather than the adoption of ability and whole-class teaching.[4]

In England the adoption of ability and whole-class teaching directly impacted upon the policies related to literacy instruction. In 1996 the Conservative Government cut funding to the New Zealand inspired Reading Recovery (RR) programme[5] and set up the National Literacy Project (NLP) which promoted the development of 'a range of practical teaching strategies based on whole-class and group teaching' and the more effective use of time through the introduction of the daily 'Literacy Hour' as two of its main aims.[6]

This marked a significant move away from teacher-devised strategies to address literacy difficulties. As we will see in the following chapter, RR aimed at targeting poorer readers and providing one-to-one instruction, coupled with the careful indoctrination of the teacher to be an 'expert' in early literacy learning.[7] The emphasis was on the specialist teachers training themselves to use systematic observation and records to probe their students' difficulties in learning in order to assess the quality of teaching in the classroom. By contrast, the NLP's emphasis is upon the management of literacy at whole-school level, through monitoring by senior staff and NFR-based researchers.

The introductory leaflet for the National Literacy Project outlined a framework of teaching objectives which set out 'clear expectations of what should be covered in each term'. It also introduced the concept of the 'Literacy Hour' that was carefully structured to ensure a balance of whole-class and differentiated-group teaching.[8] As Labour education policy developed during 1997, it became clear that many of the objectives and structures of the NLP would be kept and developed further by the new Labour Government. The Literacy Task Force initiated under the Labour Government would gather 'together a range of initiatives, many of which have already taken on life under this, Conservative, government'.[9]

In May 1996, the Labour Party announced a back-to-basics drive to improve literacy standards if it came to power in the election to be held the following year. David Blunkett noted that a recently published OFSTED report on the teaching of reading in forty-five Inner-London primary schools found that 40 per cent of Year 6 pupils had reading ages two or more years below their chronological ages. The Labour Party planned to raise standards through the introduction of a new literacy taskforce and wanted to examine ways of ensuring 'that every child leaving primary school does so with a reading age of 11 by the end of the second term of office'.[10]

In the same announcement, Blunkett, the shadow Education Secretary, stated that teachers were to 'use teaching methods which work and are not just the latest fashion'. The Labour Party's dissatisfaction with the quality of newly trained teachers also resulted in a pledge to place greater emphasis on basic skills, classroom discipline and whole-class teaching. Blunkett also stressed the use of phonics. His statement that 'It is self evident that phonics are a crucial tool for teaching children in the early stages and abilities' did not acknowledge the issues which surrounded the international debate over the use of phonics and whole language.[11]

The need to raise standards and skills was a key point in the 'New Life for Britain' document released in July that was to lay the foundations for the Labour Party's election campaign. The document promised a 'radical improvement in primary standards through focussing on the basics, better testing and assessment with target-setting of results; value-added performance tables; the reform of teacher training and the sacking of inadequate staff. It also announced that the newly formed taskforce on literacy would have its report and recommendations ready for an incoming government.[12]

The membership of the English Literacy Task Force

An academic, Professor Michael Barber, Dean of New Initiatives at London's Institute of Education, chaired the Literacy Task Force. The key role Barber played in instigating an informal network that led to appointments on these taskforces was noted in the *TES*:

> In the web that is being woven, Prof Barber has a direct route to David Blunkett, the Education Secretary, and has the key role in coordinating the work of the task forces. No less impressive is the informal network within which he operates. Prof Barber has links to Tony Blair (and his policy adviser on education, David Miliband) and has contributed to his speeches.[13]

Professor David Reynolds of Newcastle University, who chaired the Numeracy Task Force, was another key member of the taskforce. Other members on the taskforce were: John Botham, a head teacher from Greenwood Junior School, Nottingham, where he had successfully led a City Challenge Achievement Project (he would later receive an OBE for being 'one of the new, bright breed of heads who have rescued schools');[14] Anne Waterhouse and Mary Gray, also head teachers; Diane Wright, a parent; Simon Goodenough, a school governor; David Pitt-Watson, from Deloitte & Touche; and Mike Raleigh, an observer from the Office for Standards in Education. The *TES* pointed out that Barber had played a central role in choosing these minor members of the taskforces.[15]

Like Blunkett, Barber stressed the problem of low reading standards and advocated an overall strategy rather than 'ad hoc' measures such as the Reading Recovery scheme. The cost of Reading Recovery was an important factor in this decision, even though there was support for funding its continuation.[16] Barber argued that a Labour Government would provide adequate resources so that teachers would have to take responsibility for improving literacy standards.[17] In his inaugural speech at the Institute of Education, London University, Barber drew attention to the central position education played in individual economic success as well as economic competitiveness: hence the resulting need to make decisions, prioritise and monitor literacy standards:

> A government ought to establish clear priorities and stick to them. If, for example, literacy standards are to be the priority, then decisions on initial teacher education, teachers' professional development, the nature of inspection, the content of the national curriculum, the form of tests and the character of home–school agreements need to take that priority into account.[18]

Throughout 1996, Barber was reported as advocating the raising of literacy standards in schools through national testing at key stages. He also supported allowing parents access to exam performance information. Teachers, he argued, would then be forced to take responsibility for improving standards through the publication of performance data. Poorly performing teachers could be threatened with dismissal in order to stimulate professional commitment to raised standards.[19]

Barber's views were to be a major influence on the leader of the Labour education team, David Blunkett, and the formulation of Labour policy:

> The focus now is on raising standards in schools, with an acceptance that parents want the kind of information that is provided by exam performance tables. In executing the changes, Mr Blunkett has listened to a number of academics, the most influential being Michael Barber, dean of the new initiatives at the Institute of Education at London University ... much of Labour's policy on ways of improving schools can be traced to Barber.[20]

Reynolds was chosen as a key member of the Literacy Task Force because his research, in which he examined the success of basic literacy and numeracy skills for children in Taiwanese schools, had provoked debate on effective ways of organising classes.[21] In 1996, his research on school effectiveness reached an increasingly wide audience through the screening of a BBC *Panorama* documentary which highlighted his view that teachers must be held accountable for failing schools and low standards.[22]

Reynold's claims that a lack of whole-class teaching was a key element in Britain's failure to match the educational progress of Pacific Rim countries was publicly supported by OFSTED's Chief Inspector, Chris Woodhead, and by Blunkett. In an earlier BBC *Panorama* programme, which focused upon Reynold's research, Woodhead was quoted as stating that lessons directed at the whole class were 'a key factor in the strong mathematical performance of Pacific Rim countries such as Taiwan and Korea'. He also argued that 'the lack of whole-class methods is a key element in Britain's failure to match the educational progress of the Far East'. He told viewers that British primary teachers should double the amount of whole-class teaching across the whole primary school curriculum and was quoted as being concerned that only a quarter of teaching in English primary schools was directed at the whole class. Furthermore, the programme showed David Blunkett endorsing these claims by visiting a whole-class teaching experiment in the east London borough of Barking and Dagenham.[23]

By the end of 1996, therefore, the drive to teach the 3Rs to primary children had become the focus of the newly elected Labour Government's draft programmes for the next National Curriculum. These draft programmes indicated that there would be a highly detailed, prescriptive outline for teaching reading, writing and number for each term of the primary school. It was also clear that these programmes would result in a considerable increase in government control over the teaching of literacy, if the draft programmes were developed into part of the National Curriculum. Commentators noted that the draft programmes would also allow the Government to achieve its aims of increasing whole-class teaching and target setting.[24]

The context for the development of a New Zealand literacy strategy

In the early 1990s, public concern over literacy issues in New Zealand did not initially focus upon the mechanics of reading. Rather, newspaper and magazine articles tended to express concerns about 'computer'[25] and adult 'workplace literacy'.[26] Within academic circles, however, Professor William Tunmer and Professor James Chapman at Massey University, together with Associate Professor Tom Nicholson at the University of Auckland, were publishing research findings that raised serious concerns about the whole language approach that underpinned New Zealand's highly centralised and systematised approach to the teaching of reading, particularly the Reading Recovery programme (RR), aimed at early intervention, developed by Marie Clay.[27]

The onset of the literacy debate in New Zealand was to be facilitated by the growth of mass circulation magazines, a comparatively new media form in that country, expressly catering for a more affluent middle-class clientele seeking independent political, social and educational commentary. Thus, the first article claiming that literacy standards had been falling for some time was published in the popular magazine *North & South* by staff writer, Jenny Chamberlain. Chamberlain observed that reading was now big business in New Zealand, one local publisher having exported forty million school readers to twelve countries in the last twelve years. International visitors flocked to see the New Zealand approach to reading in action. Yet despite the emphasis placed on reading in primary schools, it was 'almost as though we've made a national pact with each other to ignore our illiteracy', because 'Government, teachers and those good-news merchants book publishers constantly block[ed] the literacy debate'.[28] According to Chamberlain, however, the reality was that one in four six-year-olds required remedial assistance after one year at school; 47 per cent of unemployed fourteen- to-nineteen-year-olds had no formal qualifications; one-third of school leavers went straight from school onto unemployment benefit with no post-secondary education, whilst polytechnics and universities struggled to provide basic literacy skills for their clients.

In mid-1995, the press debate moved from a general focus on the literacy standards of school leavers and university students to a more specific critique of reading methods and 'the teaching of reading' in New Zealand. In June 1995, a major newspaper reported that a report by Professor Tunmer 'questions the way NZ children are taught to read'.[29] In fact, Tunmer and Chapman were to subsequently emphasise that they were in general agreement with 90–95 per cent of what New Zealand teachers did to facilitate the acquisition of reading skills in young children. What they did claim was that the current widespread practice amongst New Zealand teachers of predicting words from context was a highly ineffective and inappropriate learning strategy. Instead, they argued that beginning readers should be encouraged to look for familiar spelling patterns first and to use context to confirm hypotheses about what unfamiliar words might be, based on available word-level information.[30]

This argument not withstanding, the popular magazine, *The New Zealand Listener*, featured an article in July 1995 by Noel O'Hare entitled, 'What's wrong with reading?' The article claimed that 'the century old debate' over how to teach reading was 'becoming a hot issue among academics in New Zealand and overseas'.[31] O'Hare added the long-standing concerns of those who supported a return to phonics-based approaches that had supposedly been at the centre of reading teaching prior to the 1970s and the advent of whole language teaching. This article alleged that the current debate over reading methods could be seen as a debate between a group of university-based academic researchers who advocated a return to the teaching of phonics, and experienced educational practitioners who defended the currently accepted use of 'whole language' and 'reading recovery approaches' to teaching reading. The latter were powerful proponents of whole language who had a vested interest in maintaining the status quo, attempting to silence those who supported the teaching of phonics both inside and outside the teaching profession through fear, ridicule and even stand over tactics.[32]

The 'most public advocate of phonics', Tom Nicholson, was regarded by O'Hare as having cast doubts on the effectiveness of current reading methods, stating that teachers were 'hanging in there', utilising a less effective approach to reading. Nicholson was cited as noting that teachers favouring the 'use of more phonics are afraid to speak out publicly for fear of being ridiculed by their colleagues'. In turning to the Tunmer and Chapman research, the article observed that:

> *Instructional Strategies for Word Identification*, co-authored by Tunmer and James Chapman, casts doubt on the work of New Zealand's reading

guru Dame Marie Clay. The central belief of whole-language advocates such as Clay – that learning to read is essentially like learning to speak – is incorrect argues Tunmer.[33]

The article concluded by claiming that research was mounting to show that the theories that supported those who supported the current use of whole language were 'wrong headed', 'flawed' and 'anti science'. New Zealand teacher educators who had written books with academics supporting the teaching profession's adherence to 'whole language' were incorrectly looking to 'good practice' based approaches to reading rather than scientifically based research-based approaches:

> In the US, whole-language advocates simply reject the research as irrelevant and damn every study as an artificial assessment of a narrow set of skills. That 'anti-science' attitude is common in New Zealand, too, says Nicholson. 'Teachers know through their gut feeling what children need.' As Smith and Elley complacently put it in *Learning to Read in New Zealand*: 'New Zealand reading methods developed largely as a result of good practice on the part of competent teachers rather than on the accumulation of research.'[34]

The growing polarisation of a reading debate that appeared to pit university-based scholars with links to the international research community against colleges of education that saw themselves as leaders of the nations' community of professional educators was to be almost immediately illustrated in a special *Developmental Network Newsletter* circulated to a readership of largely professional educators and parents. This blasted the O'Hare article as 'a new low in education reporting and academic behaviour'. Promising a series of articles in response to the issues raised, the newsletter labelled the use of the numbers of children in RR to demonstrate the failure of New Zealand approaches to reading by academic researchers as 'either an example of academic stupidity, waywardness or perversity'.[35] The newsletter questioned the appropriateness of their continued access to schools and suggested that, in future, any such access should be rigorously supervised. It advocated that someone with a leadership role in whole language and RR be appointed to guide future research. Finally, it called upon teachers to write personally to Tunmer, to Chapman, to the editor of the *Listener* and the Ministry to protest at 'this shameful episode', which was another example of 'The media, Business Roundtable and academics at it again'.[36]

In August 1995, the weekly magazine *Metro* published an article on the growing 'phonics versus whole language' debate entitled 'Adventures in the reading trade' which also attacked the established whole-language approach and the Reading Recovery programme.[37] Taken together, the publication of these articles initiated a 'reading wars' debate in the New Zealand press. In the eyes of the press, concerns over literacy became narrowly focused upon the technical procedures related to methods of teaching early literacy. A group of university-based psychologists and reading researchers were seen to have lined up on the side of phonics and phonemic instruction, while another group of professionally based supporters and their allies were identified as defending the whole-language approach.

By the second half of 1997, mounting New Zealand public interest in reading mirrored the concerns expressed in United States articles on the 'reading wars' published in locally available editions of international magazines. Overseas, the debate over the 'role of phonics in reading instruction' featured on the cover page of the April/May edition of the bimonthly newspaper of the International Reading Association (IRA). This article noted that 'the debate' had recently narrowed to a focus on 'intensive direct skills instruction as opposed to more flexible, literature-based approaches to the teaching or reading'. It had also 'moved beyond the education arena to become a hot political issue' in New Zealand as well as in the United States, Canada and Australia.[38] The IRA Board of Directors were moved to claim that they had grown increasingly concerned about the trend towards 'non-educators issuing curricular and legislative mandates that rob teachers and other educational professionals of the freedom to exercise their judgment'. They also warned that the press could be 'inaccurate and exaggerated' in their claims of poor achievement among students, often attributed to a perceived inattention to phonics in beginning reading instruction.[39]

Further articles in the New Zealand press began appearing in July 1997. Tunmer and Chapman's joint 'statement' given at the 1997 IRA international reading conference held in New Zealand was reported as indicating that 'The Education Ministry's emphasis on teaching children to read by using context rather than sound was wrong', and that 'Reading recovery programmes did not greatly improve sound processing skills in children who needed it'. They also alleged that 'reading recovery teachers appeared to be giving "highly inflated" estimates of reading levels of children finishing their programmes', and that 'assessments of reading book level' by classroom teachers are 'inaccurate'.[40]

Throughout August and September, newspaper headlines successively announced a 'fall in reading standards' and counter-claims that 'the literacy level was dropping' with the release of a report by the Otago National Monitoring Unit,[41] and the Education Review Office (ERO).[42] Detailed opinions from commentators on both sides of the debate were quoted in the *New Zealand Education Review*,[43] a New Zealand based weekly newspaper which focuses specifically upon educational topics.

The ERO report on literacy, released at the beginning of September, added a major impetus to the debate over 'poor' literacy standards. The report stated that 'poor teaching rather than a lack of resources' was to blame for 'problems with teaching reading in schools'. In her reply, The

New Zealand Principals Federation president stated that 'primary school teachers will be very aggrieved', as the 'sample [used in the ERO report] was far too small to make such sweeping assumptions'. She also reiterated the claims of whole-language supporters that 'New Zealand children scored highly in international literacy studies and reading programmes developed here [in New Zealand] were in demand overseas'.[44]

Despite such attempts to argue that little was seriously wrong with literacy standards in New Zealand, the majority of headlines such as 'New Zealand loses world crown in reading',[45] 'Poor reading claim renews dispute',[46] and 'Schools "fail to teach reading skills"',[47] gave the impression that teachers were failing to properly teach reading skills. At the end of September, the South Pacific edition of *Time Magazine*[48] published an article with the headlines: 'An Australian survey stirs debate over the best way to teach children the first two Rs.' The article reflected the New Zealand situation stating that, 'While some educators emphatically agreed with its findings, teachers' unions and state education ministers roundly criticised it'.

In October 1997, the New Zealand Business Round Table and its associated organisation, the Education Forum, entered the debate.[49] The Director of Research for the Education Forum and policy analyst for the New Zealand Business Round Table (NZBRT), Michael Irwin, linked the press coverage of 'adult literacy problems' to the debate over methods of teaching emergent literacy. This moved the focus of the debate from the methods of teaching emergent literacy to an emphasis upon the teaching profession's competence. All literacy problems could be attributed to New Zealand teachers. They had a vested interest in resisting change and their approaches to teaching literacy had 'obviously failed':

> evidence of the mediocre state of much of our education system is everywhere. If the stream of complaints from university teachers and employers about the literacy problems of school leavers is even half true, we have big problems in the teaching of English . . . That educators are still largely in denial about these problems says a great deal about the stake they have in policies and approaches that have so obviously failed.[50]

During May 1998, the New Zealand press carried reports of the British Labour government's new 'national literacy strategy'. Coverage of this topic was not limited to the daily newspapers. *The National Business Review*'s 1 May article linked the news of the British Government's 'literacy strategy' to employers' interests with this headline: 'Why your employees are illiterate: educators refuse to acknowledge that our children are struggling to read under the present system'. This article stated adult literacy problems could be directly linked to the methods used to teach emergent literacy. Advocates of the 'phonic method' for teaching reading were the main interviewees in this article which linked their side of the 'reading war' to the business sector's concerns over 'workforce literacy'. The article quoted Nicholson as having referred to the 'British' reading policy, which supported abandoning the promotion of whole language and increasing support for 'phonics':

> In Britain in March this year David Blunkett, the Education Secretary, announced all primary schools will be required to return to the traditional method of phonics, and abandon 'the present system by which children are largely expected to learn by reading story books to their teachers' once again directly linked the methods of teaching reading to the concerns over adult literacy. Here in New Zealand we encounter the defeatist attitude from some professionals that there will always be slow readers, nothing can be done about it.[51]

Nicholson and Irwin were in accord that illiteracy would 'always be with us' as long as teachers resisted using the correct method. *The National Review* article implied that the failure to teach phonics was the cause of New Zealand's 'workforce' literacy problems. The article concluded with Nicholson reinforcing the article's theme that illiteracy could be solved through the use of phonics, which was the correct method to teach reading.[52]

The beginning of May also saw the release of a 'Government consultation Green Paper' on 'Assessment for Success in Primary Schools', which proposed to make changes by 'Bringing in external, nation-wide maths and literacy tests, based on the curriculum, for students in Year 6 and Year 8'. The influence of similar policies introduced in other OECD (Organisation for Economic Cooperation and Development) countries was noted in the background to this document, with the statement that 'Similarly, education policy in the countries belonging to the OECD is also shifting to focus on the results or outcomes of education'.[53]

At the beginning of October 1998, in an article headed 'Get the Bureaucrats out of education', the Chairman of the NZBRT, Roger Kerr, was quoted as criticising the 'whole language' approach to the teaching of reading and grammar in New Zealand and supporting phonics.[54] In mid-October, headlines announced 'leaks' that New Zealand's National Government intended to follow the British initiative and develop their own 'back to basics' literacy strategy.[55] At the end of October, *The National Business Review*, in its analysis of current New Zealand educational policy, pointed out that these announcements were part of 'Recent curriculum-related school announcements' which 'fit' a 'pattern' 'of announcements in principle that can be incorporated into a manifesto for the inevitable [1999] election and its campaign trail':

> the re-affirmed emphasis upon the 'three Rs – reading "riting" and "rithmetic"'. This is a ritual of modern western culture – one can trace the political fortunes of governments by the frequency and nature of

such calls ... Suddenly without public debate the traditional big three [three Rs] are given precedence. The fact teachers complain that the new literacy announcement has been made without their involvement supports the perception that it is partly a political move, a knee-jerk reaction to some league table results. Change the coach, we have lost some tests.[56]

The New Zealand reading debate as it re-emerged during the 1990s thus reflected broader, often conflicting political forces. University-based academics, teaching professionals, the Business Round Table and all the other participants in the current public debate over 'literacy standards' in New Zealand had their own educational political agendas, sometimes resulting in alliances between disparate groups. As revealed below, the resulting controversy was to prove a political embarrassment for successive governments that could not afford the reading standards issue to become a political catch-cry that might be utilised by opposition parties and impact upon the electorate at large.

The membership of the New Zealand Taskforce

In New Zealand, the Literacy Taskforce was set up by the National Government in 1998, together with a separate Literacy Experts Group. While the English Literacy Taskforce consisted of one group of ten members, the New Zealand Literacy Taskforce report drew the expertise of thirty-three participants. *The Report of the New Zealand Taskforce* was written with contributions from two groups, the Literacy Taskforce group, which had twenty-three members, and the 'Literacy Experts' Group, which had ten members, two of whom were also members of the main taskforce group. As well as greater numbers, the New Zealand Taskforce report drew upon a greater pool of direct-experience literacy research and the development of literacy initiatives. The ten members of the Literacy Experts Group, whose own report was used to write the task force report, were appointed because of their ability to 'provide the Literacy Taskforce with advice from theoretical and academic perspectives'.[57]

At first glance, this would appear to have permitted the New Zealand Taskforce to draw upon a much larger range of experience and research expertise than the smaller English Literacy Task Force. In reality, however, the highly politicised nature of the New Zealand reading debate was to prove a key factor in the ostensibly neutral review processes and reports of the next few years. The Government's need to be seen to 'balance' sharply opposing points of view meant that political considerations were to dominate the process from the very beginning. Both the Literacy Taskforce and the Literacy Experts Group attempted to 'balance' advocates of whole-language and phonics-based programmes.[58] Perhaps unsurprisingly, the reports of both groups were essentially compromises. Further, vitriolic debate led to the setting up of yet another committee – the Education and Science Select Committee. This committee consisted of representatives from all the major political parties. The inquiry took seventeen months to complete and the select committee received 300 submissions.[59] A sub-committee was set up to hear evidence, and there were public hearings across the country. The Education and Science Select Committee Report on Reading was finally released in 2000. This report was broadly consistent with the earlier reports, but was much stronger on the need for the inclusion of phonics.[60] Such a conclusion was bound to be controversial and eventually proved to be politically unacceptable. In 2002, the Minister of Education, the Hon. Trevor Mallard, dismissed the recommendations, including one that teacher training providers incorporate the teaching of phonetic skills and word-level decoding into their programmes, declaring that these things were already being done. At the time of writing, the situation remains largely deadlocked.

An examination of the membership of the English Task Force indicates its members held coherent views on 'best practice' which conformed with clearly articulated government policy. In New Zealand, governmental approaches to the issue of raising 'literacy standards' were not so clearly defined. Academics and professionals who were invited to contribute to the New Zealand Taskforce report also held diverse and even opposing views of 'best practice'. The references to the research used to construct the Literacy Experts Group's report indicated that the members of this group also engaged in research on a range of literacy-related perspectives. They also held a range of views regarding the debates over the 'the best practice of teaching literacy' and had engaged on opposing sides in public debates over the teaching of reading.[61]

Research evidence and the Literacy Taskforce reports

On the 28 of February 1997, *The Preliminary Report of the English Literacy Task Force* was released by the Labour Government.[62] The report cited research, 'studies', 'data' and 'experience' as the basis for its conclusions. Unlike the New Zealand Literacy Taskforce, the English Literacy Task Force did not draw upon a Literacy Experts Group. The New Zealand Literacy Experts Group concluded with an extensive bibliography that provides a clear indication of the research base the New Zealand Literacy Taskforce report drew upon when constructing their report. The Literacy Experts Group's recommendations were integrated into the report of the New Zealand Literacy Task Force. Nor does The English Literacy Task Force provide appendices to explain the evaluation of educational achievement studies, as the New Zealand Taskforce report does. This makes it more difficult to trace the research base that informed the English Literacy Task Force's recommendations. Roger Beard, who was not a member of the task-force, has more recently published papers on the research that influenced the Literacy Hour.[63] In order to compare how the two original documents drew upon a research base to reach and justify their recommendations, the following discussion focuses upon the material contained within the two Literacy Taskforce reports.

Both use national and international data in the first part of their reports to arrive at recommendations for 'the best practice'. The second part of each report outlines how these recommendations will be implemented. In the second section, the two reports reach different response possibilities to the problem of an identifiable group of low achievers. An examination of the first section of the reports of the two literacy taskforces enables an exploration of how the similar sources of data were used to reach the different recommendations outlined in the second section of each report.

The Introduction to the English Literacy Task Force report stressed the contributions made by outside experts and the 'substantial consultation' which had taken place up to this point, although no details were given:

> Our aim is to draw on the huge amounts of information and thinking that have been put at our disposal to produce a final report by the end of May 1997. If we are to achieve our goal of designing a strategy which can stand the test of time, it is essential that it is founded on the best available information and commends widespread support.[64]

The target for 'reading well' and the directive to 'design a strategy' was set by David Blunkett rather than derived from a consideration of the research base:

> When David Blunkett established the Literacy Task Force, he asked us to design a strategy to meet an ambitious target; namely that: 'By the end of a second term of a Labour government all children leaving primary school . . . will have reached a reading age of at least eleven.'[65]

The 'executive summary' in the Introduction to the New Zealand Literacy Taskforce report outlines a similar target to that set for the English Task-force. Like the English Literacy Task Force, The New Zealand Taskforce endorses the Government's goal that 'By 2005, every child turning nine will be able to read, write and do maths for success'.[66] Unlike the English Literacy Task Force, however, the New Zealand Literacy Taskforce does not refer to a government directive to 'design a strategy', as political and bureaucratic sensitivities largely precluded such an option.

The introduction to the English Literacy Task Force report concluded with references to data collected by local agencies such as OFSTED and what the report referred to as 'international comparisons'. This data was seen to reinforce the 'disturbing picture of literacy achievement' described in the previous section. The international data was used to argue that there 'is evidence of the existence of a "long tail"' in the results among British schools. In the analysis of the significance of this data in the conclusion of section three, it was argued that this data showed that allowing the teaching profession the autonomy to adopt new practices was not feasible.

The New Zealand Literacy Taskforce stated it had used international data that was stated to come 'from the IEA international survey of reading of nine-year-olds' that was explained in detail in Appendix C of their report. Like the English Literacy Task Force, they used this data to evaluate New Zealand's position relative to other countries, and claimed that the studies confirmed that New Zealand children were successful readers when compared with children in countries with similar or better socio-economic conditions.

The depth of analysis of the international data varies between the reports. The New Zealand Taskforce report took the conclusions of their analysis of the data a stage further than the English Task Force. Their analysis of the IEA data included the breaking down of the data of lower-ability pupils who formed the 'long tail' of low achievement. Given the strength of the Maori political lobby, the New Zealand Literacy Taskforce used the IEA data to differentiate levels of poor achievement in relation to different cultural and socio-economic groups. They acknowledged the need to account for the existence of other languages of instruction by stating that 'there has been no systematic collection of children's progress and achievement in the medium of Maori (or any other language of instruction)'.[67]

The English Task Force placed an emphasis upon a large group of under-achievers in literacy which had been identified in the 'international studies', without specifying the specific make-up of this group. This was followed by points which targeted the failure of teachers and specific programmes to meet these needs, and the recommendations that the needs of this group had to be met by a national, systematic strategy to bring to bear pressures upon the teaching profession to address this issue. The New Zealand analysis of the IEA International Survey of Reading data identified particular factors, and therefore particular groups, who were in the low-achieving group. This analysis was used to arrive at the political palliative that particular and diverse strategies needed to be employed to reach the needs of those groups.

There was also a significant difference in the use of local data in the Introduction to both reports that also reflected the use of international data described above. The English Literacy Task Force relied upon local data from OFSTED and local agencies that focused upon national test results. The New Zealand Literacy Taskforce used local data which surveyed reading achievement in low socio-economic schools, data from the Reading Recovery scheme, and data from the National Educational Monitoring Project. The

National Monitoring Project data is gathered independently of ERO, New Zealand's equivalent of OFSTED and school-administered tests, although the validity of the data has been called into question. Nevertheless, the New Zealand Taskforce used this data to draw a detailed picture about those who were prominent in the low-achieving group and to argue that there was a need for different school-based and professionally-led responses to literacy difficulties.

An analysis of local and international data is given immediately after these introductory statements which set goals and government agendas. The difference in the amount of control governmental agendas gave each literacy taskforce to suggest response possibilities appears to have been a major influence upon each taskforce's interpretations of these studies.

The English Literacy Task Force opted to abandon the New Zealand-developed Reading Recovery scheme, arguing that because England is in the middle of the international league tables, variation must be prevented by 'putting in place a coherent strategy rather than a series of fleeting and unconnected initiatives such as Reading Recovery, the Better English Campaign, and the National Literacy Project'.[68]

Drawing upon international and local data, and understandings of 'best practice' that includes reference to New Zealand initiatives, the English Task Force claims that 'a constant national strategic approach over five to ten years' is the only possible way to bring about a dramatic improvement in literacy. They argue that this strategy 'combines what we now know about best practice in the teaching of reading with an appreciation of ten years of education reform'.[69] Their analysis of the research based on 'best practice' stresses the need to develop a national strategy that decreases the professional autonomy to develop best practice:

> The notion of professional autonomy was strongly embedded in the educational service yet there were insufficient mechanisms in place either within the profession itself or in the education service more generally to ensure either that practice was based firmly on evidence or that best practice was rapidly adopted or even adopted at all by others. As a result, practice varied hugely from school to school. At best it was excellent, at worst a matter of anything goes.[70]

The New Zealand Literacy Taskforce drew upon similar data to provide a different analysis and response. They recommended increasing the number of teachers and school-based responses to developing 'best practice':

> In New Zealand, decisions about how to teach are made at the school level – that is, teaching methods are not prescribed as part of the national curriculum, although official guidance is provided through the teacher materials outlined later in this report. The Literacy Taskforce believes

that this policy should not be changed. Decisions about teaching strategies, teaching approaches, and materials to use are professional decisions that are best made at the local school level in response to the needs of particular groups of children and individuals.[71]

Viewed politically, however, this conclusion is very similar to the claims made for professional autonomy in various educational documents developed post-Picot: claims that a number of New Zealand's educational researchers have seriously challenged. A further result in this case was merely to preserve the status quo, with neither side in the reading debate entirely happy with the outcome. Moreover, the recent (2004) release of the document, *Progress in International Reading Literacy Study* (PIRLS), comparing reading achievement across nations including England and New Zealand, has seen the reading debate renewed with fresh vigour amongst New Zealand academics. This debate has come to focus particularly on the achievement gap between middle-class and working-class children, together with the strategies for teaching reading that might help to alleviate the problem. Given the current New Zealand Labour Government's highly publicised goal of 'closing the gaps', it might be pertinent to ask whether this realignment of interests in literacy will lead to a new round of 'Reading Wars' or to a National Literacy Strategy on the current English model.

Chapter 7

Reading Recovery

A comparative case study

Introduction: the development of Reading Recovery

Reading Recovery (RR) was initially developed in New Zealand during the 1970s and 1980s. It was introduced into England in the early 1990s only after it had become widely established as the officially recognised programme for addressing literacy difficulties in New Zealand. RR's development in New Zealand was facilitated by ten years of consistent influence and guidance from Marie Clay and a small group of key initiators. As well as utilising the strengths of a tightly organised programme, these initiators were also able to respond and benefit from a centrally organised education system. In New Zealand, at least until the end of the 1980s, RR had few recognised critics, and it was supported by successive governments as well as the educational bureaucracy. During the last decade, however, there have been increasingly polarised debates between proponents of phonics and whole language/real books, coupled with intractable issues of ownership and control.

A key reason for looking in more detail at the beginnings of RR in New Zealand is that the organisation and centralisation of RR, together with the programme's apparently successful adoption in the United States and Australia, were features that originally attracted many English educators and politicians to the programme.[1] In the event, however, as we shall demonstrate, the educational and political context in England differed markedly, serving to restrict its influence so that it never became a nationwide programme to the extent that this occurred in New Zealand. The devolved nature of school funding made it difficult for LEAs to support RR in any consistent manner. Moreover, the pilot programme was originally funded under the pressure of addressing criticisms that literacy standards were falling. Hence, the authorities were unwilling to commit large amounts of government funding to a single programme for a sustained period of time.

In addition, the culture and climate within both the LEAs and the teaching profession created resistance to the adoption of a highly structured, procedure-driven programme. While there were strong supporters and advo-cates of RR amongst English teachers, educators and academics, the profes-sion and administration did not in general feel a sense of ownership built up through gradual evolution of the programme, as had largely been the case in New Zealand. Neither had RR time to adapt and evolve to fit the English situation.

The origins of RR in New Zealand

The teaching of reading in New Zealand has long been controversial. Concern over reading, post-Second World War, has been fairly continuous, rising to a peak roughly once in each decade. At such times, public and pro-fessional concern over reading represents just the visible tip of deeper issues impacting upon the schools. In the late 1940s, for instance, concern over lit-eracy among school leavers entering the new post-war job market stimulated purchase of the supposedly more scientifically organised *Janet & John Readers*.[2] In early 1960s, public and media concern over reading saw Janet and John supplanted in 1964 by the *Ready to Read* series, which de-emphas-ised the teaching of phonics in favour of a methodology that seemed more in tune with the more liberal and eclectic aspirations of the new decade.[3]

Throughout these years, the New Zealand Department of Education consis-tently maintained the myth that it did not favour any particular strategy for the teaching of reading over another, but simply allowed teachers to use a combination of approaches as the need arose. Departmental actions, however, suggest otherwise. In 1963, for instance, pamphlets were sent to every parent in the country, pointing out that the teaching of reading was a crucial and highly skilled task that the home would be wise to leave mainly to the school.[4] The accompanying handbook for the *Ready to Read* series, specially prepared within the Department by Reading Advisor Myrtle Simpson, emphasised the importance of teaching reading in the context of reading stories rather than teaching words in isolation.[5] Phonetic analysis was to occur only when the teacher saw a need for it.[6] Simpson's advice was soon supported by a new Auckland University reading researcher, Marie Clay, who argued that this method of learning to read approximated those of skilled, mature readers.[7]

The first half of the 1970s therefore saw the Department of Education becoming more proactive than ever before in changing teacher attitudes towards the teaching of reading. A 1972 editorial in the professional journal, *Education*, applauded the comprehensive range of measures that had been recently introduced to this end. They included the appointment of reading advisors to junior classes, the introduction of a Diploma in Teaching course in reading, the provision of special reading materials, libraries in primary schools and the expansion of in-service courses in reading.

The Department made available considerable resources for in-service pro-grammes.[8] At the beginning of 1976, some 2,000 Auckland teachers took the Department's 'Early Reading In-Service Course' (ERIC), receiving special leave to attend. By 1978, it was available nationwide, with teachers receiving special leave and travel concessions to complete twelve units of ERIC at special centres with facilities for the presentation of audio-tutorial units for up to one-and-a-half hours over a twelve-week period.[9] Under its director, John Slane, a seconded Auckland school inspector, ERIC aimed to promote grassroots change. Accordingly, it placed considerable importance on securing a 'generic colleague-to-colleague relationship between course members and course providers'. The ideal mode of delivery for ERIC, however, was considered to be through the centres rather than schools, and there was some concern expressed lest the learning principles become compromised in rural areas where schools became de facto venues.[10]

The Department was also active in securing assistance from private publishers. In a paper delivered to the Fourth New Zealand Conference of the International Reading Association (IRA), Beverley Randell, a writer and publisher of reading books, praised the Department for being 'very helpful to private publishers in this country by giving encouragement to the publication of supporting books and by distributing *Ready to Read* vocabulary lists'.[11]

Concern with reading in New Zealand during the early 1970s should also be viewed within a wider cultural and economic context. In this instance, the operative factors were public spending cuts introduced in order to combat a deepening economic crisis, a high youth unemployment rate and a sharpening perception of a race problem, fuelled by continuing Maori educational under-achievement. Moreover, in reading circles, new organisations such as the IRA placed a new importance on the relative decline of printed sources and the increased role of the media in shaping youth values. Domestic publishers were beginning to enter the growing market for supplementary readers. A strong media interest in illiteracy was fuelled by an increasing realisation among academics that here was a powerful means of popularising their own concerns about the teaching of reading.

RR development and expansion

It was into this complex mixture of pessimism and optimism that RR emerged in New Zealand during the mid-1970s. RR's developer, Marie Clay, envisaged it as an early-intervention strategy that involved the extension of existing whole-language approaches to the individual tuition of young children identified as having difficulties with reading. Virtually from the beginning, however, the Department of Education regarded the RR project as having developed as a joint venture between Clay, the University of Auckland and the Auckland office of the Department of Education.[12] Clay herself was later to concede that the first steps in the implementation of RR would never have been taken without the support of a District Senior

Inspector who insisted on personally visiting the project site.[13] From 1976 to 1978, the project set out to explore and describe both the range of reading behaviours and the variety of teaching responses with respect to six-year-olds considered to be experiencing reading difficulties.

These early years involved considerable clinical study, from which a draft manual of procedures was written. In 1977 field trials were carried out in five schools. The success of these trials resulted in an expansion of the RR project, involving an in-service training course in 1979 for approximately fifty teachers of junior classes. The course equipped participants to provide a programme of individual reading tuition in their schools. In each school an experienced teacher was released for two hours daily to become familiar with RR procedures and to individually instruct six-year-olds experiencing reading difficulties.[14] Clay's book, *The Early Detection of Reading Difficulties with Reading Recovery Procedures*, was published in Auckland by Heineman in late 1979, and the Department of Education contacted Auckland principals regarding a major in-service course in the region to be held in 1980. Expansion was rapid. By 1981, RR was also operating in the Hamilton region. By this time some 129 schools possessed teachers trained in RR procedures and additional funding had became increasingly urgent.[15]

Meanwhile, RR was attracting considerable professional interest. A remit from NZPTA to the Minister of Education sought Government finance to extend the programme nationally. Following a large-scale and favourable evaluation of RR in February 1980, the Department sought further Government resources for the programme early in 1981. At this time, a senior Departmental officer observed that RR enjoyed 'the full unqualified support of the Director-General, and required only an undertaking from the Government to provide sufficient finance for its expansion'.[16] The officer conceded, however, that extension of the programme involved more than finance alone. It would involve an extensive training scheme for teachers, which would limit the rate of programme expansion. In addition it necessitated a considerable shift in both teacher thinking and school organisation, neither of which would 'be accomplished quickly or evenly'.[17]

With the programme enjoying official favour, product promotion became an effective marketing ploy for many schools, whether they were actually engaged in the programme or not. This particular problem provoked the Department's Wellington-based Director of Schools Supervision, A. Gilchrist, to write to all District Senior Inspectors of primary schools in July 1981, warning them of the growing tendency for many schools to use the term 'RR' to describe their own remedial programmes. Aware that such actions could create future difficulties for the Department, he observed that it would be helpful in the future 'if they avoided using the RR name, however close to the authorized version those programmes might be'.[18]

To some extent, however, the overwhelming concentration on the 'authorized version' of RR, together with its implications for school resourcing, brought the Department into conflict with the NZEI. Briefing notes provided by the Department to the Minister of Education in December 1982, shortly before he was scheduled to receive an NZEI deputation, pointed out that the position of the Institute had been summed up in an editorial in the December issue of its magazine, *National Education*. The editorial had concluded that the value of the RR programme did not 'justify asking schools to dismantle the various successful and essential programmes now staffed by their part time hours in order to support RR training'.[19]

Ultimately, however, many teachers probably came to support RR because of its whole language/real books philosophy which they considered to empower them as professionals.[20] A further reason for the rapid success of RR lay in its centralised structure of support. Up until the early 1980s, RR was largely concentrated in the Auckland and Hamilton districts of the North Island, but in 1983 a structure was adopted that could provide a basis for nationwide implementation. Teachers were given long-term support by inspectors and specially prepared RR tutors. Close cooperation between Departmental school inspectors and tutors was regarded as a particular strength in keeping the programme operating as designed. All applicants for RR tutor positions were required to have successfully completed a recognised training course.[21] Aspiring applicants were selected by a special panel that included the Director of RR. The only recognised course was that held at the Auckland College of Education. This was staffed by RR tutors under the leadership of the Director of RR, Barbara Watson, and overseen by Clay. Both Watson and Clay were to remain adamant concerning the need for continued control over tutor training and administration in order to maintain its quality.[22]

In late 1988, the Labour Government announced economies in education. These included cuts to RR allocations in some districts, provoking impassioned defences of the programme from teachers of reading, RR tutors and Departmental officers. In the face of this reaction, it is hardly surprising that a government-commissioned (1989) report by a team headed by Professor Ted Glynn of the University of Otago, entitled 'Reading Recovery in Context',[23] which was critical of a number of aspects of RR, was itself strongly attacked by RR officials. Subsequently, the report received very little publicity and appears to have had little impact upon the continued operation, nationwide, of the RR programme. By this time successive governments were routinely pointing to the apparent success of RR and New Zealand's growing international reputation as a world leader in the teaching of reading as evidence of their own commitment to quality education. It was at this stage, in the late 1980s and early 1990s, before the programme's New Zealand-based critics had gained significant public and media attention,[24] that English politicians and educators began to consider introducing the programme to their schools.

The introduction of RR into England

In the early 1990s, English politicians saw the chance to utilise this New Zealand-developed programme to develop a reading scheme that would be the 'best available anywhere in the world'.[25] The political motivation for adopting Reading Recovery in the early 1990s was very similar to the media and public concern which had led to its initial development and adoption in New Zealand in the 1960s and 1970s. As we noted in Chapter 5, it was during 1991 that the Select Committee Report had expressed concern over HMI's findings that, in 20 per cent of schools, the 'work in reading was judged to be poor and required urgent attention'.[26] The publication in December 1991 of these 'first nationwide tests of seven year olds in England and Wales ... showed that more than a quarter had difficulty in reading'. This led to a political battle as the then-Conservative Government and Labour Opposition front benches rushed out rival plans to improve reading standards during the period immediately preceding the 1992 election.[27]

In their scramble to endorse a politically marketable solution to improve reading standards, both parties endorsed the Reading Recovery approach in January 1991. However, while both parties promoted Reading Recovery, they proposed to allocate significantly different sums to support it. The Conservative Government managed to release details of a £3 million funding project for 'poor readers', just hours before Labour was due to announce plans for a £42 million national Reading Recovery (RR) Programme.[28] Labour's education spokesman stated that his party would provide between £42 million and £70 million to establish a national RR programme for all primary children. The Conservative Government responded with an announcement that it would put £3 million into an RR programme which would target inner-city areas which had produced the worst test results amongst seven-year-olds. It also announced that it had recruited Marie Clay, the founder of RR, to run its scheme. Marie Clay, who was based at the London Institute of Education during this period, denied this claim and it was acknowledged that she would be an advisor rather than director of the initiative.[29]

Jack Straw, the Labour education spokesman, greeted the Conservative Government's capture of the RR programme with a mixture of anger and amusement and stated that he had been 'unable to find any statement by the Government about RR schemes until this morning'.[30] Straw also accused Conservative ministers of a 'panic reaction' in bringing forward their announcement to coincide with his speech and the Labour Party's announcement of its policy to fund RR.[31] The attraction for both the Conservative Government and the Labour Opposition was that RR offered a training package and a clearly articulated and well-evaluated approach that could be quickly implemented in the UK and therefore show that action was being taken to address concerns over falling literacy standards.

Marie Clay appeared to be aware that the use of RR as a political platform by both parties could have negative implications for the programme. She expressed concern that it might become the subject of a 'political row'. She was quoted as stating: 'It is exactly what could ruin our efforts'.[32] Francis Beckett noted her ability to judge political situations and to prevent RR becoming captured by a particular political party or reading 'ideologies' when he commented on her attempt to maintain a politically neutral stance and not engage in the phonics versus real books (whole language) debate, whilst successfully promoting RR during this period.[33]

While first Surrey LEA, and then the Government enthusiastically promoted the use of RR, there were concerns raised regarding the cost of RR from the beginning. Ngaio Crequer, reporting in the *Independent*, noted that it was not 'especially revolutionary' but conceded that it worked. While Jean Prance, who worked for Surrey LEA as the first English RR tutor, was reported as being 'absolutely delighted with it', some Surrey LEA staff had also noted that it was labour intensive and expensive. It was also noted that there was 'some scepticism about the effectiveness of the technique' in New Zealand as academics 'had questioned the amount of guessing involved'.[34] In addition to being an expensive method, RR posed initial problems for the Conservatives because it did not give a 'prominence to phonics' which 'many conservative politicians believed to be at the core of successful teaching'.[35]

It was pointed out, however, that there were apparently no concerns over the cost of the programme for New Zealand governments as the 'scheme's success in its native land since 1984 has made it the sacred cow of an education budget ravaged by cuts'. The New Zealand National Government had immediately reversed cuts to RR in 1991. It had given assurances that the programme would continue in the future even though, as we have noted, the 1989 report had cast doubts on the scheme's long-term effectiveness'.[36] From the English point of view at this time, however, 'the political unanimity on Reading Recovery' was 'as strong in New Zealand as it now is in Britain'.

Nevertheless, the New Zealand Government appeared more willing to meet the high costs of the programme as the English Conservative Government would 'commit itself only to 3 million pounds for a pilot scheme' and the English Labour Party had 'not put a firm price tag upon its promise',[37] but had acknowledged that they would also have to limit the use of RR to pilot schemes. Even though Labour was advocating that more should be spent on RR than the Conservative Government had designated, there were public acknowledgements even at this initial stage of the uptake of RR into government policy that cost would also be the key factor in determining the extent to which Labour would implement the programme in England. Straw publicly acknowledged this when he stated that 'Reading Recovery is an expensive method. We want to set up pilot schemes to see whether it is cost effective.'[38]

Politicians' concerns over the costs of RR and their subsequent account-ability for spending were not the only factor that led to a localised imple-mentation of RR. The localised funding of LEAs resulted in the Government paying 60 per cent of the funding for RR, however, and leaving the LEAs having to pay the remaining 40 per cent of the cost. The limited number of funded piloted programmes and short time span of the allocated funding also implied that RR would only be available to a small proportion of pupils for a limited period of time. The funding for RR, however, was only given for a three-year trial, which was due to run out in March 1994.[39] The poll-tax capping of funding was also seen to restrict Local Authorities' spending to the level which would enable them to meet local needs.[40] Despite the worries about the cost of the programme, through-out 1992 the RR programme remained popular with politicians who were becoming increasingly concerned about the rising costs of resourcing pupils' individual statements of special educational needs. As in New Zealand, politicians in England could claim that, in supporting RR, they were taking positive steps to overcome pupils' reading difficulties in a way that offered good value for money as opposed to the statementing procedure.[41]

While cost and the time-scale of the funding were the major limiting factors in the uptake of RR in England, there is also evidence of teacher and professional resistance to the importation of a programme that had not been developed within English schools. Teachers commenting upon RR in the press argued that the system was successful because it provided individual attention for children, and implied that teachers should be supported to provide more one-to-one attention in addressing reading difficulties, rather than necessarily needing to import a reading programme. The adoption of RR was also interpreted as a failure to recognise the 'invaluable' work which was already going on in primary schools in England. Some teachers even went as far as to publicly state that they were 'filled' with 'anger' at the announcement that RR was to be introduced into inner-city schools because this would cause 'the removal of thousands of remedial teachers from school staffs'.[42]

Other educationalists argued that RR was not as new 'as the politicians would have us believe', as many Local Education Authorities had already been adapting and implementing RR techniques.[43] They pointed out that, in LEAs such as Leicestershire, teachers had been trained to blend Marie Clay's methods with other teaching techniques. Yet despite these criticisms there was tacit support from the National Union of Teachers as RR was seen as positive support for one-to-one and small-group teaching.

O'Leary also commented that the adoption by the Government was a 'marked contrast' to previous educational policy and conservative educa-tional philosophies that supported a 'return to traditional methods, rote teaching and whole-class work'. Why then *did* the Tories support RR in England? Arguably, the reason lay in the programme's centralised structure,

as this was to be perceived by the English observers of RR in actual operation in New Zealand. In February 1992, the Government revealed that the
DES was undertaking a national trial of the Reading Recovery programme,
which was to be conducted with six-year-old children in some 200 inner-
city schools in twenty-one local authorities who were experiencing reading
difficulties.[44] In the opinion of the Government and of Ofsted, only New
Zealand, where the programme was originally developed, could demonstrate
RR as a coherent national system. Accordingly, given the context of
continuing national expressions of concern about reading standards in
England, two HMI were selected to spend two weeks visiting New Zealand
in 1992, 'to observe and report on RR in action'.[45] The bulk of their time
was spent observing RR lessons in schools, together with training and
continuing contact courses for RR teachers in Auckland, Wellington and
Christchurch. In addition, time was spent in briefing sessions with the Chief
Executive of Ministry of Education and Ministry staff, recently retired DSIs
who had fostered early RR development, the principal of ACE and staff
responsible for administering RR in the Auckland area, parents and former
pupils in the scheme, and university researchers at Auckland and Canter-
bury.[46] Not surprisingly, perhaps, given the export potential of the programme, HMI was presented with an official story of almost unmitigated
success in New Zealand.

The preface to the 1993 Ofsted report on the visit claimed that the RR
scheme had 'excited widespread interest both in the United Kingdom and
elsewhere'.[47] However, it is particularly noteworthy that the English
observers appear to have been most impressed, not with the method of
reading being taught, but by the degree and extent of government funding,
direction and control. HMI particularly noted the 'importance of establishing a monitoring regime to follow the progress of all pupils for whom the
programme has proved successful'.[48] On the RR lessons themselves, the visitors commented that 'This was no chance harmony of practice: it was in line
with the advice contained in *Reading in junior classes*, the handbook which
accompanies the *Ready to Read* series and which, like the series itself, is available in all schools.'[49] HMI also stressed the uniform nature of the initial
training all teachers received, and the continuing influence of two previous
national in-service initiatives undertaken in New Zealand, whose materials
remained in widespread use. This uniformity was also seen to be reflected in
the training of tutors, where all possessed a copy of Marie Clay's book, *The
Early Detection of Reading Difficulty*, the core text of the programme.[50]

Whilst the report emphasised that the visit had not been long enough or
sufficiently representative to embark on full reliable comparisons with
England, some clear professional impressions had evidently emerged. The
significant differences with England thus included New Zealand's adherence
to the same core-reading scheme throughout the nation. The *Ready to Read*
series was provided free to schools and central guidance was given on its use.

Teachers were well prepared to teach reading in the normal classroom, and the report noted that the RR programme was built on 'a very thorough approach to teaching reading'.[51] HMI field notes likewise recorded the impression (reproduced in bold type in the report) that 'literacy [was] accorded the supremely important place in the New Zealand education system, as evidenced by the time and space given to it in the daily routines of primary schools and in ITT, the resources devoted to it by government and by local boards of trustees'. Moreover, the curriculum itself had fewer competing elements, enabling teachers to concentrate far more on securing a very sound foundation of literacy in the early years. The classroom organisation of reading was thus 'generally more coherent and efficient than would normally be found in a sample of similar kind and size over a similar period of time in England'.[52] The advantages of a centrally controlled system were likewise emphasised in the conclusion to the report which asserted that 'The essential conditions for the success of Reading Recovery, as a system, lie in the coherence, the resourcing and the reach of the support and quality assurance structures which are put in place for its implementation'.[53]

Once pilot funding was gained, the programme was tested in twenty English LEAs by the beginning of 1993.[54] It quickly emerged, however, that there were key differences between the situations in New Zealand and England. English politicians and educators attempting to introduce RR into educational, political and funding contexts were markedly different from those in New Zealand. Significant changes had occurred in the organisation of English educational structures and funding mechanisms in the period immediately preceding the introduction of RR. This meant that the wider structures for implementing and funding RR were very different from the centralised structures which existed in New Zealand during the same period. RR was introduced at a time when centralised funding was being abolished in favour of devolving funding to individual schools.[55] This had led to a reduction in LEA services, and a funding system for teacher release which made it extremely difficult to pay tutors and schools as they trained teachers. This situation resulted in the non-participation by some LEAs, funding difficulties for those that did participate and schools dropping out of the programme.[56]

In New Zealand an understanding had developed between educational administrators and governmental organisations, over the time RR had evolved during the 1970s and 1980s, that the programme was to be maintained and supported as the 'one best' approach to the nation's problems with early-reading difficulties. In England it was a very different situation. English-based educators who supported RR found that the English government and educational administrators did not fully appreciate the nature and structure of the RR programme at the time it was introduced. They, therefore, had unrealistic expectations of its ability to rapidly show results in addressing the claims in the early 1990s that there had been a reduction in reading standards. The biggest misunderstanding was over the potential to rapidly expand the programme to address large numbers of pupils. Marie Clay had warned shortly after the initial granting of £1.8 million to the first inner-city project that it may not 'yield the quick results that ministers want'.[57] English educators who became involved with RR programmes found that her warning was justified. The RR system of training of tutors, tutors' training of teachers and the fact that teachers had to work with small numbers of children all reduced the ability for rapid expansion and coverage of large numbers of students.[58] New Zealand-based RR tutors who came to work with English LEAs during the initial stages of the programme also found that the LEAs they worked with had difficulties dealing with the complexities and commitment demanded by instigating RR. They felt that the LEA colleagues they worked with failed to understand that 'Reading Recovery was a package and did a whole set of things that you wanted'. The New Zealand RR tutors viewed it as a 'high tech' programme founded on scientific principles that dictated how things had to be done in order to guarantee results. From their viewpoint, it was not possible to 'fiddle' with the programme or adapt it; 'you had to take it on as it was'. They found, however, that their English colleagues tended to take on some things and leave other aspects of the programme. The centralised nature of the programme, and the difference between the English and New Zealand situation, also made it even more difficult to negotiate solutions to problems they encountered in the English context. The LEAs' lack of understanding of the programme and its standardised procedures meant that they 'didn't listen to everything' the RR initiators told them. The English LEAs had their own traditions and ways of doing things, and an approach to teaching which, from a New Zealand RR tutor's point of view, appeared 'very individualistic'. The standardised procedures which were rooted in following the certain 'scientifically researched principles' which informed RR did not fit in with their English colleagues more 'personal' approach. Given this situation, LEAs often engaged with the programme at a superficial level, by taking the funding but not following it through.[59]

By early 1993, it was becoming increasingly unlikely that RR would be introduced throughout England. Rather, it was clear that RR would continue to be tied to local authority initiatives, with little hope of finding the money to expand the programme after 1994. DfE officials were suggesting that funding for RR would have to be found in a 'single regeneration budget',[60] which implied that it would compete for funding with housing, training and other education projects. There would be no money specifically earmarked for RR. It was now evident that this would prevent RR ever becoming a national scheme as it would not give local authorities enough money to pay for RR teachers in their schools, as well as pay for the release of teachers for RR training. Nor would it cover the cost of training RR teachers.

The later 1990s in England: increasing tensions and contradictions

As we have seen from the previous chapter, the mid-to-late 1990s in England saw the development of The National Literacy Strategy[61] and whole-class teaching which can be seen to have adversely impacted upon a widespread uptake of one-to-one programmes such as RR. In 1996 the Conservative Government cut funding to RR,[62] and set up the National Literacy Project (NLP). Beard states that 'the NLP reflected many of the implications of the school effectiveness research'. The NLP was led by a senior member of Her Majesty's Inspectorate, John Stannard, who 'was not only very familiar with the inspection evidence of recent years but also with the findings from the school effectiveness and overseas literacy research'.[63]

This adoption of NLP marked a move away from the RR scheme, which had been supported by both main political parties in the early 1990s.[64] RR in New Zealand was marketed as targeting poorer readers in their first years of schooling, providing for one-to-one instruction together with the careful induction of the teacher to be an 'expert' in early literacy learning.[65] There is also an emphasis on the training and utilisation of specialist teachers able to utilise systematic observation and records to probe their students' difficulties in learning. These RR tutors then link with the classroom teacher in order to raise the quality of teaching in the classroom. RR therefore focuses upon individualised tuition which, in turn, feeds into classroom practices and pedagogical approaches. The NLP's emphasis was upon the management of literacy at a whole-school/whole-class level through monitoring by senior staff and National Foundation for Educational Research (NFER) based researchers.

The NLP also introduced a 'Framework for Teaching' and the Literacy Hour which 'were earlier versions of what were subsequently to be found in the NLS'.[66] As Labour's education policy developed during 1997, it became clear that many of the objectives and structures of the NLP would be kept and further developed by the new Labour Government. In May 1996, the Labour Party announced a back-to-basics drive to improve literacy standards if it became the government in the election to be held the following year. The Labour Party planned to raise standards through the introduction of a new literacy task force and wanted to examine ways of ensuring 'that every child leaving primary school does so with a reading age of 11 by the end of the second term of office'.[67] Labour party dissatisfaction with the quality of newly trained teachers also resulted in a pledge to place greater emphasis on basic skills, classroom discipline and whole-class teaching and the use of phonics.[68]

In February 1997, *the Preliminary Report of the English Literacy Task Force* was released by the Labour Government. The Literacy Task Force report reflected the tensions that were building between the avocation of whole-class instruction for efficient, centralised control of teaching practices and the need for individual approaches to teaching reading for those who experienced difficulties in learning to read. At the beginning of the introduction to the report, the New Zealand strategy, which utilised Reading Recovery for addressing reading difficulties, was praised as the way forward for English literacy policy. Yet, in paragraph 36, at the conclusion of the section, Reading Recovery was rejected as part of 'fleeting and unconnected initiatives' which were difficult to implement across the range of English schools.

This tension is apparent throughout the 1997 Literacy Task Force report. Paragraph 45 suggested that the emphasis would be upon whole-class as well as individual tuition. It stressed 'carefully sequenced whole-class, group and individual work to focus upon strategies and skills, with the teacher combining instruction, demonstration, questioning and discussion, providing the structure for subsequent tasks and giving help and constructive response'. In the section of the document entitled 'Children with Special Educational Needs', Reading Recovery was mentioned as providing a model for these needs. This section also noted the need for 'an individualised learning plan' and the role of special educational needs coordinators (SENCOs) in diagnosing children's particular needs.[69]

The release of the National Literacy Strategy, launched in August 1997, was followed by the Framework for Teaching[70] which came into operation under a quasi-statutory status in all state primary schools in England in September 1998. This document set out the teaching objectives in literacy for pupils from reception to Year 6 and outlined the format of a Literacy Hour as a daily period of time throughout the school which would be dedicated to 'literacy teaching time for all pupils.'[71] The tension between the need for individualised instruction for children *experiencing difficulties in literacy* and the avocation of whole-class teaching was also embedded in this document. Critics argued that the Framework for Teaching could be seen to emphasise 'interactive whole-class' teaching, which reflected the influence of school improvement literature that had been espoused by influential members of the Literacy Task Force.[72] There was also criticism of its lack of acknowledgement of individualised instruction and failure to cater successfully for children with special educational needs.[73]

Chapter 8

Conclusion

Reading debates and educational policy

This book has sought to fill a gap in existing research by seeking to examine broader questions concerning the origins and the contexts of national literacy policy, with reference to a defined historical period in English educational history. The central question we sought to address in this study was: 'What role did public debates over reading play in the shaping of the NLS in England?' In answering this question we were drawn to a consideration of the historical role that public debates over reading standards have played in precipitating the changes in literacy policy that took place in England between the end of the Second World War and the mid-1990s. The beginning of this period was characterised by a largely decentralised curriculum where reading was a matter for local authorities, schools and teachers. Over the next sixty years, the literacy curriculum in England became increasingly centrally controlled, through the introduction of national testing, the assessment of reading skills, the development of the NLS, accompanied by a growing preoccupation with international league table comparisons.

As we reviewed the historical sources available to us, we began to grapple with the issue of what commentators at various times have meant by terms such as 'standards', 'literacy' and 'illiteracy'. Indeed, the subtitle of this book, *Children Still Can't Read!*, encapsulates a powerful accusation that has been wielded by successive generations of concerned newspaper editors, politicians, reading researchers, teachers and parents. By attempting to shift the argument away from such narrow parameters, we are not necessarily dismissing what are quite legitimate concerns about children's reading. However, a historical study of the reading standards debate in England reveals that for various reasons it is extremely difficult to prove whether literacy standards across time have significantly risen or fallen. It therefore follows that, in the absence of clear-cut evidence one way or the other, we are drawn, as historians, to search for other explanations for the major and demonstrable impact that reading debates have undeniably had on educational policy formation in England during the post-Second World War period.

Our historical examination of the public debate over reading standards, and in particular its impact on policy in England, has led us to endorse the conclusion already reached by critical literacy theorists that literacy is an intensely political activity and that literacy instruction can be seen to be linked to particular ideologies.[1] There is also evidence for the view that, since the Second World War, there has been an assumption that there is a need to address 'illiteracy' and raise 'reading standards' to increase the drive to further economic interests and living standards. Debates over reading standards have also led to a withdrawal of public confidence and contributed to increasing standardisation and centralisation. In addition, the book has sought to enhance our understanding of the way in which reading standards debates can drive the development of the intervention policies that lie at the heart of so many sub-sequent curriculum policy initiatives in English education – a central theme identified and critiqued in the broader work of Stephen Ball, Roger Dale, Ken Jones, Christopher Knight and Brian Simon.[2]

In undertaking detailed historical study, however, we became increasingly aware that we needed to account for and explain the complex dynamics that made for shifting allegiances between politicians, newspaper commentators, professionals and others who were visible participants in the public debate over reading standards. As we became more familiar with the variety of views expressed by the various participants, it became clear that groups and individuals often shared common concerns such as anti-progressivist views, but nevertheless had different motives, and sometimes offered different solutions. Whilst we share the view of critical theorists that the result has been an increasing accent on the surveillance and centralisation of literacy teaching, we have attempted in this book to better clarify the diverse nature of the forces that eventually determine these outcomes.

As we came to outline and understand processes and dynamics which shaped the public debates over reading standards, we began to question the traditional Left–Right dualism implicit in much literacy theory and, instead, to embrace the more complex and dynamic Kliebardian conceptualisation of curriculum as a contested area. The English contexts demonstrates that, as reading debates become more public and more visible, the media, professionals and politicians, often with widely differing agendas, seek to utilise growing public concern in order to influence policy. More specifically, we illustrate the ways in which reading debates are intensified through being linked to both wider educational concerns over progressivism, and to governmental attempts to increase national efficiency. Hence, throughout the book, we have examined not only the impact on reading debates of reports such as the *Bullock Report*; documents such as *Crisis in the Classroom*, the Black Papers and Turner's *Sponsored Reading Failure*; published reading test scores, party politics and allegedly failing schools such as Tyndale and Culloden; but also the way in which public impressions and media portrayal of these actively contributes to power to influence policy.

Chapter 2 of our book reveals, somewhat surprisingly, that expressions of concern over reading standards were very frequent, even in the early post-war years. The chapter goes on to demonstrate that this concern did not have a direct impact on policy, concluding with a consideration of the various factors which prevented this process from occurring. Part 2 of the book examines the way in which heightened public, media and political concern over reading standards subsequently became crucial in creating a political climate where government intervention in the teaching and assessment of reading was considered desirable by both major political parties. Hence, this section emphasises the cumulative impact on policy of successive public debates over reading standards.

Part 2 also demonstrates not only a growing public concern over literacy, as evidenced by the increasing frequency of newspaper articles critical of literacy standards, but also the tendency of debates over reading standards to become linked to wider controversies over the impact of progressive educational methods on academic achievement. This tendency is linked with social concerns such as unemployment and industrial decline and cutbacks in funding to schools. The outcome of these trends proved to be highly significant. They included: the adoption of regular testing and assessment with a view to monitoring the trend of national reading standards; the realisation by politicians and political parties that educational standards in general and reading standards in particular were potentially important election issues; and the increasing willingness of governments to intervene in curriculum matters.

The opening chapter in Part 3 of the book builds upon our understandings of the way in which public debates over reading standards in England from the late 1960s on helped to create a climate of opinion that supported regular monitoring procedures and government intervention in response to national expressions of concern. It goes on to demonstrate how the NLS was introduced against a background of an increasing external control exercised over the curriculum and teaching styles. These public debates set the contexts for the revision of the National Curriculum in England, which was first introduced in the 1988 Education Reform act. This Act introduced a prescriptive and detailed curriculum with statutory national testing in the primary school at ages seven and eleven. It also encouraged an inspection system controlled by OFSTED. These initiatives would in turn provide a context which would fuel yet another literacy crisis over 'falling literacy standards' and a backlash against progressive teaching methods.

Coldron and Smith argue that there are three 'significant general features' that arose from their analysis of the key documents which implemented the national literacy and numeracy strategies. These significant features are: a 'central concern' over the 'behaviour of teachers in the classroom'; an 'assumption abroad that change was necessary' which was accompanied by a common consensus that literacy standards were low and falling; and finally that it was possible to bring about change and address falling standards through the 'science' and 'technology of teaching' rather than changing practice through 'reflection' and 'reflective practice'.[3]

Fisher's comments highlight the way in which early childhood educators are facing difficulties with the NLS emphasis upon literacy standards which fails to acknowledge the dominant child-centred and child-development orientation of early childhood educators.[4] Hilton argues that 'the National Literacy Strategy is a deskilling initiative which itself is based on unsubstantiated claims that its proposals are more effective than other methods'. She sees it as enshrining 'a mythology that teachers do not teach literacy effectively and need to be retrained to do so' and notes that 'there are no research findings of any validity whatsoever to support it'.[5]

Reading debates, of course, are by no means confined to England, as the international comparisons we provide in our book clearly demonstrate. Thus, in addition to considering the immediate context that led to the NLS and the Literacy Hour, we also examined the ongoing debate over literacy in New Zealand before turning, in Chapter 7, to the adoption of the RR early-intervention programme by its original homeland, New Zealand, and subsequently, by some English local authorities. One reason for this comparative approach is that it permits us to reflect on both the similarities and the differences between national contexts. Another reason for the choice of New Zealand for the purposes of comparison is that, in England, the teaching of reading and the development of reading policy in New Zealand is frequently viewed in idealised terms as being somehow 'non-political'. This book, however, suggests that, as in England, New Zealand debates over reading remained highly politicised, as well as having been sustained over a considerable period of time. To be sure, there are also significant differences between the two countries. New Zealand curriculum decisions have long followed a centre–periphery model where decisions are made at the centre and filtered through to the periphery by a variety of techniques.[6] Thus, whilst the trend in England has been towards centralisation and surveillance, the teaching of reading in New Zealand has been not so much characterised by the gradual onset of centralisation and surveillance, but rather by their maintenance.

A comparison of the development and content of the English *Literacy Task Force Preliminary Report* and the New Zealand *Report of the Literacy Taskforce* highlights the way in which differing wider political contexts, membership and governmental 'vision' can influence policy outcomes even when they are informed by a similar research base. The choice of specific instructional recommendations in the English Task Force fitted accepted governmental policies and a directive to develop 'a strategy'. Examinations of policy development in the United States show educational policy can be motivated by a process of agenda-setting advocacy.[7] When policy is formed in this way, the outcomes have often been increasingly specific and pedagogically restrictive legislation.

Both the English and New Zealand governments played a significant role in the concern over literacy standards, providing an opportunity for advocates to shape educational policy and practice through the development of new standards and approaches to teaching and learning. The outcome and shape of the English recommendations was largely predetermined by limited numbers and common viewpoints of influential members on the English Literacy Task Force, whose interests and research supported the policy agendas of the Labour Government.

In New Zealand, the possibilities for change were opened up, but there was no directive to recommend a new strategy. Unlike the English Literacy Task Force, the large membership of the New Zealand taskforce represented a wide range of agendas and viewpoints. However, the underlying political realities of opposing expert viewpoints, the New Zealand Ministry of Education's assumption of the role as a supposedly neutral arbiter, and the continuing need for successive governments to avoid the potential alienation of any significant section of the electorate, almost entirely nullified this apparent advantage.

In both countries, major issues are raised through the use of research by governmental and quasi-governmental bodies to fit a preset agenda. As Loveless notes, 'researchers' reputations can be enhanced when their ideas are realised in legislation or regulation'. The use of researchers' work in policy initiatives can also result in the legitimation and stamp of scientific approval for the causes they champion.[8] Commenting on this issue, Allington and Woodside-Jiron point out 'that by selecting like-minded scholars as the "experts," one can produce a research consensus document that can be used as a policy lever'.[9] In the New Zealand context, Nicholson has underlined the opposite problem of attempting to 'reconcile' what are, in effect, opposing viewpoints.[10] In each case the result may be the adoption of a simple solution to a perceived crisis, effectively preventing the exploration of more complex issues in literacy.

The adoption of more complex views on literacy have also been hindered during the 1990s by increasing public debate over reading standards, which has served to intensify competition amongst those offering rival methods. In England, the increasing preoccupation with NLS and with national assessment reflects the trend towards seeing reading only as the coding of print. Throughout this study, we have been careful to avoid any suggestion that one method of teaching reading is intrinsically superior to another. In fact, the adoption of Reading Recovery programmes in New Zealand, the United States and, to a lesser extent, by local authorities in England provides further confirmation of the increasing tendency to view reading as being largely synonymous with the mechanics of breaking code in order to read text. Thus, as Lankshear and Knobel observe, 'Approaches like Reading Recovery appear to operate on the assumption: "We will take care of code breaking. It's up to others to look after the rest".' Our study provides support for their further contention that much of the subsequent debate over Reading Recovery in New Zealand remains effectively at the level of ascertaining whether Reading Recovery or some other programme does this job better.[11] The same might be said of the Literacy Hour in England. This, we suggest, further encourages a very narrow view of literacy.

Where to from here?

Whilst this study has relied largely on evidence from newspapers, parliamentary debates, official reports and various secondary sources, we acknowledge McCulloch and Richardson's call for a multi-sourced approach to literacy history that can help overcome the built-in bias that can afflict documentary research.[12] Such an approach might include interweaving documentary material with other forms of evidence such as oral interviews with key figures in reading debates, with reading researchers, and with teachers.

The debate over reading encompasses a number of sites, and this study has concentrated on the public debate largely for reasons of space. A further fruitful line of inquiry would seek to review a mix of professionally orientated and theoretically orientated reading and literacy journals over time. Particular note could then be taken, not simply of the various debates that took place between researchers and other professionals over methods of teaching reading, and over the interpretation of findings concerning reading standards, as revealing as these might be, but also of the intersections between these 'in-house' professional concerns and the frequently more public concerns expressed by politicians and the media. The result would permit us to better compare and contrast the 'outsider' public debates with which this book has largely been concerned with the 'insider' debates between professionals, researchers, and teachers. In this way, it might be possible to arrive at a deeper understanding of the many ways in which outsider and insider concerns can intersect, thereby contributing to the shape, structure and outcome of reading debates.

The debate over dyslexia, together with the subsequent legislation requiring all schools to make provision for teaching dyslexic children, and the introduction of government funding to deal with the issue, is a highly significant development that we have not been able to explore in this book for reasons of space. Once again, we would argue for an approach that both critically examines the political dimensions of the dyslexia debate in England, and compares this with what has occurred elsewhere in the world. In New Zealand, for instance, various political and social factors have combined to discourage the development of a significant dyslexia lobby.

There is also an obvious need to more closely examine the ways in which debates over reading standards intersect with debates over related curriculum areas such as language, spelling and grammar. This linkage might also be widened to include debates over numeracy as well, given that 'literacy and numeracy' are often run together as a single catch-cry by the public and by politicians.

Appendix I

A READING REVOLUTION: HOW WE CAN TEACH EVERY CHILD TO READ WELL

The Preliminary Report of the Literacy Task Force Chaired by Professor Michael Barber

Published for Consultation
on 27th February 1997

MEMBERS OF THE LITERACY TASK FORCE

Michael Barber (Chair)
John Botham
Ken Follett
Simon Goodenough
Mary Gray
David Pitt-Watson
David Reynolds
Anne Waterhouse
Diane Wright
Observer
Mike Raleigh (OFSTED)

Contents

PREFACE

SECTION ONE: THE TASK
OUR VISION: WHATEVER IT TAKES
THE TARGET
MEASUREMENT OF PROGRESS TOWARDS THE TARGET

SECTION TWO: THE PRESENT
THE EVIDENCE FROM NATIONAL ASSESSMENT
THE EVIDENCE FROM OFSTED AND ABROAD
EXPLANATIONS

SECTION THREE: THE STRATEGY – PHASE ONE 1997–2001
PRECONDITIONS
THE TEACHING OF READING: WHAT WORKS
THE MANAGEMENT OF LITERACY AT SCHOOL LEVEL
MANAGEMENT OF THE NATIONAL STRATEGY
TEACHER DEVELOPMENT
THE ROLE OF LEAs
RECOGNITION
IMPLICATIONS FOR OTHER ASPECTS OF POLICY
CHILDREN WITH SPECIAL EDUCATIONAL NEEDS
PARENTAL RESPONSIBILITIES
FAMILY LITERACY
ADDRESSING DISADVANTAGE
LITERACY FOR BIILINGUAL LEARNERS
THE NATIONAL YEAR OF READING
IN THE MEANTIME
SECONDARY SCHOOLS

SECTION FOUR: THE STRATEGY – PHASE TWO 2001–2006
THE PROCESS
LIKELY FEATURES

CONCLUSION

RECOMMENDATIONS ARE SHOWN IN BOLD TYPEFACE

Preface

The Literacy Task Force was established on 31st May 1996 by David Blunkett, Shadow Secretary of State for Education and Employment. It was charged with developing, in time for an incoming Labour government, a strategy for substantially raising standards of literacy in primary schools in England over a five to ten year period.

Since the group was established, we have met monthly. A number of outside experts and representatives of important strands of opinion have made contributions to those meetings. The Chair has had over 40 further meetings with other individuals arid groups. Hundreds more have submitted views in writing.

We have been very encouraged by the widespread welcome for the idea of a steady, consistent strategy which is sustained over a long period and by the almost unanimous agreement that raising standards in literacy ought to be a central priority for the education service as a whole.

Our aim is to draw on the huge amount of information and thinking that have been put at our disposal to produce a final report by the end of May 1997. If we are to achieve our goal of designing a strategy which can stand the test of time, it is essential that it is founded on the best available information and commands widespread support. By publishing a substantial document for consultation at this stage, setting out our thinking, we hope to be laying strong foundations for our eventual recommendations.

Section one: the task

Our vision: whatever it takes

1   In the society of the 21st century, knowledge and information will be the keys to success or failure. Only the well-educated will be able to act effectively. Young people who fail in the education system will be all too likely to become part of a group of people living in our society but not of it, unable to act as employees, citizens or even, perhaps, parents. In the society of the future, a good education will surely become a basic human need – as basic as food, shelter and warmth.

2   Only if everyone is well-educated and able to learn continuously will we be able to reap the benefits of this emerging society and ensure that they are fairly distributed. Seeking to create these circumstances has implications for a wide range of policy areas, but few would doubt that an essential first step towards its creation, should be to ensure that, by the end of primary education, all children can read and write well.

3   It is not after all an accident that we call reading and writing 'basics'. That is what they are. Along with acquiring the habits of mind on which learning depends, they are the building blocks on which all

further learning is predicated. Yet our practice has not been to treat them as basics. Indeed, throughout the 20th century, it has been accepted that a proportion of children would pass through the education system without mastering them. This is not just a recent phenomenon. Among 16 and 17 year old conscripts to the fray in the first year of the second world war, for example, virtually a quarter were illiterate. Much more recent figures from the Basic Skills Agency suggest that as many as fifteen per cent of twenty-one year olds have limited literacy skills. Data from the Secondary Heads' Association published in 1995 revealed similar concerns among eleven year olds. Meanwhile the NFER suggested, when it reviewed the situation for the National Commission on Education in 1993, that standards in literacy are much the same now as they were 30 years ago. Given the rate of progress in other spheres of activity and in other countries over the same period, this is a disturbing conclusion.

4   It is the view of the Literacy Task Force that we need to begin to take the term **basics** literally and to design an education system which ensures that all children are taught to read well by the age of eleven. Put another way, the education service should do whatever it takes to make this possible. This is the first step towards the creation of a truly literate nation and a prerequisite of a learning society.

5   The realisation of this ambitious vision is, in large part, a responsibility of the education service. The proposals in this report are designed to enhance its capability to do so and to contribute to the creation among teachers of a culture of continuous self-improvement. We do not believe that the education service on its own, however good it becomes, can fully realise this vision because we believe that the culture of this country itself needs changing too. Parents, business and the media also have significant roles to play in raising literacy standards. Indeed, the realisation of our vision will require a crusade in which everyone plays their pan. In addition to setting out a strategy and making practical proposals, we appeal – unashamedly – to the idealism of everyone involved. We have to put behind us both complacency and the all-too-prevalent British tendency to slough off responsibility onto others. We are convinced – not least by the overwhelmingly positive response to our work so far – that the time is ripe to develop a new culture with new high expectations of what is possible.

6   That is why our report, in addition to making proposals for the education service, also makes recommendations for ensuring that parents and schools work closely together and suggests how business, publishers and the media can play their pan.

7   It is our firmly held belief that, if all these groups take their responsibilities seriously, then the dramatic progress necessary to meet our ambitious target is possible. Indeed, we would like to be able to guarantee to

parents that if they play their full part in collaboration with the school, then their children will learn to read well. The achievement of this goal across the society will not happen overnight. It will happen only as a result of a coherent strategy, broadly supported and consistently applied over a period of years. That is what our proposals are designed to put in place.

The target

8   When David Blunkett established the Literacy Task Force, he asked us to design a strategy to meet an ambitious target; namely that:

> 'By the end of a second term of a Labour government, all children leaving primary school ... will have reached a reading age of at least eleven.'

9   The target is clear. Less clear is the question of how progress towards it should be measured. The reading tests that provide reading ages generate a normal distribution around an average which is then described as the reading age of the cohort. There is clearly a difficulty about basing an absolute target on this kind of norm-referenced testing approach. For this reason, we have chosen to 'translate' our target into National Curriculum terms. Under the National Curriculum, Level 4 is the standard expected of eleven year olds. On this basis, performance in the reading component of the Key Stage 2 (KS2) English tests could therefore provide a fixed reference point. It will do so, of course, only if the School Curriculum and Assessment Authority (SCAA) and its successor body, the Qualifications and National Curriculum Authority (QNCA) are rigorous in ensuring that Level 4 is fixed. We recommend that the target should become:

> 'By the end of a second term of a Labour government, all children in primary school will achieve at least Level 4 in reading in the National Curriculum by the age of eleven.'

10 We would hope that practically every child will achieve this target, although we recognise that a small proportion of children may not be able to do so because of their special educational needs. The experience of, for example, New Zealand and Victoria, Australia is that this proportion will be significantly less than five per cent.

Measurement of progress towards the target

11 At the moment, there remains a degree of uncertainty among teachers about precisely what Level 4 in English means. As with other aspects of the National Curriculum, the level descriptors leave considerable room for interpretation and teachers come to understand the Levels through experience. In practice, Level 4, at least in reading and writing, is being defused more tightly through the Key Stage 2 tests. There have only been two full runs of these tests – 1995 and 1996 – and the tests varied slightly from one year to the next.

12 There seems to be an acceptance that the 1996 tests were an improvement on their predecessors. We anticipate that, as the testing system becomes established, a common understanding of the standard represented by Level 4 in English will be established among teachers and other relevant groups.

13 **We recognise that, although the target is confined to the reading component of English, reading and writing need, in practice, to be taught together in a mutually reinforcing way and that the two skill areas are integrally linked.**

14 SCAA's analysis of the 1996 KS2 English tests proves this point. It suggests that there is a very close correlation between pupil performance in the reading component of the KS2 tests and English as a whole (correlation 0.84) and that 58 per cent of pupils achieved Level 4 in the reading component of English in 1996 compared to 57 per cent in English as a whole. **For our purposes, it is essential that the reading component of English is published separately from English as a whole.** SCAA recommended that this should be done in 1996 but the government – mistakenly in our view – turned this recommendation down.

15 **Teacher assessment results should also be made publicly available along with results from the tests and used by schools to inform their targets and strategies for moving towards them.** Over time, we would anticipate that the results of the externally marked tests and the teacher assessment results will in any case converge.

16 **We also believe that there ought to be some milestone targets on the way to the ultimate target which, seen from the present, may appear to many to be unachievable. We believe two such milestone targets would be beneficial.**

  i A target relating to the percentage of eleven year olds who have achieved the ultimate target. In 1995, 48 per cent did so. In 1996, 57 per cent did so. We intend to set an interim target of 80 per cent or more doing so by 2000–2001.

  ii Targets relating to the performance at age 7 of the cohort who will become eleven in the year 2006. If they are to come close to the ultimate target, then well over 90 per cent should be achieving Level 2 of the reading component of English in the KS1 National Curriculum tests.

17　Finally on targets, we are conscious of the motivational force of individual school targets set by the schools themselves. We recognise that schools will have different starting points in terms of standards and that for schools with socially disadvantaged intakes, the national target will be more difficult to achieve. Some of our proposals later on address disadvantage in a practical way. **At this point, we simply want to urge that as schools move towards the national target, they should want to establish targets for themselves based on the notion of improvement against previous best. Any school recording year-on-year improvements will be contributing to the achievement of our national target.** This approach will help schools with disadvantaged intakes to gain the recognition and sense of achievement they will need.

18　**It is important that information about primary school performance is published and reported to parents. In addition, national progress towards the national target should he reported annually to Parliament by the Secretary of State for Education and Employment.**

19　In addition to ensuring that parents and the public are well informed, **we believe that each primary school needs to he given data which enable it to compare its performance in both reading and English as a whole to national performance, to other local schools and to schools with comparable intakes.** We welcome the work that SCAA/QNCA is currently undertaking to provide for every school high quality comparative data, based on the national test results. We believe that such information is an essential prerequisite if primary schools are to set their own improvement targets and monitor progress towards them as we believe they should.

Section two: the present

The evidence from national assessment

20　Clearly, it is important to establish how the education service is performing currently before going on to describe the nature of a strategy for improving it. Given the target we have set ourselves, the best starting point for examining the current situation is an examination of the KS2 English test results.

21　International comparisons of children's achievements in reading suggest Britain is not performing well, with a slightly below average position in international literacy 'league tables'. Most studies show also a long 'tail' of underachievement in Britain, and a relatively poor performance from lower ability students. Whilst general societal factors (such as the status given to school learning or the prevalence of television viewing amongst adolescents) may be responsible for some of the poor British performance, most are agreed that the educational system bears the main responsibility.

22 The results for KS2 English in 1995 and 1996 show how far there is to go in relation to the target we have set:

Level	1995	1996
Absent/No level	4%	5%
1	1%	1%
2	7%	6%
(level expected of the average 7 year old)		
3	39%	30%
4	41%	45%
(target level for 11 year olds)		
5	7%	12%
Total on or above target	48%	57%

Figure 1

23 For the reasons given above, detailed data have not so far been made available nationally on the results in the reading component of English alone, but performance in the reading component of English is very close to these figures for English as a whole. As Figure 1 reveals, the percentage reaching the target level we have set has risen from 48 per cent in 1995 to 57 per cent in 1996. This substantial step forward is due to a combination of factors including a clearer understanding among teachers of the nature of the tests, better preparation of the pupils for the test and most importantly better teaching from teachers now able to give more attention to the basics after the considerable broadening of the primary school curriculum in the early 1990s.

24 It is encouraging that there has been progress over the last year or so, on which our strategy can build. Nevertheless, there is no room for complacency. More detailed analysis reveals just how far there is to go. The analysis that follows is based on the 1995 KS2 English results but it is already clear that in-depth analysis of the 1996 results will confirm it.

25 Figure 2 (below) examines the relationship between the percentage of pupils in a school achieving Level 4 and the percentage of pupils who take up free school meals. Free school meal uptake is generally agreed to be the best proxy available for social disadvantage.

26 Firstly, in 1995, only in somewhere between 300 and 400 primary schools did 100 per cent of pupils achieve Level 4 in the KS2 English

tests. The analysis of the 1996 results is sure to reveal an improvement but it is unlikely to show that more than 5–10 per cent of primary schools at best have achieved the target. This demonstrates on the one hand that the achievement of our target is possible but, on the other hand. just how far there is to go. **The first strategic lesson therefore is that expectations and overall performance need to be substantially raised.**

27 The second strategic lesson is the dramatic and profoundly disturbing range of performance among schools with similar intakes. For example, when those schools with fewer than 5 per cent of pupils on free school meals (I.e. with a highly disadvantaged intake) are examined, some have 100 per cent of pupils achieving Level 4, while at the other end of the

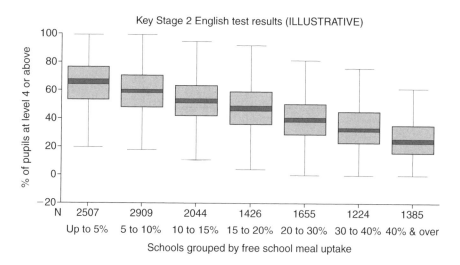

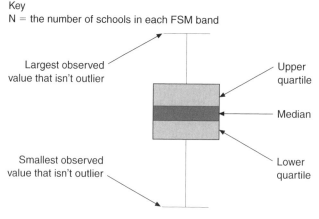

Figure 2 Performance at KS2: the impact of inconsistency and disadvantage.

scale, in some of them as few as 20 per cent of pupils are achieving the same level. In other words, the best schools in this group are already achieving our target while some comparable schools are falling far below it and indeed below the average of the most disadvantaged group of schools. Many parents in leafy suburbs and wealthy county areas will find this state of affairs profoundly disturbing. Meanwhile, among the most disadvantaged schools, the range is from 70 per cent achieving Level 4 to zero per cent. The graph shows a similar dramatic and unacceptable range across all primary schools, irrespective of their intake. It is important to note that on this graph, outliers have been deleted. The real variability is therefore even greater than appears here. In short, at present, whether children learn to read well is a lottery in both advantaged and disadvantaged areas. **Thus, the second lesson is that any strategy must address the issue of consistency how to encourage all schools to achieve in line with the best schools with comparable intakes.**

28 Thirdly, it is clear that, generally speaking, the higher the levels of disadvantage, the smaller the percentage of pupils who achieve Level 4. The slope of the bold black lines the average in each case – represents this fact. The graph therefore makes plain that if our target is to be met across the country there is, on the whole, much further to go for schools with disadvantaged intakes. **The third lesson, therefore, from our analysis is that – since we are determined that society should have the same high expectations of all its pupils – our strategy needs to include practical proposals to enable schools with more disadvantaged intakes to succeed.**

The evidence from OFSTED and abroad

29 Evidence from OFSTED inspection reports reinforces concern about the variation of performance among schools. For example, OFSTED suggests that reading standards at KS1 are low in about 9 per cent of schools, with many pupils in those schools having a weak grasp of the necessary skills and little understanding of what they read. Standards at KS2 are low in 13 per cent of schools, with many pupils having poor skills and a narrow experience of reading. In writing, standards at KS 1 are low in some 16 per cent of schools, with many pupils demonstrating uneven development in some 16 per cent of schools, with many pupils demonstrating uneven development in their work and making inadequate progress. Standards at KS2 are poor in over 20 per cent of schools, with weak spelling and sentence construction, limited vocabulary and lack of attention to improving work through redrafting, being t' ¬ain problems.

30 Inspection findings confirm, as might be expected, that a coher/

founded approach to the teaching of literacy is the major factor affecting standards of achievement.

31 In spite of these concerns, OFSTED suggests that standards in reading are satisfactory or better in over 90 per cent of schools at KS I and 87 per cent at KS2. This suggests that performance which inspectors currently describe as having 'a balance of strengths and weaknesses' is certainly not sufficient to ensure that most, never mind all, pupils achieve Level 4. **If we are even to approach the target we have set, then expectations of what is considered 'satisfactory', and indeed 'good' by OFSTED, need to be substantially raised across the system.**

32 As we have seen, international comparisons reinforce this data. It is clear that Britain is outperformed by a group of countries (e.g. Finland, United States, Sweden, France, Italy, New Zealand, Norway) and is located within a 'middle' group (including Germany, The Netherlands, Ireland, Belgium, Spain etc.) which is in turn ahead of a 'bottom' group (including Indonesia and Venezuela). Most disturbing in international studies is evidence of the existence of a 'long tail' in the results among British schools, since performance of lower ability pupils is substantially below that of other countries.

33 There is a long way to travel over the decade ahead. **We shall only achieve the progress necessary if, in addition to ensuring that the whole society contributes to the literacy strategy (as we urged in the opening section of this document), government and the education service explicitly and practically address the problems of overall standards and consistency and disadvantage which this analysis has revealed.**

Explanations

34 Before we are in a position to recommend how to put right this evidently unacceptable state of affairs, it is necessary to examine briefly how it came about.

35 Concerns about literacy standards were expressed from the rrid-1970s onwards, most notably in James Callaghan's speech at Ruskin College in 1976. However, prior to 1988, no systematic attempt was made to deal with the problems that Callaghan and others identified. The prevailing culture was voluntaristic with the extent of change depending on the extent to which local education authorities, headteachers or teachers chose to become involved in it. The notion of professional autonomy was strongly embedded in the education service, yet there were insufficient mechanisms in place either within the profession itself or in the education service more generally to ensure either that practice was based firmly on evidence or that best practice was rapidly adopted or even adopted at all by others. As a result, practice varied hugely

from school to school. At best it was excellent, at worst a matter of anything goes. Since there was little or no published intonation about primary school performance and inspection practice varied from LEA to LEA, the pressure for change from outside schools was limited. Meanwhile. standards of and approaches to initial teacher education varied dramatically.

36 The reforms from 1988 onwards changed this state of affairs but replaced the old problems with new ones. The National Curriculum, for example, was so broad and detailed across ten subjects that it distracted primary teachers, at least for a while, from the 3 'R's. Worse still, while government ministers highlighted problems with the teaching of literacy in their rhetoric, they put in place not a coherent strategy but rather a series of fleeting and unconnected initiatives such as Reading Recovery, the Better English Campaign and the National Literacy Project. Each of these had intrinsic merit but no attempt was made to link them together. Instead of sewing the seeds of a new, more productive harvest, they clutched at straws.

37 Meanwhile, the National Curriculum, national tests and OFSTED inspection provided growing evidence – on which this report has drawn – of the character and extent of the problem. Primary teachers found themselves, as a result, the target of extensive public criticism from politicians and the media but, even up to the present, no systematic attempt has been made to ensure that all primary teachers acquire the skills to teach reading in the way the most successful teachers do. In spite of ten years of radical reform, the capacity of the education service to disseminate best practice remains fatally flawed.

38 In the future, we have to do better, much better, than this. The strategy we set out in the remainder of this document combines what we now know about best practice in the teaching of reading with an appreciation of the lessons of ten years of education reform. Tony Blair has repeatedly drawn attention to the fact that effective change results from a judicious balance of pressure and support. Without too much exaggeration, it would be possible to describe the history of the last 30 years as 20 years of support without pressure and ten years of pressure without support. If we are able to transform literacy standards in the decade ahead, we shall certainly need both.

Section three: the strategy – phase one 1997–2001

Preconditions

39 We recognise that our target is ambitious. We also believe that our evidence – both national and international – suggests it is achievable. **Bringing about a dramatic improvement in literacy standards is**

therefore possible, but only if there is a consistent national strategic approach over five to ten years. This in turn demands a new, mature, active partnership. All those involved, including teachers, parents, governors, government, the media, publishers and business must accept their part of the responsibility for taking up the challenge.

40 Clearly Labour's literacy strategy will be embedded in its overall crusade for higher standards. We do not wish to spell out again all the elements of that strategy here but we would point out that our plans assume the implementation of important Labour commitments which are relevant to the work of the Task Force. These include:

    i the introduction of pre-school education for all four year olds whose parents want it and the progressive extension of nursery provision to three year olds as resources become available;

    ii the provision of funding to enable infant classes to number no more than 30 through phasing out the Assisted Places Scheme;

    iii Labour's standards agenda with its emphasis on school improvement, target-setting, the provision of comparative data, enhanced leadership, home–school agreements, improved discipline and a focus on the improvement of teaching and learning, which should combine to encourage all schools to perform in line with the best, thus bringing greater consistency and reliability;

    iv an emphasis on zero tolerance of failure and therefore focused intervention in schools which have failed or are heading towards failure;

    v the implementation by local education authorities of their education development plans in which literacy should be a high priority;

    vi the plans for a new deal for the teaching profession, including the introduction of a new General Teaching Council, advanced skills teachers and the provision of paraprofessional support;

    vii the investment of a greater proportion of GNP in education by the end of the first term of a Labour government than is currently the case, particularly if the growth is predominantly focused on primary education;

    viii the repair and maintenance of school buildings, especially in disadvantaged areas, through the public–private sector partnership proposed by David Blunkett in April 1996.

41 The successful implementation of these policies will provide the kind of positive context in which our literacy strategy can be put into practice.

The teaching of reading: what works

42 The core of our strategy necessarily relates to improving the teaching of reading in primary schools. It is only through doing so that the prob-

lems of consistency mentioned above and the overall standards of reading in primary schools which we have identified can be addressed.

43 There have been few more vigorous educational controversies in the last decade than the one over how reading should be taught. Opposing sides in a vigorous national debate took to the barricades with banners proclaiming their loyalty to 'phonics' or 'real books'. But while this debate has raged, research and the understanding of 'best practice' have moved on. We now know a great deal about the best technologies for the teaching of reading and that they include a recognition of the critical importance of phonics in the early years. The chief strategic task is to ensure that primary teachers and schools are well-informed about best practice and have the skills to act upon it.

44 There are a number of general factors which characterise effective teaching in general:
- ensuring a good 'match' between curriculum, teaching and the learners' varied needs;
- good management of time, involving maximising learning time and pupils' levels of 'time on task' in classrooms, and minimising the time spent on administration or control;
- high levels of teacher 'higher order' interaction with classes, High frequency of questioning and frequent provision of feedback;
- structured classrooms, with a limited range of activities being pursued at any one time and a limited range of lesson goals in any session.

45 Meanwhile, evidence from both OFSTED and research suggests that the successful teaching of literacy in general:
- makes initial and continuing progress in reading and writing for all pupils a central objective of the school;
- involves parents in positive and practical ways through discussions at school and work with pupils at home;
- is based on a teaching programme which is thoroughly planned, with clear learning objectives, and provides direct teaching and careful assessment through to the end of KS2;
- capitalises on pupils' enthusiasm for communication to make reading and writing challenging and enjoyable;
- teaches all aspects of literacy explicitly, directly and intensively in their own right, and creates deliberate opportunities in the teaching of other subjects to extend experience and consolidate skills;
- appreciates what pupils already know about language, and teaches them about the system of written language and how to recognise and correct their own errors;
- shows good understanding of techniques for beginning reading and writing, of how to select and combine them and how to judge their impact;

- uses carefully sequenced whole-class, group and individual work to focus on strategies and skills, with the teacher combining instruction, demonstration, questioning and discussion, providing structure for subsequent tasks, and giving help and constructive response;
- makes use of systematic records of progress to monitor pupils' strengths and weaknesses, to intervene in a discriminating way and to plan the next stage of work;
- follows clear procedures for the early identification of pupils with difficulties and gives them targeted and positive support;
- makes good use of classroom assistants and volunteers, briefing them on how to work with pupils and to record what they do.

46 The successful teaching of *reading* in particular:
- equips pupils at the earliest stage to draw on the sources of knowledge needed when reading for meaning, including phonic knowledge (simple and complex sound/symbol relationships), graphic knowledge (patterns within words), word recognition (a sight vocabulary which includes common features of words), grammatical knowledge (checking for sense through the ways words are organised) and contextual information (meaning derived from the text as a whole);
- continues the direct teaching of reading techniques through both key stages, building systematically on the skills pupils have learnt earlier in, for example, tackling unfamiliar words, deduction and using texts to find information;
- provides a range of reading material, usually based around a core reading programme, but substantially enriched with other good quality material, including information texts, used selectively to deepen reading experience and to provide choice at each level:
- encourages library usage;
- extends pupils' reading by focused work on challenging texts with the whole class or in groups, and involves frequent opportunities for pupils to hear, read and discuss texts and to think about the content and the language used;
- gives time for productive individual reading at school and at home, and opportunities for pupils to share their response with others.

47 The National Literacy Project (NLP), established by the government last year, has developed a framework for teaching based precisely on this evidence. Our plans will build on its valuable work.

The management of literacy at school level

48 However well teachers are capable of teaching reading, they can only succeed fully if they are supported by effective school management. There is extensive evidence of the management strategies that work in

educational and other organisations. Assuming there is a clear national view on how best to teach literacy, there is no reason to consider the management of literacy in primary schools any different from the management of other key educational priorities.

49 The following characteristics are crucially important in creating the setting for the development of literacy:

    i a well-informed headteacher who understands effective approaches to literacy, sets high expectations and provides consistent leadership;

    ii a systematic school approach to the professional development of teachers and other staff involved in the teaching of literacy;

    iii effective arrangements, which take account of national standards, for monitoring the progress in literacy of both individual children and the school as a whole;

    iv targets for each child, including those with special educational needs.

    v high expectations of what children are able to achieve in school and through regular homework;

    vi a strong climate of 'academic push' in which high levels of achievement are reflected both in a school's 'mission' and the use of regular homework;

    vii effective systems for communicating with parents about the performance of their child, the performance of the school as a whole, the teaching approach used by the school and the ways in which parents can help the school and especially their own child or children to achieve their literacy goals;

    viii the consistency and cohesion of the school's organisation;

    ix understanding how to ensure that money spent on books and other reading materials is spent wisely providing a range of graded levels of books, both fiction and non-fiction.

50 Clearly, ensuring that all schools benefit from such effective management must also be a key part of our strategy. In addition, it is important that governing bodies recognise the centrality of literacy and support the development of a strategic approach to it. It will be essential, through existing governor training programmes and other means to heighten governor awareness of the importance of literacy and to promote among governors the skills they need to oversee the strategy at school level.

51 In addition to gathering the evidence above, we have examined a number of literacy programmes both here and abroad. In particular, we studied programmes in both Western Australia and Victoria, which seem to be soundly based in the research evidence and broadly consistent with the OFSTED and research findings listed above. We have also paid close attention to the literacy strategy adopted in New Zealand which is generally recognised to have been one of the most successful English-speaking countries in terms of teaching literacy.

52 We have considered, too, the principles behind Robert Slavin's impressive Success for All project in the United States and have arranged discussions with him in order to learn more from a project which is internationally acknowledged as having been remarkably successful in raising literacy standards. The four key principles underpinning Slavin's approach can be summarised as:

   i prevention is better than cure;
   ii intervention should be early and intensive;
   iii a belief that **all** students can succeed is crucial;
   iv relentless determination to pursue the planned intervention is essential. We intend to apply each of these principles in the strategy we put forward.

53 We have also examined in depth the materials developed by the recently established National Literacy Project (NLP) in this country which currently involves schools in 13 LEAs and is led by John Stannard. The NLP's framework for teaching is firmly based on the OFSTED data, research evidence and international experience. It has the major additional advantage of having the active support of the DfEE and each of the major agencies with an interest in teaching methodology. The central features of the NLP's approach are:

- a requirement that each participating school will provide literacy lessons, timetabled for an hour a day. During this 'literacy hour' the project requires that for at least 60 per cent of the time pupils are working with the teacher either in whole class work or in groups;
- a clear focus on literacy instruction during the hour. The teachers in the project are required to develop the range of teaching strategies this requires. clarity about three 'strands' of the reading programme which are as follows:

word level	phonics, spelling and vocabulary
sentence level	grammar and punctuation
text level	comprehension and composition

54 As participating schools only began to implement the carefully planned programme in January 1997, it is too early to be certain of its effects. However, given its firm grounding in both international research and the evidence from OFSTED inspection and the central place it gives to systematically teaching phonics, we believe it has a sound basis in evidence of what works.

55 As it is implemented, those responsible for the NLP will surely learn from experience and be able to refine their plans. We wonder, for example, on the basis of comparison with the programme in Victoria, whether the NLP encourages teachers to assess pupils sufficiently on a day-to-day basis and to use such assessment to inform instruction.

56 Minor caveats notwithstanding, **the work of the National Literacy Project seems likely to make a major contribution.** There is nothing to be gained from a new government coming in and over-turning good work which is already in progress. On the contrary, the National Literacy Project provides a helpful beginning from which we can develop our strategy.

Management of the national strategy

57 Our overall strategy should be overseen by a Literacy Strategy Group chaired by a senior DfEE official based in the enhanced Standards and Effectiveness Unit in the DfEE which Labour intends to create. **It should include senior representatives of OFSTED, SCAA, TTA, BSA and the NLP, as well as experienced educators and a representative from the No. 10 Policy Unit.**

58 The Literacy Strategy Group should commission an independent evaluation of the NLP as soon as possible after an election. It should involve comparison of the participating schools with a control group. It should be undertaken with the specific goal of showing how the model could be refined and built upon to form the basis of a national approach to the teaching of literacy in primary schools. It would need to examine not only the details of where the approach works well and where it needs improvement. It would also need to draw on other innovative primary school approaches such as target-grouping, the use of trained classroom assistants and effective home–school collaboration, Reading Recovery methods and the use of information technology, each of which, we believe, has a contribution to make. Above all, it should consider the strategic policy implications of spreading the approach from a relatively small number of volunteer schools to large numbers and ultimately to all schools.

59 This evaluation of the National Literacy Project's work, alongside the evidence from other strategic literacy interventions such as 'Success for All' in the USA, and those in Western Australia and Victoria, would provide the basis for the next and perhaps most important step in our strategy, the teacher development programme.

60 We hope that **as the teacher development programme outlined below is implemented, the NLP will continue its work in those areas where it is already established. It will provide a vital source of experience and knowledge for the second phase of our strategy from 2001 onwards and continue in the meantime to make a con-tribution to raising standards of literacy in areas of disadvantage.**

Teacher development

61 The ability of primary school teachers to teach reading is by far the most important factor in whether or not children learn to read well. If all primary school pupils are to read well, then all primary teachers need to learn how to teach reading well. Obvious though this may seem, it is not the case at present. There is substantial evidence, as we have seen, that standards in the teaching of reading vary hugely from school to school. Many primary teachers have not had systematic opportunities to update their skills to take account of the evidence described above. This means that their teaching approach is often based upon a distant recollection of what they learnt when they trained and their experience since then. As we have seen, this is an unacceptably haphazard state of affairs. Primary teachers have found themselves a target for criticism, particularly in relation to the teaching of reading over the last few years. Yet the system has not done nearly enough to enable them to change what they do.

62 Amazingly, there has never been a major national initiative to enable all primary teachers to learn the most effective methods of teaching reading and how to apply them. The government has not created the structures or incentives to ensure that all schools learn from the best practice of the most effective schools. Instead, there has been a series of unconnected initiatives which, while usually worthy in themselves, have neither been interlinked nor had the scope or ambition necessary to tackle the problem across the country. If teachers are to change, they need opportunities to learn the best approaches and incentives to adopt them. Ultimately, we need a culture in which primary teachers themselves expect to adopt the best methods as a matter of professional pride.

63 The ambitious strategy we propose will, we hope, offer them the opportunity to do so cost-effectively and provide incentives to ensure they are taken up. If what we propose is implemented, it will be the most ambitious attempt ever in this country to change for the better teaching approaches across the entire education service. Our teacher development plans have two elements. The first relates to the initial training of teachers; the second to the professional development of teachers already in the profession.

i) Initial Teacher Education (ITE)

64 The training of student primary teachers is currently governed by Circular 14/93 which sets out in some detail the course requirements and establishes a long list of 'competences' which aspiring teachers are expected to acquire by the time they complete the course. Its weaknesses are that it is too broad and fails sufficiently to prioritise. The government, through the Teacher Training Agency. has recently pub-

lished for consultation a National Curriculum for teacher education to be published early in 1997. We have not yet had time to examine it in detail but it appears to be a major advance on the arrangements currently in place. It also appears to be consistent with the approaches to the teaching of reading in the National Literacy Project.

65 We are certainly persuaded that under the present Circular, primary teacher training courses are prevented from giving sufficient attention to the teaching of reading. In New Zealand, for example, the amount of time devoted to reading instruction is double the 50 hours devoted to it here. **We believe that in future every course of initial teacher education for primary teachers should give the highest possible priority to ensuring that all trainee teachers are taught – in accordance with nationally established criteria – how to teach literacy, and that the amount of time devoted to it should be substantially increased.**

66 The New Zealand experience also provides another important insight. There, the student finds that teaching practice in school reinforces what has been learnt in the higher education institution (HEI) because there is a consistency of approach between schools and HEIs. Here, even when the HEI prepares students excellently, there is no guarantee that the student will find a similar approach to the teaching of reading being followed in the school, where they spend two-thirds of their time. The result can be confusion for the student. As our overall strategy is implemented and variation of performance among schools is reduced, the room for confusion should be reduced too. In the meantime, it is an issue to which HEIs and their partner schools should give careful attention. **We recommend that the TTA should encourage those universities which have been found, through inspection, to be good at preparing students in the teaching of reading to play a part in training teachers in partner schools too.**

67 Finally, **we welcome Labour's plans to reintroduce the probationary year and urge that priority is given during it to ensuring that beginning primary teachers continue to develop their skills in the teaching of reading.**

ii) Professional development

68 In 1995–96, just under 15,000 people were recruited to primary ITE courses. Thus altering ITE, while crucial in the long term, does not bring substantial change in the short or medium term. The key to our strategy, therefore, must be to provide the 190,000 or so serving primary teachers with the skills they will require. **A programme of professional development in the teaching of reading for all ordinary teachers is therefore essential.**

69 Four groups, each with different development needs, will be targeted in our strategy:

   i all primary teachers who require the skills not just of teaching reading to beginners but of teaching those who can read to read with fluency and discrimination;

   ii literacy/language co-ordinators – those teachers in primary school with a responsibility for reading across the school – who require, in addition to the above, knowledge and understanding of how to devise and implement a coherent literacy strategy for the school;

   iii primary headteachers who need to understand the leadership and management implications of the policy we intend to propose;

   iv primary school governors who need to understand the implications of the literacy strategy for their work.

70 Logistically as well as professionally, providing high quality, cost effective training for each of these four groups presents a substantial challenge. Given the variation in the background, knowledge and expertise of the primary teaching force, the huge variation in primary school performance and the diversity of background and experience among school governors, the question is both complex in nature and large in scope. We are aware that many primary teachers will be cautious about yet another major strategic change affecting their work. However, we believe that by basing the change on evidence of what works and ensuring that the training is of the highest possible quality, we will be providing them with the incentive to participate enthusiastically in the training and to change their practice. The fact that the training will be based on what successful primary teachers are already doing and that the Literacy Strategy Group at the national level will involve successful practitioners will provide further incentive. Above all, the fact that primary teachers will be seen to be publicly responding constructively and systematically, to the literacy challenge will surely boost their public standing and enhance their status. We have consciously timed the main drive to retrain primary teachers during the National Year of Reading (see below) to enable this point to be emphasised. Instead of finding themselves the beleaguered targets of public criticism, we hope primary teachers will come to see themselves as playing a leading part in a major social transformation.

71 The constraints on implementing a major professional development strategy for primary teachers are as follows:

   i few primary teachers have any non-contact time;

   ii individual primary schools' professional development budgets are tightly constrained, especially in small schools;

   iii a wide variety of attitudes to change exists among primary schools, ranging from constructive, thoughtful response at one extreme to a suspicion of anything new and externally promoted at the other.

72 However, there are opportunities too.

i Each year there are five training days on which teachers are required to work and pupils are not in school.

ii There is evidence that increasing numbers of primary schools are becoming effective in managing their own affairs and therefore better at implementing change.

iii There is evidence that increasing numbers of schools are anxious to be provided with good practice – based on evidence – on which they can build rather than being expected to invent it for themselves.

iv Local education authorities such as Newcastle-upon-Tyne, West Sussex and Birmingham are in many cases providing an excellent infrastructure for the promotion of change and development in schools, particularly at primary level.

v There is substantial expertise among the national agencies and organisations such as the Open University in the preparation and dissemination of information and distance learning materials.

vi Labour's plan to provide a 'Teachers' Centre' accessible through the internet will, in the long run, provide a new and powerful means of disseminating information and spreading best practice.

73 **The professional development strategy we wish to put forward is designed to take advantage of these opportunities. The broad timetable for it is set out below.**

By When?	What?
End September 1997	Management structure for strategy including Literacy Strategy Group in place. Evaluation of NLP in progress. Specification for distance learning materials prepared.
End April 1998	National distance learning materials being commissioned and prepared. These would draw on the work of the National Literacy Project, the evaluation of its work during 1997 and other research evidence and take account of the National Curriculum. The materials would include training activities, reading materials, video, CD Rom etc. Four modules would he included • Awareness Raising: The Nature of the Challenge • Teaching Reading to Beginners • From Functional Reading to Fluency • The Management of Literacy

By When?	What?
	Special educational needs and the need for teachers to extend their own knowledge about language should be taken into account in each of them. The preparation of these materials would be put out to tender by the Literacy Strategy Group and the cost of them covered by existing budgets for 1997–98 of OFSTED, SCAA and TTA. The development of the materials should involve a trialing stage
End April 1998	Through the existing Literacy Centres, between two and rive 'consultants' in each LEA (depending on size) would he trained and prepared for the implementation of the national strategy. The possibility of linking LEAs in regional consortia for this purpose should be considered. The cost would he met from within the existing GEST budget.
End Summer Term 1998	All primary schools would be expected to devote one of the five training days to awareness raising on the issues involved in the new national literacy strategy. This session would be for all staff and open to governors. They would be supported by the first module of the distance learning materials and the trained consultants.
End Autumn Term 1998	All primary headteachers and literacy co-ordinators should receive two days' training in the management of literacy. The head and literacy co-ordinator from each school would attend the same training sessions. It would be based on the module in the distance learning materials and provided across an LEA by the trained consultants. The training materials would, in addition, be available through the 'virtual' Teachers' Centre, assuming it is in place by then. Appropriate parts of it could also be made available through the BBC's Learning Zone. Funding for all this would be provided within the 1998–9 GEST grant. Headteachers would be asked to make a major input to their next governors' meeting on the implications of the strategy for the governing body
End Summer Term 1999	Over the Spring and Summer terms of 1999, schools would be expected to devote four of their training days to training in the teaching of

By When?	What?
	literacy. This would coincide with the planned National Year of Reading which would be urging everyone, not just teachers and parents, to promote reading. The training would be based on the nationally developed distance learning materials. LEAs would be asked to devise and implement plans – drawing on inspection evidence – to support that training among those schools which needed it most. This would avoid the problem identified in the Alexander, Rose & Woodhead report of underperforming schools 'recycling their own inadequacy'. Small schools would be urged to cluster in order to share expertise and benefit from economies of scale.
During School Year 1999–2000 and thereafter	In the year following the major training initiative, its impact would be evaluated by OFSTED and others, using a rigorous approach based on hard outcome data and involving valid comparison of before and after.
	All primary schools would be expected to devise individualised training plans in the teaching of literacy for any newly qualified teacher and to devote at least one of the five training days each year to the teaching of literacy.
	The LEA consultants would be charged with following through the training that had taken place the previous year.
	From time to time, new distance learning materials would be devised to support this process to ensure that all teachers kept up to date with the latest evidence of what works.
	The GEST grant which covered the training costs in 1998–9 would he sustained at the same level for at least two further years to provide sustained support for schools in disadvantaged areas.
1998–2000	The Teacher Training Agency would he asked to examine its entire professional development framework, including HEADLAMP, the NPQH and subject leader qualifications to ensure they prioritised the national literacy strategy.
2000–2001	The impact of the strategy so far would he evaluated and the second phase of the strategy refined to take account of the lessons learned.

74 These plans will be costed in detail but overall represent a highly cost-effective way of carrying out as rapidly as possible an essential task. It is our view that they could be paid for from within the existing GEST programme and grants to the relevant national agencies, OFSTED, TTA and SCAA.

The role of local education authorities

75 At various places in this report, reference is made to the crucial role of local education authorities in implementing the literacy strategy. The purpose of this section is to bring together and summarise the contribution they will be expected to make.

76 Labour's overall standards agenda has given LEAs a vital role. In Excellence for Everyone, the following roles are emphasised:

'The local education authority will become a raiser of standards rather than a chain of command ... LEAs have an essential role in helping struggling schools, Providing advice and support – and intervening to raise standards. LEAs should become champions of children, providing information to parents and schools and developing local networks to help improve standards. But the most important new role for all LEAs will be to set Education Development Plans.

Labour will expect all LEAs to set strategic Education Development Plans on a three year rolling basis detailing how standards will be raised in schools in their area. Such education development plans will form the basis of each locality's contribution towards the national drive for rapid and radical improvement in standards and effectiveness across the country. EDPs will reflect the development plans and targets drawn up by individual schools, and they will be developed in partnership with representatives from education networks bringing together parents, governors, the business community, colleges and universities, and diocese and voluntary sector representatives. The plan will set clear targets to raise standards and increase participation in education both pre- and post-16. They will be subject to the approval of the Secretary of State for Education and Employment.'

77 These plans will need to give high priority to literacy. The Secretary of State, to whom the plans must be submitted for approval, should he especially concerned to see the cogency and clarity of the literacy element of them in reaching decisions on whether to approve them. In addition, inspection of LEAs should give high priority to the quality of the LEA's support for the national literacy strategy.

78 The most important task for LEAs will be to appoint and make effective

use of the literacy consultants who would be funded through GEST for three years (1998~2001). In 1998–9, their chief responsibility would be to implement the national training programme in their area, focusing especially on those schools which, because of their small size or for other reasons, are likely to need most assistance. In the following two years, their efforts would be concentrated on supporting continued improvement in literacy in the most disadvantaged schools.

79 A wide range of LEA-based factors will have a crucial impact on the success of the strategy including, among others:

  i the quality of the LEA's preparation for the National Year of Reading and especially its capacity to motivate and involve communities, teachers and parents in the event;

  ii the quality of the LEA's services and its capacity to work in partnership with schools, colleges, TECs and businesses;

  iii the LEA's provision of nursery education;

  iv the LEA's LMS formula, the age weightings in the formula and the extent to which the LEA is able to provide a steady resource framework within which primary schools can operate confidently;

  v the quality of comparative performance data provided by the LEA.

Recognition

80 After the pressures of the last decade, there is a risk that any major national initiative such as the one we are proposing will be received with scepticism by primary teachers. The benefits to them of playing an active part in implementing the planned strategy need to be made explicit. The first point to make is that our plans are designed to give all teachers access to the best practice that only a minority have had the opportunity to learn from so far. The message we have heard loudly and clearly from primary teachers is that they are desperately keen to teach reading as well as possible and would welcome a programme which enabled them to do so. In addition, we are strongly of the view that the sense of being part of a strategy involving all the education service, and indeed the whole society, could be inspiring and motivational to primary teachers. Above all, if the strategy is ultimately successful and major progress in literacy across the country is demonstrable, primary teachers will surely then get the recognition and status in society that they deserve.

81 We believe that if a school is managing and teaching literacy well, this fact should be recognised. We would hope that, as our training and development programme is implemented, many more schools will be carrying out this central task well and will therefore have earned the recognition, which surely would provide an additional incentive for schools. We also hope that individual teachers will be able to gain

accreditation towards Diploma or MA qualifications for completing the training programme and relating it to their day-to-day practice.

82 The Basic Skills Agency (BSA) has recently developed a Basic Skills Quality Mark for primary schools. It has been developed in consultation with other government agencies, LEAs and representatives of teachers. In its present form, it recognises 'the ability to read, write and speak in English and use Mathematics at a level necessary to function and progress at work and in society in general'. We shall ask them to consider the possibility of separate recognition of literacy and numeracy.

83 Certainly, we fully endorse the ten criteria which the BSA have established for schools which want to gain the quality mark and which are consistent with the strategy we are developing (see box).

1 A whole school action plan to improve performance in basic skills.
2 An assessment of pupil performance in basic skills in the school.
3 A target for the continuous improvement of the school's performance in basic skills.
4 A basic skills improvement plan for pupils under-attaining in the school.
5 Regular review of the progress made by each pupil under-attaining in basic skills.
6 A commitment to improving the skills of staff in the school to teach and extend basic skills.
7 The use of appropriate teaching styles and approaches to improve basic skills.
8 The use of appropriate teaching and learning materials to improve basic skills.
9 The involvement of parents in developing their children's basic skills.
10 An effective method for monitoring the action plan and assessing improvement in performance in basic skills.

84 At the moment, the BSA intends to leave assessment of whether a school meets these criteria entirely to the discretion of LEAs. While we do believe that there should be a degree of local discretion and that LEAs should implement the scheme, **we urge the BSA to ensure that clear national standards – based on the inspection framework – are built into the Quality Mark to ensure it maintains its credibility. We believe that a validated self-review approach, based on national standards, is likely to be the most effective means of deciding whether a school merits the award. The proposed training programme and the associated training of primary headteachers and literacy co-ordinators should be explicitly linked to the Quality Mark idea.**

Implications for other aspects of policy

85 We are strongly of the view that primary schools will only be able to give steady priority to literacy over a number of years, if the literacy strategy is placed at the heart of education policy as a whole and becomes consistent with it. This section of the report sets out our thinking on the implications of the literacy strategy for other important areas of policy.

i) National Curriculum

86 It is a generally held view among primary teachers that the National Curriculum, even following Sir Ron Dearing's review in 1993, is both too broad and too prescriptive, especially in Key Stage 2. There is some evidence that this 'clutter' reduces both the time available for the basics and the priority which teachers feel able to devote to them. We share this criticism of the National Curriculum.

87 In the full-scale review of the National Curriculum which will begin in 1998 to enable changes to be in place by the year 2000, the highest possible priority should he given to ensuring that high standards of literacy and numeracy – which compare well with those in other advanced societies – become an entitlement for all pupils. We recommend that the National Curriculum for primary schools should clearly prioritise the basics – and especially literacy – and that, to make this possible, it should become less prescriptive in the other subjects, giving schools and teachers greater discretion. Nationally laid-down minimum times per week on literacy for each key stage should be written into the National Curriculum.

88 These recommendations, however, could only be implemented in the year 2000 since any sudden or piecemeal revision of the National Curriculum before the end of the promised five-year moratorium would do more harm than good.

89 Primary schools should not have to wait that long for a clear signal on a government's central priority. **We recommend, therefore, that as soon as possible, the chairman of SCAA/QNCA and Her Majesty's Chief Inspector of Schools should write jointly to all primary schools urging them to give priority to literacy and numeracy and to use their professional judgement about the implications of doing so for the rest of the National Curriculum. Inspection teams would be required to take this letter into account in reaching their judgements.**

90 The combination along these lines of an immediate, clear statement of national priorities under a new government and the endorsement of professional judgement could be a powerful motivational force among teachers.

ii) National assessment

91 We have already commented on national assessment in the section on our target. From our point of view, **it is essential that the national tests at the end of KS2:**
  i test reading effectively;
  ii provide detailed information on reading performance;
  iii ensure public credibility;
  iv are consistent over time.

92 The achievement of these objectives demands that the SCAA/QNCA subjects its own test development and marking procedures to external scrutiny and evaluation. **If the test system is refined over time – and clearly ten years is a long time – we would urge that the core measure on which we are basing our target is nevertheless sustained.**

93 **The achievement of our objectives would also be served by the introduction of 'baseline' assessment for five year olds entering school and by the continuing refinement of KS1 tests in English.** These would enable schools to set individual targets for progress and enable early intervention where problems are identified. This is particularly important in relation to children who have or might develop learning difficulties. They would also provide primary schools with comparative, value-added and improvement information on which to base targets and other management decisions.

94 SCAA/QNCA has begun to develop software packages for schools which enable much more sophisticated analyses of pupil performance in National Curriculum tests than has been possible in the past. For example, they make it possible for schools to look at performance in comparison to other schools and by gender or race and to analyse performance in different questions on the test. We believe that the provision of tools such as these, which enable schools to analyse their provenance, is crucial to the achievement of our target. The training in the management of literacy suggested above should include training in the use of these kinds of data.

iii) Inspection and school self-evaluation

95 The combination of the OFSTED inspection cycle and the emphasis in the DfEE's School Effectiveness Division on the five stage cycle of school improvement is already helping to generate both a climate of self-review in schools and a healthy focus on outcomes.

96 The revised OFSTED inspection framework, implemented as recently as 1st April 1996, already gives a strong emphasis to the core subjects of the National Curriculum, including English. **We would recommend**

that in the next revision of the inspection framework it should be modified to ensure that inspectors seek evidence of a whole school strategy for the improvement of literacy standards, including the use of training and promotion of literacy across the curriculum in both primary and secondary schools. In the meantime, clear guidance should be prepared for inspectors on these issues.

97 We believe that the inspection framework and the Basic Skins Agency Quality Mark referred to above should he brought into alignment and, indeed, that successful inspection should become a route to the achievement of the Quality Mark.

98 We are also keen to ensure that all those who inspect primary schools are well informed about the teaching and management of literacy. We recommend that all those involved in the inspection of primary schools should, at their own expense, participate in training on literacy in primary schools to ensure that they understand the details of the proposed strategy.

99 The inspection system will play an essential part in ensuring that the professional development strategy is in practice followed up in every school. We urge that, in addition to the normal cycle of inspections, experienced OFSTED inspectors should examine the impact of the literacy strategy in a substantial representative sample of primary schools (i.e. at least 10 per cent) in the year 1999–2000. The notice period for such inspections should be no more than a month.

iv) The National Professional Qualifications Framework

100 The Teacher Training Agency is currently developing and piloting the NPQH. Labour intends to make the achievement of this qualification a requirement for all those who want to become headteachers. We recommend that an explicit requirement of that qualification should be assessment and, where necessary, training for all aspiring headteachers, secondary as well as primary, in the management of literacy. As the TTA's National Professional Qualification for Subject Leaders is developed and implemented, we would urge that priority is given to Literacy Co-ordinators in primary schools.

v) Reading Recovery

101 Reading Recovery works by enabling teachers to diagnose reading difficulties among six year olds and providing them with targeted one-to-one support to enable them to catch up with their peers before they fall irrevocably behind. We wish to emphasise the importance of such early

intervention to our strategy. The evidence suggests that any remedial approach introduced once a child is eight or more is likely to be both much less effective and much more costly.

102 The Reading Recovery scheme – based on the work of the New Zealander Marie Clay was introduced in this country with cross-party support in 1992. In 1995, the government withdrew funding for the scheme. Yet the evaluations of its impact – the most recent one published in December 1996 – suggest that for those pupils who have fallen behind their peers at age six, it has been successful in bringing about pupil progress. For example, four out of every five pupils involved in 1996 successfully caught up with their peers. This British finding is consistent with international evidence on its impact. The programme has also improved diagnostic and teaching skills among the staff involved. Twenty-eight LEAs working with the Reading Recovery National Network based at the Institute of Education, London have continued to support Reading Recovery even after the withdrawal of central government funding because of this proven beneficial impact.

103 The strategic problem between 1992 and 1995 was that Reading Recovery was introduced independently of any coherent attempt to ensure that the vast majority of children learnt to read quickly and effectively through being taught in the best possible way. In New Zealand, the assumption is that 80 per cent of pupils will learn to read first time through the normal teaching programme – the so called first wave – with Reading Recovery picking up over three-quarters of the remainder in what they describe as the second wave.

104 **As our strategy is implemented, we see Reading Recovery playing the part it was designed to play in New Zealand, namely addressing the specific reading difficulties of those who, in spite of being taught well, fall behind. In its proper strategic place, it could also play a vital part in dealing with pupils with special educational needs.** The statements of special educational needs of the vast majority of pupils in late primary and secondary schools relate to literacy and are enormously expensive to manage and implement and, over time, cost much more than Reading Recovery. There is, therefore, a powerful case for investing in Reading Recovery on the grounds that prevention is better than cure. Evidence shows that it is a sound medium to long term investment. **We recommend that Reading Recovery is kept under review with the aim of both refining it over time and seeing if its outcomes can he achieved more cost effectively through, for example, more systematic use of the staff and volunteers already working in many primary schools.** If this is to be done, it is important that the existing network and infrastructure are maintained. Given the many pressures on education expenditure, however, we recognise that a major development of Reading Recovery

may not be achievable until economic growth brings additional funds into education. In the meantime, we urge that any resources for Reading Recovery are targeted at areas of disadvantage where the need is greatest and that those LEAs which have chosen to sustain it are encouraged to do so.

Children with special educational needs

105 In New Zealand, as we have seen, the 80 per cent who learn to read First time are referred to as the first wave and those who catch up through Reading Recovery as the second wave. This still leaves in the region of 5 per cent of pupils who are known as the third wave. It would be disastrous to write off this group by excluding them from the target. Many of them, although they will have identified special educational needs, can nevertheless learn to read well. Each of them needs an individual learning plan and we recommend that, under the present Code of Practice arrangements (and any refinement of them in the future), plans are made to meet their literacy needs. The introduction of universal baseline assessment should help. Assuming that the success levels expected of the first two waves are achieved or exceeded, there is no reason why such individual plans should be prohibitively expensive, especially if interventions are structured and early. The problem at present is that in many cases, intervention is too late and, in addition, many pupils who ought to learn through either the first or second wave are becoming unnecessarily caught up in the special educational needs procedures.

106 We acknowledge the crucial role in this context of each school's special educational needs co-ordinator (SENCO). SENCOs diagnose children's needs and devise (and advise on the implementation of) specific learning programmes for children and liaise with the multi-disciplinary agencies to support them. The TTA's plan for a National Professional Qualification for SENCOs is welcome. In addition, we believe the place of the SENCO in the school needs to be an aspect of the professional development strategy outlined above.

Parental responsibilities

107 Parents have a vital role in supporting and encouraging children's learning, perhaps most of all in helping their child learn to read. The National Year of Reading will help to draw attention to this role. If our literacy strategy is to succeed, then a key element of it must focus on enlisting parents in it and enabling them to play their full part in it. Almost all parents are desperately keen to see their child learn to read. We expect that they will be enthusiastically supportive of our strategy

and keen to play their part in realising it. We make a number of proposals to enhance the role of parents in helping their child learn to read
from birth through to his/her completion of primary education.

108 The learning a child does between birth and age three or four is known
to be extremely important, particularly in the acquisition of language.
Children who are read to regularly, hear stories, sing or learn nursery
rhymes, look at books, visit libraries and so on, are much more likely to
learn to read easily. We have been impressed by the work done by
Birmingham education authority to encourage parents to provide these
opportunities for young children.

109 **We believe there are a number of strategies an incoming government could follow which would emulate at national level what
Birmingham and some others have done locally. These should
include:**
   i finding cost effective means of getting advice to parents via
the health visitor network and doctors' surgeries;
   ii evaluating the success of the Basic Skills Agency's proposed
parent helpline;
   iii urging businesses that are in regular contact with parents –
banks, stores and supermarkets, for example – to participate
in promoting the importance of reading. At busy times supermarkets, for example, could employ staff to provide entertain-
ing reading-related activities for small children while their
parents shopped in peace;
   iv a high-profile media campaign encouraging parents to
support their children's reading. Discussions with major
broadcasting organisations and with those companies who use
television and radio advertising extensively should begin as
soon as possible.

110 We believe the National Year of Reading, which we describe below,
will provide a good stimulus to such activity but recognise that the
kind of campaign we have in mind needs to be sustained over a longer
period. It would provide a positive and constructive climate in which to
press ahead with the literacy strategy.

111 On its own, however, a campaign of this kind would not be enough.
There needs, in addition, to be a systematic approach to linking
home and school. Labour is committed already to introducing
home–school agreements. At primary level, we believe these
should emphasise not only attendance, punctuality, good behaviour and the school's responsibilities but also the potential of
work at home to support a child in learning to read. They should
be discussed with parents before their child or children start at a school
and then build on it at parents' meetings, which ideally should take
place at least twice a year. **The ultimate goal should be the estab-**

lishment of clear targets for the improvement of each child's progress over a six month period, with both parents and school being clear about what their respective responsibilities are in ensuring the target is met. We believe that support for and the improvement of reading among all children, and especially those with special educational needs, could be greatly assisted by this approach.

112 In relation to reading, very often the best homework is simply for the parent or someone else from home to spend 20 minutes or so each day either reading to their child or hearing him or her read. This is important not only while the child is learning to read but also once the child can read so that his/her fluency is improved and range extended. This would not generate marking for teachers, nor place an intolerable burden on the vast majority of parents. National guidance from the DfEE on home–school agreements and homework should encourage it for children in both KS1 and KS2. The 20 minutes reading should be seen as part of the half an hour's homework a day which Labour intends to recommend in guidance on homework.

113 We have seen the documentation produced by Greenwood Junior School and its partners in an inner city school improvement project in Nottingham. The director of the project, John Botham, is a member of the Task Force. The model of 'home study' developed there appears to have been highly successful, not least because in addition to being educationally sound, it is eminently practical. The homework tasks have been designed to link with the National Curriculum. They are also constructed so that they do not generate extensive marking which could overwhelm already heavily burdened teachers. The school realistically recommends four home study sessions a week. We recommend that the Literacy Strategy Group should also examine the production of home study guidance, drawing on the experience of Greenwood and other forward-thinking primary schools. The distance learning training materials should recommend home study as part of the approach to improving reading standards.

Family literacy

114 The involvement of parents in helping children learn to read is predicated, of course, on the notion that parents themselves are literate. Given levels of adult illiteracy, this is not always the case. There is therefore a need to link efforts to improve literacy among adults to our proposals for improving reading standards in primary schools. Much of this lies outside our terms of reference. We do wish, however, to draw attention to the success of the Basic Skills Agency Demonstration Projects in Family Literacy. There were four Programmes based in areas of multiple deprivation in Cardiff, Liverpool, Norfolk and North Tyneside.

Each provided courses which lasted 96 hours over 12 weeks, and involved children aged 3 to 6 and their parents (96 per cent of participating parents were mothers). On entry, the parents had low levels of literacy, and many of their children were severely disadvantaged for learning by low development in vocabulary and in emergent reading and writing. Parents worked on their own literacy, built on home literacy activities and beamed how to extend the help they gave their children. Meanwhile, the children were given intensive early years teaching, with a strong emphasis on writing and talking as well as reading. There were also joint sessions in which the parents worked with their children and used the strategies they had been taught for helping them.

115 The evaluation of these by the NFER published in 1996 found that the children made greater-than-expected average improvements m vocabulary and reading during the courses and in the 12 weeks after them, while in writing, they also made substantial gains. For example, the proportion whose lack of vocabulary would leave them severely disadvantaged for learning fell from 17 per cent to six per cent, while the standardised mean score for reading rose from 84 to 92, where 100 is the average.

116 In addition, both the literacy levels and the ability of parents to help their children to read was boosted. There were substantial increases in literacy-related home activities, and these became fully embedded in family practice. Parents also reported substantial increases in their ability to help their children with language and literacy and in their confidence in doing so.

117 All the evidence therefore suggests that family literacy is both beneficial and cost-effective.

118 We strongly welcome the government's decision to fund a number of family literacy projects recommend that an incoming government sees family literacy as a central part of its approach to reading standards in disadvantaged areas and provides continuing support for these projects, with a view to expanding them as and when resources become available.

Addressing disadvantage

119 In the opening sections of this report, we point out that in addition to raising overall performance and improving consistency, our strategy would have explicitly to address disadvantage. This section draws together the strands of our strategy which are designed to do that. **We believe that early action to implement Labour's existing commitments to providing nursery education for all four year olds and reducing class sizes for five, six and seven year olds would be**

most beneficial in areas of disadvantage, where research shows they are likely to have the most effect and where there is most distance for schools to go if our target is to be met. We also recommend the continuation and, if funds allow, extension of the NLP as a significant contribution to raising literacy standards in LEAs where it has been established.

120 In addition, we propose that through a continuation of GEST funding at the level necessary for the professional development programme in 1998–9 for at least two further years, resources would be targeted at schools with disadvantaged intakes to ensure that, in addition to teaching well, they could provide extra support through proven school improvement strategies. **The details of how this should be done need further consideration but we believe that the American 'Success for All' programme offers a powerful model. Adapted to English circumstances, it would imply that:**

   i   schools would have to meet nationally agreed criteria on social disadvantage;

   ii schools would have to express a willingness to adopt in full proven school improvement strategies. In addition to governors' approval, 80 per cent of the professional staff of the school would have to vote for participation;

   iii any additional resources would be carefully targetted.

121 The international research evidence suggests that a programme at this level could ensure substantial progress among participating schools. If it were applied solely to the most disadvantaged primary schools, then it could be funded comfortably from within the planned GEST programme.

122 **We welcome the idea of providing, with Lottery funding, study support centres at which young people in disadvantaged areas can do homework and other assistance with their learning. We believe that the needs of primary pupils should be borne in mind as these plans are constructed.** Indeed, in many communities, primary schools themselves are likely to be ideal locations for such centres. Adult volunteers, university students and indeed many secondary school pupils could provide reading support to primary pupils in these and other after-school settings at very little cost. There is also a growing body of experience in the use of volunteers and business mentors, on which we could usefully build.

123 As we have already suggested, the family literacy programme and a revived Reading Recovery scheme should focus on areas of disadvantage too.

124 We believe hard-pressed teachers in schools in such areas would be greatly assisted in achieving their goals, if they had more systematic support from trained classroom assistants. We are encouraged by the

success of the government's programme for training specialist teaching assistants (STAs) and by the teacher unions' recognition of their potential benefits. **We believe that the training of STAs should continue and that primary schools in disadvantaged areas should be encouraged to employ them, particularly to support the teaching of reading.**

125 We are aware that, compared to many other developed countries, the amount we spend on books for each primary school child is low. We would like to encourage projects such as Bookstart in Birmingham, which has used health visitors to raise awareness of books and reading among the parents of very young children. Training of headteachers and literacy co-ordinators should include approaches to book purchasing, as we have suggested.

126 Finally, we would like to see a series of targeted experiments in the use of IT to support literacy sited in areas of disadvantage. These should build on the evaluations the NCET has already undertaken of Integrated Learning Systems, the impressive work of the Technology Colleges Trust and the early success of the Docklands Literacy Project. Schemes such as these should be funded through public–private partnership. **We believe that in areas where there are secondary schools with Technology College status, they might be expected to enhance the use of IT to support literacy in their feeder primary schools.** In the long run and especially in the second half of our ten year strategy, we believe IT may enable us to go beyond the levels of achievement envisaged currently. The Literacy Strategy Group should monitor developments in the use of IT in the teaching of literacy closely.

127 **We recognise that there is an overall resource constraint and that there is no prospect of rapid growth in education expenditure. However, Labour is committed to increasing the proportion of GNP which will be devoted to education over the lifetime of a government. If, through reducing welfare expenditure, additional resources become available without any need for taxation increases, we urge that a highly cost-effective use of them would be to enable primary schools in disadvantaged areas to appoint additional teaching assistants and buy more books. We recommend that, in any review of education funding and LMS formulae, this suggestion is taken into account.** This would contribute to an overall strategic need, identified by (among many others) the House of Commons Select Committee on Education, to bring per pupil levels of expenditure in primary schools up towards those in secondary schools.

128 **Some primary schools have been able to improve greatly their adult/pupil ratios, not just by employing teaching assistants but**

also by becoming recognised training bases for NVQ Level 3 qualifications in, for example, child care. We believe consideration should be given to building on this model through piloting it in a number of areas of disadvantage. Groups of people aged 16 and over from local areas who have very basic qualifications (i.e. 2/3 GCSEs) could be involved. They would work in groups based in primary schools and be trained at their school base. They would train to NVQ Level 3 in a new qualification comparable to the existing childcare qualification but focusing on the skills of teaching reading/literacy. Those who did not already possess it would be required to retake GCSE English through evening classes. Schools that chose to participate would appoint a senior member of staff to co-ordinate the scheme. This person would oversee the work of the trainees when they were in school and arrange for their assessment. Small schools could participate in consortia. At the end of a training period, this qualification could be used in conjunction with the GCSE's, and would provide a strong platform for seeking employment in a range of possible lines of work.

129 A scheme of this kind would offer a real chance to local young people and contribute to raising reading standards. We urge government and the NCVQ/QNCA to begin work on developing it as soon as possible.

Literacy for bilingual learners

130 The issues covered in this report clearly have implications for the teaching of bilingual pupils. Bilingual pupils are not, of course, an homogeneous group. In some cases, they are from families long established in this country who are very familiar with English and with English schools; other may be the first generation to attend school and perhaps the first to develop literacy in those languages. For bilingual learners, fluent literacy in English takes time to learn, but we believe that it is right to expect that most pupils with full experience of primary education in English can reach the Level 4 target in reading and writing by age eleven. Children who have arrived recently from abroad may need longer to reach the target with a special programme planned by the school.

131 In either case, we believe that our overall proposals will facilitate their acquisition of literacy as rapidly as possible. The emphasis in the proposals on maintaining the direct teaching of skills and strategies through to the end of KS2, on individual target-setting and on home–school collaboration are likely to be of particular benefit.

132 Successful work over a number of years points to the characteristics of effective provision for bilingual learners. In the best practice issues about the teaching of bilingual pupils are thoroughly explored and integrated within general school policies; the contribution of support

staff, whether teachers or teaching assistants, is well managed; a careful analysis is made of the language demands of the curriculum and of how bilingual learners at different stages can be helped to meet them; there is particular attention to the links between the learning of the spoken and the written language; close help is given on reading for meaning and on models of written language for more advanced learners; additional resources such as visual aids, talking books and dual language materials are intelligently used.

133 We intend that the distance beaming materials for school staff and governors which we are proposing will reflect this successful experience. We also expect that the training of teaching assistants, referred to elsewhere in this report, will encompass those who work particularly with bilingual learners.

134 We recognise that, in the next phase of our work, we need to examine this issue in more depth and would welcome views from those with an interest and expertise in this field.

The national year of reading

135 The bulk of our report has necessarily concentrated on reforming the education service so that primary schools and teachers are better equipped to teach reading effectively and parents are enabled to play their part in supporting a child's reading.

136 However, as we made plain earlier, we are convinced that for our strategy to succeed, it is necessary for the whole society to assist teachers and parents in their respective tasks. If there were a national sense of everyone, both inside and outside education, working together to raise literacy standards it would help to transform expectations and to ensure that primary teachers felt that they were part of a wider movement with broad support. While we believe that some of the criticism of primary schools' performance over the last generation has been legitimate – as the picture we have painted of the current state of affairs makes clear – we also recognise that very often primary teachers currently feel they are swimming against a cultural tide which threatens to overwhelm them and their best efforts. We recognise that the teaching profession will be in no position to take on the challenge we have set if it is totally demoralised and that our strategy must provide teachers with the encouragement and support to take on the challenge ahead.

137 For these reasons, in addition to changes we have recommended in the education service, in this section we make proposals designed to turn the cultural tide so that teachers and schools feel they are swimming with it. The National Year of Reading originally proposed by David Blunkett in his speech to the 1996 NAHT conference – is central to our plans for achieving this objective.

138 The school year 1998–9 – the last full school year of the millennium – will be designated 'The National Year of Reading'. Along
with the changes we plan in the education service in that year, we
hope there will be a huge media campaign and a series of events
aimed at urging:

   i parents and all other adults to support schools in their
    efforts to raise reading standards
- for example, every company or organisation could urge those of
its employees who are also parents to read with their children.
Some n-light give employees half a day off for this purpose
during the year;
- there could be a nationwide appeal for volunteers to help with
reading. In Tower Hamlets, over 200 business people read with
primary school children on a regular basis and companies have
offered a further 400 such mentors since a Newsroom South
East item in January 1997.

   ii adults with poor literacy skills to try to improve them *
- the Basic Skills Agency could link up with television – as it has
done in the past – to promote adult and family literacy;

   iii the media to recognise its influence and to seek imaginative
    means of encouraging children and young people to read
    and parents and other adults to support them in doing so *
- television schedules could include both short 'advertising' slots
and longer programmes urging parents to support children's
reading and showing them how;

   iv publishers and booksellers to contribute to the campaign to
    raise reading standards, not least because it will clearly be in
    their commercial interests to do so *
- publishers and booksellers could organise events in schools and
libraries, sponsor television productions and produce advice for
schools on book-buying;

   v business to play a part through, for example, partnerships
    with the public sector *
- businesses could vary advertisements from time to time to
promote reading (e.g. BT: 'It's good to read'); *
- existing business mentoring schemes could be extended; *
- supermarkets could promote reading among customers and
provide, as we have suggested above, literacy events on site for
children while parents shop in peace.

   vi the experience of the public library services to be drawn
    upon in promoting reading in communities.

139 The National Year of Reading will only work if it achieves a very high
profile indeed. Its goal must be to engage the interest of every single
citizen and the activity of many millions. **The initial soundings we**

have taken indicate great enthusiasm for the National Year of Reading among publishers, booksellers and librarians. WH Smith, Britain's leading bookseller, has expressed keen interest as have several publishers including Macmillan and Random House, as well as the public relations agency Colman Getty, which publicises the Booker Prize, among other things. The Library Association has also expressed strong support. The climate of opinion appears to be entirely right for such an initiative. The entire event could be an innovative and exciting example of public–private partnership related to a national priority.

140 If it is to take place in 1998–9, then preparations need to begin as soon as possible. **We recommend the establishment of a planning group – with high level representatives of all the key interests – as soon as possible after the election to start this process, with either the National Literacy Trust or the Basic Skills Agency or both jointly acting as host to it.**

141 We hope that the gains made in the year will be sustained and that the National Literacy Trust, the Basic Skills Agency and other organisations will prepare in advance to build upon it well into the next millennium.

In the meantime

142 We believe the strategy we have outlined in this report so far 's comprehensive, ambitious and likely to make a substantial impact on literacy standards. However, we recognise that even if the strategy proved entirely successful in meeting our long-term target, there would be children in the short term who reach the end of primary education without the literacy skills necessary to take advantage of secondary education.

143 For this reason, David Blunkett announced at the Labour Party Conference that Labour would pilot Literacy Summer Schools for Year 6 children whose reading level was below Level 4. Their purpose would be to give a boost to these children's reading performance before they started secondary schools. He announced that resources would be made available within the GEST budget for this purpose.

144 We intend to give further consideration to the best way to organise and provide these summer schools in time for our final report. We are, at this stage, open about the best means of organising them and flexible about approaches and the appropriate ages to involve pupils. **At this stage, we believe that in order to gain experience and evidence of the likely impact of Literacy Summer Schools, an incoming Labour government should:**

1 evaluate a number of different models that are already

planned for the summer of 1997 by LEAs and other organisations;

2 on the basis of the evaluation, develop a number of models of summer school support which have been demonstrated to work;

3 under the GEST scheme, invite proposals to run schemes in 1998 according to the established criteria;

4 on the basis of the 1998 schemes, consider the development of a national scheme which could include a variety of approaches to be launched and delivered in 1999 during the National Year of Reading.

Secondary schools

145 Our chief focus, given the nature of our target, has been on primary education. However, we are aware that literacy is as much an issue for secondary schools as it is for primary schools.

146 In the short term, secondary schools are faced with substantial numbers of young people who join them with inadequate literacy skills and are therefore at risk of being disaffected and/or disruptive. In the longer run, if our strategy is successful, there will be far fewer such pupils. Even so, it will be important for secondary schools to build on the efforts of primary schools and work consistently across the curriculum to enhance literacy levels so that all pupils leave school articulate, confident and able to express themselves orally and in writing. We have been impressed by the Western Australia Stepping Out materials which are aimed at secondary schools and build on the First Steps approach to literacy in primary schools.

147 We have not, in the time available to us, been able to do justice to the issue of literacy m secondary schools, although we recognise that it is of major importance. The Task Force would need additional members and a further consultation exercise to develop a way forward.

148 **We recommend that, once an incoming government has embarked on its literacy strategy for primary education, it should seek to develop a programme showing how secondary education might build upon it and making proposals for how in the meantime they might address the substantial literacy challenge they face. We hope, with the support of some additional secondary colleagues, to begin work on this task in the next phase of our work.**

Section four: the strategy – phase two – 2001–2006

The process

149 In the foregoing section, we have set out a detailed and comprehensive strategy for the years 1997–2001. Broadly, the plans we have described would form the work of the full term of a government. We are confident that, if this first phase of the strategy is adhered to, it would dramatically raise literacy standards and our interim targets would be met or exceeded.

150 However, we also recognise that, if we are to reach our ultimate target and sustain it, and if we are to ensure that secondary and tertiary education build systematically on the foundations laid by primary schools, then the drive for improved literacy standards will need a second phase.

151 Clearly, it would be foolish to be too prescriptive at this stage about a policy strategy to be pursued in the early years of the next century. It is essential that, in thinking that far ahead, we are flexible and in a position to build on the thorough evaluation of the first phase of the strategy which we have already recommended.

152 We are, however, in a position to set out the process through which phase two of the strategy win emerge. The Literacy Strategy Group, which we have recommended should oversee the first phase of the strategy, should, from the start, have in mind the need to prepare for the longer term future.

153 This perspective should inform its monitoring and evaluation of the first phase of the strategy. It should seek constantly to gather data, information and ideas for the second phase. The evidence gathered by OFSTED and major research projects will be of particular importance, as will evaluations of the impact over time of the NLP. In order to keep close to teacher and parental opinion on the effect of the strategy, the Group ought also to use focus groups and other polling techniques periodically. Above all, the Group needs to develop and sustain good links with similar strategic approaches to literacy in other countries. We believe that, increasingly, such international crossfertilisation can make a vital contribution both in providing ideas and approaches and in ensuring that standards here match the best in the world.

Likely features

154 We anticipate that the second phase of the strategy will involve some or all of the following features:
  i considering the evidence of the impact of IT on approaches to teaching literacy and, in the light of the evidence, deciding how to make effective use of it;

ii improving the diagnostic and pedagogical skills of teachers in relation to pupils with various specific reading difficulties;

iii building on the experience of the first phase of the strategy to enhance home-school links;

iv building on the experience of the first phase of the strategy to make greater and more effective use of trained classroom assistants;

v continuing to improve links between primary and secondary schools on literacy;

vi enhancing the capability of all primary teachers to assess children, to analyse data from assessment and apply it in the teaching process; in particular we anticipate considerable progress in the capability of IT to enhance the capacity of schools in assessment;

vii above all, building on the growing capacity of primary schools to improve themselves, a capacity which should be substantially enhanced by a sustained drive for school improvement and much greater consistency across the education service.

155 From these strands, we anticipate the Literacy Strategy Group will be in a position by around 1998–9 to set out in some detail the strategy to be pursued in the years 2001–2006. We expect this will be consistent with and supportive of the strategy for improving literacy at secondary level, which we would expect to be in place by then.

Conclusion

156 This interim report has set out in some detail our thinking on the strategy necessary to transform literacy standards. We hope, on the basis of responses to this report, to refuse and develop our thinking so that when we publish our final report in May, it can command widespread support. Any written responses should be clearly marked 'LTF' and sent by mid-April at the latest to:

Professor Michael Barber
Institute of Education
20 Bedford Way
London WC1H OAL

Appendix 2

Report of the Literacy Taskforce

Advice to the Government on achieving its goal that:

'By 2005, every child turning nine will be able to read, write, and do maths for success'

A report prepared for the Minister of Education
March 1999

Executive summary

The Literacy Taskforce endorsed the Government's goal that 'By 2005, every child turning nine will be able to read, write, and do maths for success.'

The taskforce agreed that the goal provides a focus for the whole community to support children's learning both in and out of school. Defining the goal through providing a rich description of the knowledge, understandings, skills, and attitudes that nine-year-olds should demonstrate when they are reading and writing for success will set clear national expectations that everyone – teachers, parents, and children – can understand and work towards.

The Literacy Taskforce believes that the goal can be achieved by ensuring that all children receive the best possible teaching in their first four years at school. This means that teachers must be well prepared for their challenging jobs through high-quality teacher education that includes a strong focus on developing the skills and knowledge necessary to implement best practice in the teaching of reading and writing. It means that teachers should be supported by strong professional leadership in their schools, through ongoing access to quality professional development opportunities, with appropriate classroom materials, and with the support of effective interventions when they identify children who need a period of intensive specialised teaching.

The Literacy Taskforce agreed that children's learning is enhanced by effective partnerships between school and home and that people and organisations in the community can support children's learning in a range of ways, many of which are simple yet effective.

The recommendations of the Literacy Taskforce are directed towards this end.

Background

The Government's Literacy and Numeracy Strategy

Although most New Zealand children do well at reading, writing, and mathematics, there is evidence that some do not. Of special concern are a wide gap between the highest and lowest levels of reading achievement and significant differences in performance in all areas between particular groups of children. With the objective of raising overall achievement, particularly in maths, and closing the gap between the lowest and highest achievers, particularly in reading, the Government has adopted the following goal:

> 'By 2005, every child turning nine will be able to read, write, and do maths for success.'

Student achievement is influenced by personal, cultural, family, and school factors. Feelings of personal success and capability, as well as personal interests and liking for a subject, have a strong bearing on progress and learning outcomes. The expectations and support of people who matter in their lives and their opportunities and experiences both in and out of school are also important influences on children's achievement. Finally, the quality of the curriculum – its content, design, and the way in which it is taught and monitored – is also a significant influence on children's achievement.

Success in learning is most likely when effective teaching practices and an appropriate curriculum encourage and build on the learner's motivation and interest. Both learner interest and an appropriate curriculum are informed and complemented by good communication between home and school and by shared understandings and expectations of goals. Achieving ongoing improvements in outcomes for all students depends on the involvement of parents, communities, early childhood education services, and schools, in addition to support and leadership from the Government.

The Literacy and Numeracy Strategy includes:

- ensuring that the goal for nine-year-olds is well understood in the education sector and by parents and the wider community;
- working out the most effective way to measure the progress of individuals and groups towards the goal;
- supporting the best possible teaching of all children;
- ensuring that government interventions to support children's learning in literacy are as effective and efficient as possible;
- providing extra support for programmes through a special proposals pool;
- encouraging parents and the wider community to support children's learning at school and in early childhood through a public information campaign.

The Literacy Taskforce

As a key input into the development of the Literacy and Numeracy Strategy, the Government established the Literacy Taskforce to provide advice on how the goal should be defined, how progress towards it should be measured, and the ways in which literacy learning could best be supported. The taskforce was asked to make specific recommendations to improve teaching and learning for children in their first four years at school, to identify those aspects of current practice that need affirming or reinforcing, and to indicate programmes or practices that need reviewing.

Because the development of literacy is a fundamental role of schools, the Minister of Education wanted the taskforce to comprise mostly principals or teachers who are working successfully with those children considered most at risk of failure. Appendix A sets out a full list of the Literacy Taskforce members and their initial terms of reference.

A sub-group of the Maths and Science Taskforce was reconvened to provide advice on the mathematics part of the goal. Their advice is reported separately.

The Literacy Experts Group

The Secretary for Education convened a ten-member Literacy Experts Group to provide the Literacy Taskforce with advice from theoretical and academic perspectives. A list of the members of this group is included in Appendix A.

Process

The Literacy Taskforce met as a whole group for three working sessions over a three-month period. In between sessions, members discussed issues with their colleagues and sought and considered information relevant to the terms of reference from a wide range of sources. Their report is as follows.

Defining the goal

The Literacy Taskforce agreed that defining the goal, that 'By 2005, every child turning nine will be able to read, write, and do maths for success' provided an opportunity for everyone – schools, parents, the community, and the child – to share an understanding of what it means to read, write, and do maths for success.

The taskforce considered the tension between stating minimum standards that all children should be expected to reach and providing indicators of success that motivate students to 'soar'. The Literacy Experts Group's advice was that care needs to be taken not to set minimal competency levels. These have been abandoned by most states in the United States because they were found to have lowered standards. The taskforce is aware that the literacy strategy is about both raising achievement for all students, including the gifted and talented, and closing the gap between the lowest and highest achievers.

The taskforce was adamant that the expectations of the achievement of all children should be the same, regardless of the language of instruction or their ethnicity. However, it is clear that some children, for example, immigrant children who at nine years old might have had only one year's instruction in English, will need more assistance than others. The taskforce also agreed that although the goal is relevant and appropriate to children in Māori-medium education, the procedures and approaches for achieving the goal may well be different from those in English-medium education.

For students with special education needs, the idea of learning to read and write for success is individual to them and should be expressed through their individual education plans.

The Literacy Taskforce was strongly of the view that defining a goal for reading and writing should not result in the production of an alternative national curriculum. The taskforce considers that it is the proper purpose of the national curriculum to set out the levels of expected achievement and that the literacy goal should reflect those objectives. The members agreed that most nine-year-olds will be achieving at level 2 in English in the New Zealand Curriculum, some will be achieving at level 3, and some will be working at between levels 1 and 2. Children in Màori-medium education will be working to the appropriate levels specified in Te Reo Màori i roto i Te Marautanga o Aotearoa.

In providing advice on defining the goal, the taskforce therefore prefers the development of a description of the knowledge, understandings, strategies, and attitudes that nine-year-olds should demonstrate when reading and writing for success. The taskforce considered that developing such a set of descriptors alongside some examples of text that children are reading and of children's writing will serve to set national expectations for teachers and parents.

There are many general features of learning to read and write that apply across countries, but others are specific to New Zealand; for example, our cultural context includes recognition of the educational and language needs of both Màori and non-Màori deriving from obligations under the Treaty of Waitangi and such official policies as the recognition of both English and te reo Màori as official languages.

Reading and writing

Reading and writing are complex activities. The Literacy Experts Group's approach to providing advice on defining the goal was to use oral language as a basis.

> 'In general, successful reading for children at age nine means comprehending in print much of what they are expected to comprehend when listening to spoken language. Successful writing means expressing in print much of what they are expected to express when speaking.
>
> These statements refer to the child's language of instruction, for example, they refer to the Màori language for children who are developing bilingually in the Màori medium.
>
> The goal to read and write for success should provide an effective platform for the subsequent development of biliteracy.'
>   – Literacy Experts Group's advice to the Literacy Taskforce

Successful reading and writing have several features that a child is able to demonstrate across multiple text types. The primary features are text comprehension (for reading) and text construction (for writing), with further features of accuracy, fluency, and the self-motivation to read and write.

The Literacy Taskforce agreed that the School Journals (Parts 1 and 2) provide the only existing national examples of reading material most likely to be used by teachers in their day-to-day teaching practice with nine-year-olds. There are no national indicators for children's writing.

The junior Màori readers used in Màori-medium education have been organised into levels of difficulty (Ngà Kete Kòrero framework). All remaining Màori readers have yet to be fitted into this framework. When this work is completed, it should provide national indicators for reading in Màori-medium education.

> The Literacy Taskforce recommends that a description of the know-ledge, skills, and attitudes that nine-year-olds demonstrate when they are reading and writing for success, together with a description of the features of appropriate texts, be developed and promulgated to teachers and parents.[1] (A possible model of the descriptors is provided in Appendix B.)

The taskforce agreed that reading and writing for success at nine is essential for further progress both in and out of school. However, further progress is dependent on continuing effective education as well as ongoing practice beyond formal schooling.

The current situation

What do we know about the progress children are currently making towards the goal?

The Literacy Taskforce acknowledged that currently we know only about the achievement of students learning in the medium of English. There has been no systematic collection and analysis of data of children's progress and achievement for learning in the medium of Màori (or any other language of instruction).

International and local studies confirm that, in general, New Zealand children are successful readers and writers compared with children from countries with similar or better socio-economic conditions. However, the same studies highlight a wide variation in performance in reading tasks of particular groups of New Zealand students.[2]

The IEA international survey of reading of nine-year-olds (1990) showed that Màori performed significantly below the international average, and Màori

1   This proposal will need to be explored further for Màori-medium education.
2   These studies were the IEA Reading Literacy Study, 1990; the International Adult Literacy Study, 1997; the NEMP Report 6 Reading and Speaking Assessment, 1996. Initial disparities are reported in School Entry Assessment/Aro matawai Urunga-à-Kura, The First National Picture – July 1997–May 1998.

boys performed at a level below that of Màori girls. A further analysis of the data shows significant differences in word recognition and comprehension between children whose home language was English compared to children whose home language was not. Many of these were Pacific Islands children.

The evidence suggests initial disparities that then continue to grow over the first four years of schooling between Màori and Pacific Islands children on the one hand and Pàkehà children on the other, as well as disparities between children in low-decile schools and those in other schools. It was noted that there is a high proportion of Màori and Pacific Islands children in low-decile schools.[3]

Analyses of school leaver qualifications data and the International Adult Literacy Survey show lower levels of performance for Màori and Pacific Islands people than for Pàkehà, which suggests that later learning has not redressed these problems. This clearly has further implications for generational effects on children's literacy learning.

Reading Recovery identifies, through its diagnostic survey, about 20 percent of children who, compared with the other children in their classroom, are making relatively limited progress after one year of instruction. However, the performance of that 20 percent in any one classroom could be above, at, or below the national average. The taskforce noted that it appears that this convention of identifying children using the diagnostic survey has led to the widely expressed claim that 20 percent of children are failing in their literacy learning in New Zealand schools.

A third small group[4] of 'hard to teach' students is identified by such interventions as Reading Recovery and the Resource Teachers of Reading service.

A summary of the studies referred to above is attached in Appendix C.

Implications

The studies suggest that our literacy strategies are more effective for most students than those in many other similar countries. However, the evidence also suggests that our teaching is far less effective for the underachieving groups described in the previous section. The taskforce agreed that there is also sufficient evidence to show that boys are not doing as well as girls in our school system. The taskforce agreed that the challenge is to ensure that our teaching practices are equally effective for all children.

In many classrooms, children who might be expected to make limited progress because they fit the profile of the underachieving groups in fact make excellent progress. But the taskforce was concerned that not enough is known about the particular teaching strategies and approaches in New

---

3   Initial disparities are reported in School Entry Assessment/Aro matawai Urunga-à-Kura, The First National Picture – July 1997–May 1998.
4   This group represents around 1–2% of six-to-seven-year-olds.

Zealand that bring about these results, and it recommends that more research be undertaken so that better guidance can be given to teachers.

Effective teaching

The taskforce agreed that, in general, with adequate support systems in place, the following factors contribute towards success for all children:

- the highest quality teaching is available to all children, regardless of the medium of instruction;
- there is a culture of high expectations for all children;
- the whole school is a community of learners;
- there is a close partnership between home and school;
- the cultural identity of children is recognised and affirmed.

Best practice for teaching reading and writing

In New Zealand, decisions about how to teach are made at the school level – that is, teaching methods are not prescribed as part of the national curriculum, although official guidance is provided through the teacher materials outlined later in this report. The Literacy Taskforce believes that this policy should not be changed. Decisions about teaching strategies, teaching approaches, and materials to use are professional decisions that are best made at the local school level in response to the needs of particular groups of children and individuals. However, the taskforce was concerned that, given the evident under-achievement of some children, 'more of the same' will not be good enough.

The Literacy Taskforce endorsed the following principles of best practice in whichever medium of instruction:

- a sound understanding of the learning process that underpins all teaching;
- the expectation that all children will become successful readers and writers;
- language programmes that acknowledge the interrelationship and reciprocity of oral, written, and visual language;
- planning for teaching that will build on the child's existing skills, knowledge, interests, and individual needs and that will acknowledge the role of the child as an active learner;
- teaching that takes account of children's linguistic and cultural backgrounds;
- teaching that uses a range of explicit and implicit instructional strategies appropriate to the learner, including small-group or individual instruction where appropriate;

- regular and purposeful monitoring – children's progress in reading and writing being monitored regularly (using running records, teacher conferencing, observation, and other methods) for clear purpose and for use in subsequent teaching;
- the development of positive attitudes to reading and writing, including the willingness to take risks;
- the use of a wide range of interesting material, fiction and non-fiction, in a range of media and appropriate to the instructional levels, including repetitive texts, rhymes, poems, and songs, to enhance children's print and phonological awareness;
- access to a wide range of interesting and stimulating material, fiction and non-fiction, in a range of media;
- teachers who are readers and writers.

The taskforce also considered that a statement of best practice needs to be quite specific about what comprises appropriate instructional approaches, particularly in the light of the public debate about phonics and whole language. Although the debate has brought important issues about the teaching of reading to the surface, the taskforce felt that it had been conducted by the media in a way that polarised views. The taskforce strongly believes that such polarisation has been unhelpful[5] when the focus of attention should be on ensuring that instructional approaches include an appropriate mix of strategies.

The Literacy Experts Group's advice on appropriate instructional approaches was based on a concern they expressed that teachers may not always select appropriate strategies, particularly when working with struggling readers. There is sound research that indicates that children should not rely on context as the primary or only strategy for working out unknown words but should develop the use of word-level skills and strategies. For some struggling readers, teachers may need to place a stronger emphasis on the development of word-level skills and strategies than for those children who quickly develop alphabetic awareness and are able to use language prediction skills such as context much more readily.

The taskforce agreed that it is essential that all teachers be skilled and able to use a wide range of strategies with children, selecting those that are most appropriate at the time rather than trying to provide a balance or following a particular approach.

---

5   The taskforce was concerned that some schools' response to the phonics/whole language debate has been to move towards using reading programmes that place a heavy emphasis in teaching subskills in isolation – that is, the 'skill and drill' approach, whereas others seem to have moved towards an exclusively whole-language approach with no systematic teaching of phonological awareness.

> The Literacy Taskforce recommends that a statement of best practice be drawn up and promulgated to schools. This statement should also guide the development of curriculum materials for both teachers and children developed and distributed by the Ministry of Education and guide schools' purchase of materials.

The national curriculum

The national curriculum for reading and writing in general classrooms is outlined in English in the New Zealand Curriculum and in Te Reo Màori i roto i Te Marautanga o Aotearoa for Màori-medium education.[6] The Literacy Taskforce believes that although the curriculum objectives in the English curriculum are deliberately broad and therefore often need further elaboration to be successfully implemented, they do not need to be changed.[7] The taskforce supported the Ministry of Education's proposals to develop exemplars to give further guidance.

Members of the taskforce thought that the curriculum for Màori-medium education, Te Reo Màori i roto i Te Marautanga o Aotearoa, might need further consideration in the light of experience being gained through its implementation.

The taskforce was concerned at the way in which a balanced curriculum has been interpreted by many schools to mean that equal time should be given to each of the essential learning areas. It considered that schools should be given clearer direction to emphasise literacy and numeracy in the early years. However, this emphasis does not necessarily mean allocating more time to language programmes than is currently usually given in the junior school but using that time more effectively and actively reinforcing the development of literacy and numeracy through the rest of the curriculum.

Such an emphasis could be issued through modifying the National Administration Guidelines (NAGs).

The taskforce was concerned that the way in which the NAGs' requirements to 'monitor student progress against the national achievement objectives' and to 'assess student achievement, maintain individual records, and report on student progress' have been interpreted and implemented are not reasonable. The taskforce was aware of teachers being required to gather large amounts of detailed data to record the progress of individual children across the curriculum at the expense of quality instruction time. It is

6   The national curriculum statements are available on-line at http//www.minedu. govt.nz/curriculum.
7   The taskforce was informed by the Ministry of Education that the national curriculum would be fully evaluated over the next year or two once the current cycle of development had been completed.

difficult for teachers to maintain an emphasis on literacy and numeracy in these circumstances. The taskforce believes that all the essential learning areas are important, particularly for those children in the target groups because of the rich experiences they provide, for example, in art and physical education, but that the workload associated with monitoring in this way often intrudes on quality teaching and learning time.

> The Literacy Taskforce recommends that the requirement on schools to provide the broad curriculum, as laid out in the New Zealand Curriculum Framework, should continue but that the monitoring requirements of the National Administration Guidelines be modified for the early years to focus on student achievement in literacy and numeracy.

Curriculum materials for teachers and children

The Ministry of Education provides schools with both teacher materials, and materials for children to support literacy learning. Most of these materials, such as The Learner as a Reader and Dancing with the Pen, which are guidelines for teachers, and the Ready to Read series and the School Journals are published for the Ministry by Learning Media Limited. Ngà Kete Kòrero, a levelled reading series for children in Màori-medium classrooms, is published by Learning Media Limited and Huia Publishers. The Literacy Taskforce believes that although schools buy materials from other providers, materials provided by the Ministry are essential to ensure that all schools are provided with best practice guidelines and models.[8]

The taskforce agreed that teachers need more assistance than is currently available through the materials provided. This does not mean step-by-step instructions for teachers to follow but more detail to help them to select and use appropriate instructional approaches and strategies, particularly those to be used with children who are in underachieving groups.

The taskforce would also like to see more material for limited-progress children as well as a greater awareness being given to ensuring that the Ready to Read series includes texts that provide more support for struggling learners.

> The Literacy Taskforce recommends that priority be given to:
> * developing a video that illustrates taking and analysing running records in English and in Màori and using this data to inform the teaching programme;[9]

8 A list of current materials provided to schools can be found in the Ministry of Education 1998–99 Catalogue: Learning Materials for New Zealand Schools, which is also available on-line at http//www.learningmedia.co.nz.
9 The proposed video could be part of the self-directed professional development package that is also recommended.

- revising Reading in Junior Classes;
- developing teacher guidelines for teaching reading and writing in Màori-medium education;
- ensuring that the series for children include adequate suitable material for struggling readers;
- positioning te reo Màori readers to fit Ngà Kete Kòrero framework levels (levels 1 to 3);
- developing guidelines for schools to use when selecting materials for their literacy programmes.

The Literacy Taskforce strongly supported the development of a professional development package. This package is discussed later in this report.

Teacher education

Members of the Literacy Taskforce expressed concern about the widely reported variability in the skills and knowledge about literacy learning that they and their colleagues have noticed in graduates from current teacher education providers. For example, some members reported instances of teachers who have begun their teaching careers this year not yet able to undertake such fundamental procedures as running records or with little apparent knowledge of the procedures for guided reading. Even taking into account that two years of support and guidance will be provided by schools before they are registered, some beginning teachers do not appear to meet the relevant interim standards developed for the Performance Management System.

The taskforce was concerned that it was difficult to find out about current teacher education programmes and how they prove their suitability for teacher registration purposes. Not enough appears to be known in an area of critical importance to the quality of teaching and thus to the achievement of children.

The Literacy Taskforce recommends that the Government investigate how and why teacher education programmes, particularly in respect to literacy learning, are approved for the purposes of teacher registration.

Professional development

Throughout its discussions, the Literacy Taskforce kept reiterating the importance of professional development for teachers. The taskforce was concerned that not all teachers have the same high level of skills and knowledge in respect to literacy learning as that which is demonstrated by leading teachers. Such demonstration of best practice is particularly evident when leading teachers are working with children most at risk of underachievement. The taskforce believes that it is essential that all teachers be engaged in regular, quality professional development and that improving teacher capability in literacy learning is seen as a priority in the professional development plans in primary schools. The taskforce acknowledged that this priority creates a tension in schools having to address the implementation of new curriculum statements.

The taskforce was also very concerned that the Government's intended policy of devolving the funding currently used for the Teacher Support Service to schools could result in teachers not having access to quality advice and support. Members considered that this is a serious equity issue affecting rural and lower decile schools in particular.

The taskforce recalled the effectiveness of ERIC, the in-service training programme that was once available to teachers.[10] Members would like to see the development of a new professional development package for the Màori as well as the English medium. The package should use such media as videos and printed material, which could be available for teachers to use either independently or as part of a formal professional development programme facilitated by an expert literacy adviser or the school's literacy leader. It would be essential that such a package focused on best practice and included explicit instruction on the approaches needed to work effectively with children who are underachieving.

> The Literacy Taskforce recommends that the Ministry of Education develop a comprehensive professional development package to assist teachers to implement best practice in their teaching of reading and writing.

Literacy leadership in schools

The taskforce discussed the importance of literacy leadership within the school – a teacher or teachers with expertise in literacy learning having responsibility to provide guidance and support in classrooms as well as in the staff meetings that are part of the regular professional development of teachers.[11] To do this, literacy leaders need a thorough understanding of best practice, including the theoretical ideas that underpin best practice and their evolving status.

---

10   ERIC (the Early Reading In-service Course) was a comprehensive package available to junior school teachers and supported by the Reading Advisors and in-service courses for teachers.
11   The taskforce recognised that the literacy leader could be the principal. In Màori-medium education, the literacy expert might be an external advisor, given the current expectations on Màori teachers.

A particular responsibility of the literacy leadership should be to evaluate the effectiveness of literacy programmes[12] at the classroom level and for those children needing additional support. The taskforce was concerned that it is possible for schools to be using many different literacy programmes without knowing enough about their effectiveness in meeting the needs of children and suggests that literacy leaders develop the expertise needed to do this evaluation.

> The Literacy Taskforce recommends that support and advice be provided to develop literacy leadership in schools. The taskforce considers that such support is best provided through a nationally co-ordinated service.

Professional leadership in schools

The professional leadership in the school is responsible for setting goals and aspirations. Members of the taskforce felt the need to make the point that this leadership must include the principal, who, as professional leader, should have a thorough understanding of how learners learn as well as the ways in which the school should be organised and the teachers supported to achieve the best results possible. For example, the taskforce considered that only in the most exceptional circumstances should beginning teachers be given new entrant classes because of the particular skills and experience needed to teach these children.

In considering the role of the principal in relation to literacy learning, the Literacy Taskforce expressed its concern about the particular pressures faced by principals of lower decile schools.

> The Literacy Taskforce recommends that appropriate materials and opportunities be provided for principals to allow them to update their understanding of literacy learning.

Specific interventions

The Literacy Taskforce agreed that, even with best practice in every classroom, effective intervention programmes are still needed for children who will benefit from more intensive, specialised teaching. This need is most

12 The generic term 'programme' includes teaching approaches, materials for children, and total packages (for example, computer-assisted learning programmes) as well as the sequence of activities that the teacher plans for the class, a group, or an individual.

likely to arise in the first year of instruction but may arise later for some children, particularly those with poor oral skills in the language of instruction.

The taskforce stressed that intervention is not inoculation, and its success depends on ongoing effective teaching in the classroom. The presence of effective intervention programmes must not lessen the importance of best practice in the classroom.

Current interventions that provide specialist assistance include Reading Recovery, Resource Teachers of Reading, Resource Teachers of Màori, and the Resource Teachers: Learning and Behaviour. The taskforce focused on the first two of these, although it acknowledged the significance of the latter two. In particular, some members of the taskforce stressed that their preference was for the Resource Teachers: Learning and Behaviour to focus as much on learning as they did on behaviour – particularly since most of their work in learning was concerned with developing literacy skills in limited-progress children. The taskforce also acknowledged that the Resource Teachers of Màori carry a significant workload in that they are expected to provide advice and support across all essential learning areas of the curriculum.

Reading Recovery

Reading Recovery is internationally recognised as one of the most successful acceleration and intervention programmes to support children making limited progress in reading. The Literacy Taskforce acknowledged the strengths of Reading Recovery and agreed that it must remain an essential feature of New Zealand's education system.

However, members of the taskforce raised several issues about the programme itself and the way in which it is currently implemented. These issues were as follows:

The Reading Recovery programme is used with the lowest 20% of children compared with their cohort in an individual school. The taskforce believes that, in order to make the best use of available resources, Reading Recovery should be targeted to children with the greatest need, particularly those in lower decile schools. Further, the taskforce was concerned that a combination of factors can lead to higher decile schools having more Reading Recovery trained teachers than lower decile schools, thus compounding the problems of accessibility for children most at risk of underachieving.

The taskforce also considered that the stage at which Reading Recovery is delivered could be more flexible. For some children, it might be beneficial to participate in the programme earlier than the end of the first year of instruction; others might take longer than this first year to develop their oral language skills to a point where they can make the maximum gains from the programme.

For Màori children in general classes, the taskforce emphasised that cultural affirmation by Reading Recovery teachers is an important element of the teaching.

Members of the taskforce believe that some children with learning difficulties have specific needs that cannot be met through Reading Recovery. Although Reading Recovery can identify these children, they need a different programme.

Despite Reading Recovery being heavily researched overseas, the taskforce was concerned that only two research studies have been carried out on the programme in New Zealand independently of the programme's own monitoring and research. This is considered to be insufficient to identify any trends indicating the need for refinements or improvements.

The taskforce considered that a literal translation of an English intervention programme such as Reading Recovery is inappropriate for Màori-medium education. Instead, an effective, appropriate intervention needs to researched and developed for this medium.[13] The taskforce agreed that it is critical that Màori initiate, develop, trial, and implement this intervention.

Resource Teachers of Reading

The Literacy Taskforce affirmed the work of the Resource Teachers of Reading, agreeing that the service is a critical intervention for those children who are hardest to teach. The taskforce noted with concern that the current level of resourcing is insufficient to meet demand.

Members of the taskforce also noted that there is variability in the qualifications and experience of Resource Teachers of Reading because of the way in which they have been appointed to their positions. Despite working with the hardest-to-teach children, Resource Teachers of Reading are not required to have specialist training. The taskforce believes mandatory specialist training should be considered.

A nationally co-ordinated system

The Literacy Taskforce believes that a nationally co-ordinated and managed system of second- and third-phase interventions is the most effective and efficient way of providing consistent, specialised instruction for the children most at risk of failing to learn to read and write for success. Such a system would also provide a way of gathering reliable data for monitoring progress towards the goal. The taskforce considered that the current nationally funded interventions, Reading Recovery and the Resource Teachers of Reading, should form the basis of this system but that changes would need to be considered to the programmes and operation of each to ensure consistency in targeting and equity of access.

13   Time is needed first to implement recently developed assessment procedures.

This system should articulate with services being provided to schools by the Resource Teachers: Learning and Behaviour.

> The Literacy Taskforce recommends that a nationally co-ordinated system of interventions targeted at those most in need be established by reviewing and building on the interventions that already exist, in particular, Reading Recovery and the Resource Teachers of Reading.

Parents and the community

Learning is enhanced when teachers know something of children's home language experiences. Partnerships between school and home are not one-way, and schools should be seeking information from children's homes as well as providing parents and whànau with information. The taskforce acknowledged that getting parents involved in school activities is a priority, although it can also be a challenge, particularly if parents are not successful readers and writers themselves, their experiences at schools have been mostly negative, or their home language is different from the language of instruction for their children.

Helping parents to gain confidence in their own abilities to help their children's literacy is important. However, the school is not necessarily the best environment in which to do this. For this reason, the taskforce supported the proposed public information campaign and was pleased to contribute to the development of its themes and messages.

The Literacy Taskforce was also concerned about the impact of such social conditions as health and housing on children's learning. The ability of many children to learn is affected because they are hungry or sick, have conditions such as glue ear, or are not regularly attending the same school. The taskforce therefore supported the alignment of broader social policy and better co-ordination between the social agencies supporting the families most at risk.

The Literacy Taskforce also affirmed those schools that are facilitating links with the early childhood services in their areas so that children's transition to school is as smooth as possible.

How should progress towards the goal be measured?

Monitoring progress towards the goal has three aspects:

teachers' monitoring of individual children's progress towards the goal;
schools' collective monitoring of their pupils' progress to ensure that their teaching and learning programmes will best enable individual pupils to reach the goal;

the Government's monitoring of the system's progress toward this goal over the period to 2005 and beyond.

Teachers' monitoring of individual children

The literacy levels of individual children are strongly influenced by the quality of the interaction between the child and the teacher. Good teachers carry out monitoring, analysis, and reflection as an integral part of their teaching.

The taskforce was therefore concerned about the wide range of teacher expertise in monitoring and assessment. If monitoring is to be useful, then it must not only be used by teachers to diagnose and report on children's strengths and weaknesses but should also inform them about their own teaching practice and interactions with children in both individual and group instruction. Anecdotal evidence indicates that although detailed data is gathered, it may not be analysed or used to improve teaching programmes.

The taskforce believes that monitoring and assessment must be ongoing so that children having difficulties can be identified and helped. Any assessment must be informative to the teacher and parents and it must therefore be carried out on tasks appropriate to children's capabilities. So that assessment data can inform a new school when children move, the taskforce would like the Ministry of Education to investigate the possibility of having cumulative records travel with a child from school to school.

As with all students, teachers' monitoring of Màori and Pacific Islands students must also be sensitive to, and affirm, their prior knowledge and experience. The taskforce noted that diagnostic tools and monitoring procedures are being developed for use in Màori-medium classrooms, but that these need more research and development. However, the taskforce noted that there have been no externally referenced assessment tools developed for use in Pacific Islands languages education.[14]

The Literacy Taskforce notes that monitoring and assessment of individual children is an ongoing and integral part of teaching practice and therefore recommends that assessment be an essential component of teacher education.

The Literacy Taskforce recommends that research be undertaken to support the development of diagnostic tools for use in Màori-medium education.

---

14   The taskforce noted that the priority for development in Pacific Islands languages is the development of reading materials for children.

Schools' collective monitoring of their pupils' progress

Currently, there is no common system throughout New Zealand for assessing reading and writing. In reading, such common tools as running records are used and analysed by teachers in a variety of ways.

Externally referenced assessment tools enable schools to see where their children are in relation to other children of the same age. The taskforce considers that it is important that schools use such tools and that they analyse and collate the data they collect so that they are very clear about the progress and achievement of their students and are able to report on this to parents as well as using the information to develop appropriate instructional programmes.

The taskforce supported the Ministry of Education's proposal to develop exemplars for the achievement objectives related to reading and writing in English in the New Zealand Curriculum so that teachers are clearer about the standards that should be achieved at each level of the curriculum.

The taskforce reiterated that providing a description of the knowledge, understandings, strategies, and attitudes that nine-year-olds should demonstrate when they are reading and writing for success, along with examples of texts that children are reading and of children's writing, will help clarify expectations of student achievement.

> The Literacy Taskforce recommends the development of further externally referenced assessment tools so that they are available to assess progress and achievement in literacy in each of the first four years of instruction.
>
> The Literacy Taskforce recommends that externally referenced assessment tools be developed for use in Màori-medium education.

The Government's monitoring of the system's progress

Standard procedures and appropriate assessment tools, in both English and Màori, are necessary if progress towards the goal is to be measured.

The Literacy Taskforce would prefer to see the further development of externally referenced tools that would enable light sampling to take place as well as provide information to schools about how their students compare with the national cohort rather than a national testing regime for all students.[15] The taskforce considered the possibility of the National Education

15 Externally referenced assessment tools currently used by schools include School Entry Assessment/Aro Matawai Urunga-à-Kura (SEA/AKA), Six Year Diagnostic Survey (6 year net), Burt Word Recognition Test, and Progressive Achievement Tests (PATs).

Monitoring Project (NEMP) being used for such monitoring but decided that it does not meet this purpose.[16]

Diagnostic surveys, such as that used to screen children for Reading Recovery (the 6 year net), also provide useful data at a national level.

> The Literacy Taskforce recommends that schools be required to use externally referenced assessment tools on an annual basis and that this data be sampled to monitor the system's progress towards the goal.

Reading, Writing, and Mathematics Proposals Pool

The Government asked the Literacy Taskforce to recommend criteria for the distribution of funds available to schools from the Reading, Writing, and Mathematics Proposals Pool. The funds are to assist schools to meet the set-up costs of programmes that they are sure will meet the particular needs of children identified as making limited progress. Furthermore, it is the Government's wish that such programmes involve parents and the community.

The Literacy Taskforce was concerned that schools do not add more literacy programmes without being very clear about the way in which they will make a difference to the progress and achievement of their students. There is evidence now that some schools are using programmes without adequately evaluating their effectiveness. The taskforce considered that this not only wastes the school's resources but, in particular, is also not a good use of children's time, especially when they need to make rapid progress to close the gaps in achievement.

The taskforce would prefer that Government funds to support literacy learning be used to develop teachers' expertise, for example, through the development of literacy leaders or a self-directed professional development package, or be used to expand the specialist resource available to work intensively with children, especially for decile 1 and decile 2 schools.

Because decisions about appropriate programmes are best made at the school level, the taskforce did not accept the task of determining a list of programmes that are deemed to be suitable. However, members were concerned about aspects of the approach and quality of some of the programmes and materials currently being marketed to schools. This concern reinforces their earlier recommendation that schools be provided with statements of best practice to guide them in their decision making.

16 The NEMP uses soundly based assessment methods in a sample range of schools, but it is not administered on an annual basis. It reports on actual, not expected, performance. It would therefore need modification for more frequent monitoring of reading, written language, and mathematics and include assessment items that have been agreed to be appropriate indicators of the goal having been met.

The taskforce was also concerned that decile 1 and decile 2 schools currently face such pressures that the system for submitting proposals must be as straightforward as possible.

> The Literacy Taskforce recommends that the Reading, Writing, and Mathematics Proposals Pool be limited to decile 1 and decile 2 schools in this financial year, opening out to other schools in the following years but with priority being given to lower decile schools. The criteria for funding are listed below.

Criteria to be met for funds from the Reading, Writing, and Mathematics Pool

The Reading, Writing, and Mathematics Proposals Pool is for programmes to be used with students in years 1 to 6 in primary schools. Proposals must:

provide evidence that the needs of the target group have been clearly identified;
provide a rationale for how the programme will meet the needs that have been identified;
describe how the programme reflects best practice;
describe how the programme will further develop teacher expertise;
describe how the programme will be sustained (bearing in mind that schools will be eligible for funding for a maximum of two years);
provide evidence of the commitment and involvement of parents and the community.

Schools that have received extra Crown funding for similar purposes, for example, through the School Support Project or the Innovations Pool, will not be eligible.

Appendix A

Members of the Literacy Taskforce

Jan Baynes, Mt Cook Primary School, Wellington
Linda Bendikson, Nawton Primary School, Hamilton
Mere Berryman, Specialist Education Services, Tauranga
Gaye Byers, Teacher Support Services, Kaikohe
Garry de Thierry, Malfroy Primary School, Rotorua
Henare Everitt, Learning Media Limited, Wellington
Christine Fernyhough, The Alan Duff Charitable Foundation, Auckland
Annette Hill, Wharenui Primary School, Christchurch

Jenny Hodgkinson, East Taieri Primary School, Dunedin
Dr Libby Limbrick, Auckland College of Education, Auckland
Gail Loane, Waikato University School of Education, Thames
Dr Stuart McNaughton, The University of Auckland
Terry Martin, West Spreydon Primary School, Christchurch
Helen Parsons, Lynmore Primary School, Rotorua
Liz Patara, Clyde Quay School, Wellington
Feofanaki Pocock, Mangere Central Primary School, Auckland
Cath Rau, Consultant, Ngaruawahia
Noeline Skeet, Manurewa Primary School, Auckland
Lois Thompson, Learning Media Limited, Wellington
David Whalley, Education Review Office, Auckland

Convenor: Howard Fancy, Secretary for Education
Officials: Sue Douglas, Ministry of Education
             Diane Crew, Ministry of Education

Terms of reference

The initial terms of reference for the Literacy Taskforce were to:

provide advice on how the literacy goal should be defined;
provide advice on how progress towards the literacy goal should be measured;
identify and provide information to the Ministry and Minister on effective
initiatives to improve reading literacy and written language, particularly for
groups that are not doing as well as others (Màori children, Pacific Islands
children, and those for whom English is not the home language);
consider whether any additional curriculum support materials are needed
and provide advice on those materials;
develop criteria for programmes and resources that can be accessed by
schools through the reading and mathematics proposals pool.

Literacy Experts Group

Associate Professor Stuart McNaughton (Chair), The University Of Auckland
Professor James W. Chapman, Massey University
Cedric Croft, New Zealand Council for Educational Research
Professor Ted Glynn, The University of Waikato
Margie Kahukura Hohepa, The University of Auckland
Dr Libby Limbrick, Auckland College of Education
Associate Professor Tom Nicholson, The University of Auckland
Dr John Smith, Dunedin College of Education
Dr G. Brian Thompson, Victoria University of Wellington
Professor Bill Tunmer, Massey University

Appendix B

Reading for success

Successful reading at age nine means reading appropriate texts fluently, independently, and with comprehension. In an instructional setting (with teacher guidance), readers may cope with more difficult texts. For example, a scientific article may contain specialist vocabulary, and the teacher may introduce these in a discussion with students before the reading.

A nine-year-old reading for success:

- has the habit of reading for meaning well established
- has clear concepts about print and an understanding of the form and structure of written texts, for example, punctuation, use of paragraphing, tables of contents, indexes, and lists
- has a good reading vocabulary, that is, a thorough grasp of high frequency words (such as some, like) and is continually expanding their personal bank of words
- has the skills to decode (work out) words that may be familiar in spoken vocabulary but not in print using phonics (letter-sound relationships)
- uses a range of sources of information in the text to gain meaning, for example, the context or setting, illustrations, diagrams, and captions
- knows how to use their own background knowledge and experience to bring meaning to text
- can apply an understanding of how language works to develop the meaning of text, for example, is familiar with the order of words/ grammar
- can predict, check, confirm, and self-correct while they are reading
- has the confidence to take a risk when reading, that is, will 'have a go'
- is enthusiastic about reading a wide range of texts
- reads for both enjoyment and information
- sometimes reads from choice when there are other recreational options
- thinks critically about what is being read, that is, can get under the surface of the words, analyses and interprets what the author is saying
- can share and discuss their thoughts and reactions to a range of texts confidently, for example, how they felt about a character in a story
- recognises that authors and illustrators have different styles and will often have developed preferences and be able to say why
- can read aloud with expressions and fluency
- can retell something they have read and identify the main idea of a piece of writing and a sequence of events
- can gather information on a topic from a variety of sources, such as catalogues, libraries, and encyclopedias, and uses dictionaries and other reference tools

Texts for nine-year-olds may include:

- whole pages without illustration
- some complex sentences and varied vocabulary, for example, compound words such as 'wheelchair'
- some complexity in the story and illustrations
- technical or specialist content
- a combination of narrative text, diagrams, and explanatory notes
- themes involving other times and places.

Children's understanding of what they read is affected by their background of experience – they relate more readily to the text they are reading if they are familiar with the setting, for example, a farm, a sporting event such as kirikiti, a marae, a tangi, or an inner-city highrise.

The Literacy Taskforce recommends that the description of the goal includes examples of the types of texts that nine-year-olds should be reading.

Writing for success

After four years at school, a writer is well versed in the way in which language 'works'. The child knows that what he/she thinks or says can be written down – but is also aware of the transformation in taking oral language to a written form. They have a knowledge of grammar, of punctuation, and of the way in which other writers use language for different purposes and for impact. They are aware that writers write for audiences. To this end, they are able to select appropriate forms for their writing and include such elements as interesting leads (story beginnings), strong endings, appropriate verbs and adjectives, and appropriate vocabulary for the form and develop their writing with the reader in mind.

A nine-year-old writing for success:

- has a bank of high-frequency words and experiments with words outside this bank
- continually adds new words to their vocabulary bank
- consistently makes informed attempts at spelling
- understands written language features (comma, full stop, capital letters, paragraphs, and exclamation and question marks)
- is developing an awareness of the purposes of quotation marks
- recounts an event and writes instructions and explanations
- can write from a personal point of view about their experiences and observations
- writes on a variety of topics
- writes using a variety of forms, for example, stories, poems, letters, and recipes

- chooses a form of writing appropriate to the purpose and the intended reader
- can use language to express imaginative and creative ideas
- is beginning to set out ideas in a logical way (to argue a point of view or to persuade the reader)
- is beginning to use the power of language through similes and manipulation of sentence structure
- sees the sharing of writing as a way of getting feedback from the reader
- has the confidence to take a risk during the writing process (to 'have a go')
- is enthusiastic about writing in a range of forms
- is able to add, change, delete, and reorder the language to make sense, for grammar and for impact
- understands some parts of speech (word classes) and their functions, for example, noun, verb, adjective, pronoun, preposition, and adverb.

The Literacy Taskforce recommends that the description of the goal include examples of the types of texts that nine-year-olds should be constructing.

Appendix C

The International Association for the Evaluation of Educational Achievement (IEA) Reading Literacy Study (1990)

The IEA international reading survey (1990) showed that, overall, New Zealand students at age nine perform well above the international average in literacy achievement, but deeper analysis of the overall results shows that there are significant disparities between sub-groups.

There is a wide gap between the highest and lowest levels of reading achievement and a significant difference between the average performance of Màori and Pacific Islands students and that of others. Màori performed significantly below the international average, and Màori boys performed at a level below that of Màori girls. On average, Màori students outperformed Pacific Islands students. Wagemaker (1992) reports that on three comprehension tasks, there were large significant differences between Pàkehà and Màori children (mean differences of around eleven percent items correct), and Pàkehà and Pacific Islands children (mean differences of around fifteen percent items correct). Differences were not present on the word recognition task.

Children whose home language is not the language of instruction have markedly lower literacy levels than other children. Out of thirty-two systems of education, New Zealand has the largest gap in achievement between children who are learning in their home language and those who are not (many of whom were Pacific Islands children). A reanalysis by

Wilkinson (1998) revealed significant differences between these children on both comprehension and word recognition. The differences remained after controlling for socio-economic status. Pàkehà students had significantly higher scores on comprehension and word recognition after controlling for socio-economic status. Limited relationships between word recognition and comprehension were found, and socio-economic status was significantly related to both measures.

New Zealand also had the second largest score difference between gender groups when compared with other countries in the study.

Wagemaker, H. 'Preliminary findings of the IEA literacy study: New Zealand achievement in the national and international context.' Educational Psychology 12 (3&4) 1992, : pp. 195–214.
Wilkinson, I.A.G. 'Dealing with diversity: Achievement gaps in reading literacy among New Zealand students.' Reading Research Quarterly 35 (2), 1998. pp: 144–168.

International Adult Literacy Survey (1997)

This survey, which was the first comprehensive study of its type in New Zealand, was conducted in March 1996 as part of a series of international surveys known as the International Adult Literacy Survey. It surveyed a random sample of 4223 adults ranging in age from sixteen to sicty-five years and used a wide range of prose, document, and quantitative literacy texts containing the type of information that people encounter in everyday circumstances.

The results show that around one in five New Zealanders is operating at a highly effective level of literacy, able to manage abstract concepts and employ specialised knowledge in interpreting information. Over half of New Zealand adults are operating at a level considered to be a requirement to meet the demands of 'everyday life'.

However, of particular concern is the high concentration of adults with very poor literacy skills (around one in five New Zealanders). There are, overall, poorer literacy skills among the unemployed. Poor literacy was also found to be concentrated within the Pacific Islands and other ethnic minority groups and within the Màori population. Results for Pacific Islands and other ethnic minority groups were reflected in the relatively poor English skills of those for whom English was not their first language.

Ministry of Education. Adult literacy in New Zealand: Results from the International Adult Literacy Survey

National Education Monitoring Project (Monitoring Report 6: Reading and Speaking Assessment Results, 1996)

The results of this project confirmed the lower performance of Màori compared with non-Màori on reading tasks. It also found examples of inverse relationships between performance and the proportion of Màori on school rolls. Schools with Pacific Islands students were in a similar situation. In addition, the project found that, in general, there were significant differences in performance between students in the low-decile grouping (deciles 1 to 3) and those in the middle- and high-decile groupings.

Approximately twenty percent of the national sample in NEMP were below 'expected bands' in oral reading on measures of decoding and comprehension. (Whereas ten percent were considered to be just below expected bands, a further ten percent were of particular concern.) Significant differences were found between schools (decile 1–3 versus the rest), and significant differences were found between Màori and non-Màori on all ten oral and silent reading tasks and on one of four speaking tasks. Significant differences between Pacific Islands and non-Pacific Islands children are indicated, based on school comparisons.

Flockton, L. and Crooks, T. Reading and Speaking Assessment Results 1996: National Education Monitoring Report 6. Wellington: Ministry of Education. 1997.

Notes

1 Introduction

1 J. Chall, *Learning to Read: The Great Debate*, New York: McGraw-Hill, 1967.
2 G. McCulloch and W. Richardson, *Historical Research in Educational Settings*, Buckingham: Open University Press, 2000, pp. 5–6.
3 A. Luke and P. Freebody, 'Critical literacy and the question of normativity', in S. Muspratt, A. Luke and P. Freebody (eds), *Constructing Critical Literacies: Teaching and Learning Textual Practice*, Cresskill, N.J.: Hampton Press, 1997, p. 2.
4 See, for example: A. Luke and C.D. Baker, 'Towards a critical sociology of reading pedagogy: an introduction', in C.D. Baker and A. Luke (eds), *Towards a Critical Sociology of Reading Pedagogy*, Amsterdam and Philadelphia: John Benjamins Publishing Company, 1991, pp. ix–xxi; A. Luke, 'The social construction of literacy in the primary school', in U. Unsworth (ed.), *Literacy, Learning and Teaching: Language as Social Practice in the Primary School*, Melbourne: Macmillan Education, 1993, pp. 1–54; Muspratt, Luke and Freebody (eds), *Constructing Critical Literacies: Teaching and Learning Textual Practice*.
5 H.M. Kliebard, *The Struggle for the American Curriculum 1893–1958* (second edn), New York: Routledge and Kegan Paul, 1995, p. 8.
6 S.J. Ball, *'Educational Reform: A Critical and Post-Structural Approach*, Buckingham: Open University Press, 1994.
7 S.J. Ball, 'You've been NEFRed! Dumbing down the Academy: National Educational Research Forum: A National strategy-consultation paper: A brief and bilious response', *Journal of Education Policy*, 16(3), 2001: 265–268; B. Carter and H. Burgess, 'Testing, regulation and control: shifting education narratives', *Journal of Education Policy*, 1(2), 1993: 233–245.
8 Carter and Burgess, 'Testing, regulation and control', 1993, p. 233.
9 Foucault, M., 'The subject and power', in L. Dreyfus and P. Rainbow (eds), *Foucalt: Beyond Structuralism and Hermeneutics*, Chicago: University of Chicago Press, 1983, p. 184.
10 Department for Education and Employment (DfEE). Standards and Effectiveness Unit. *The National Literacy Strategy: Framework for Teaching*, London: DfEE, 1998.
11 J. Coldron and R. Smith, 'The construction of reflective practice in key policy documents in England', *Pedagogy, Culture and Society: Journal of Educational Discussion and Debate*, 7(2), 1999: 305–320; R. Fisher, 'Developmentally appropriate practice and a National Literacy Strategy', *British Journal of Educational Studies*, 48(1), 2000: 58–69; M. Hilton, 'Raising literacy standards: the true story', *English in Education*, 32(3), 1998: 4–16.

12 Report of the Central Advisory Council for Education, *Children and Their Primary Schools (The Plowden Report)*, London: HMSO, 1967.
13 Luke, 'The social construction of literacy in the primary school', p. 3.
14 Ibid.
15 A.R. Welch and P. Freebody, 'Introduction: explanations of the current international "literacy crises"', in P. Freebody and A.R. Welch (eds), *Knowledge, Culture and Power: International Perspectives on Literacy as Policy and Practice*, London and Washington, D.C.: Falmer Press, 1993, p. 8.
16 As argued in, for instance, S. Arnowitz and H.A. Giroux, *Education Still Under Siege* (2nd edn), London: Bergin and Gavey, 1993.
17 R. Aldrich, 'Educational standards in historical perspective', in Harvey Goldstein and Anthony Heath (eds), *Educational Standards*, Oxford: published for the British Academy by Oxford University Press, 2000, pp. 39–68.
18 Ibid., p. 40.
19 Ibid., pp. 40–41.
20 C. Burt, 'The education of illiterate adults', *British Journal of Educational Psychology*, xv (February 1945), part 1: 20–27. *British Journal of Educational Psychology* hereafter cited as *BJEP*.
21 Ibid., p. 20.
22 Ibid., p. 21.
23 Ministry of Education, *Reading Ability: Some Suggestions for Helping the Backward*, Pamphlet no. 18, London: HMSO, 1950.
24 Ibid., pp. 10–11.
25 Ibid., p. 11.
26 Ibid., p. 14.
27 Ministry of Education, *Standards of Reading 1948–1956*, Pamphlet No. 32, London: HMSO, 1957.
28 Ibid., p. 2.
29 Aldrich, 'Educational standards in historical perspective', p. 43.
30 G. Brooks, 'Trends in standards of literacy in the United Kingdom, 1948–1996', Paper presented at UK Reading Association conference, University of Manchester, July 1997, and at the British Educational Research Association conference, University of York, September 1997.
31 Ibid., p. 3.
32 Ibid., p. 4.
33 Ibid., pp. 11–12.
34 Chall, *Learning to Read: The Great Debate*.
35 K.S. Goodman, *In Defense of Good Teaching: What Teachers Need to Know About the 'Reading Wars'*, New York: Me, Stenhouse Publications, 1998; R.T. Vacca, 'Who will be the winners? Who will be the losers?', *Reading Today*, 14(2), 1996: 3.
36 R.L. Allington and H. Woodside-Jiron, 'The politics of literacy teaching: how "research" shaped educational policy', *Educational Researcher*, 28(8), 1999: 4–12.
37 R. Beard, 'Influences on the Literacy Hour', *Reading: A Journal about Literacy and Language in Education* 33(1), 1999: 6–12; R. Beard, *National Literacy Strategy: Review of Research and Other Evidence*, Leeds: School of Education University of Leeds, 1999; Literacy Task Force, *A Reading Revolution: How We can Teach Every Child to Read Well, The Preliminary Report of the Literacy Task Force*, London: Institute of Education, 1997.
38 Literacy Taskforce, *Report of the Literacy Taskforce*, Wellington, Report prepared for the New Zealand Minister of Education, 1999.

2 Re-emerging debates over methods and standards, 1945–1965

1 J.M. Morris, *Reading in the Primary School: an Investigation into Standards of Reading and their Association with the Primary School*, London: Newnes Educational Publishing for NFER, 1959, p. 1.
2 J. Chall, *Learning to Read: The Great Debate*, New York: McGraw-Hill, 1967.
3 Ibid.
4 J.M. Morris, 'Introduction', in J.M. Morris (ed.), *The First R. Yesterday, Today and Tomorrow: a Selection of Papers from Conferences of the United Kingdom Reading Association*, London: Ward Lock Educational, 1972.
5 Ministry of Education, *Reading Ability: Some Suggestions for Helping the Backward*, Pamphlet No. 18, London: HMSO, 1950.
6 A.E. Sanderson, 'The idea of reading readiness: a re-examination', *Educational Research*, vi, November 1963: 3–9.
7 P. Cunningham, *Curriculum Change in the Primary School since 1945: Dissemination of the Progressive Ideal*, London: Falmer Press, 1988, p. 9.
8 C. Burt, 'The education of illiterate adults', *BJEP*, xv, February 1945, part 1: 20–27.
9 W.D. Wall, 'Reading backwardness among men in the Army', *BJEP*, xv, 1945: 28–40.
10 F.J. Schonell, 'Problems of illiteracy: an examination of present needs', *Times Educational Supplement*, 23 February 1946: p. 87. *Times Educational Supplement* hereafter cited as *TES*.
11 Ibid.
12 Ministry of Education, *Reading Ability: Some Suggestions for Helping the Backward*, Pamphlet no. 18, London: HMSO, 1950, Preface, pp. 7, 47.
13 Ibid., pp. 47–48.
14 Educational Correspondent, 'Illiterates and backward readers: conditions in England since the War', *The Times*, 13 February 1953, p. 7.
15 See Morris, *Reading in the Primary School*, pp. 1–8, for a full discussion of these studies and their results.
16 *Hansard Parliamentary Debates*, Commons, 5th ser., vol. 511 (1953), col. 2420. All subsequent references are to the Commons unless otherwise noted.
17 Ibid., col. 2436.
18 Ibid., cols 2496–2497.
19 Ibid., col. 2459.
20 Ibid., col. 2434.
21 *Journals to the House of Commons*, vol. 208 (1952–1953), p. 365.
22 See, for instance, the 21 April 1967 debate over the introduction of ITA, *Parl. Deb.*, 5th ser., vol. 745 (1967), cols 1053–1061.
23 G. Eden, 'Impressions of Parliament', *Punch*, vol. ccxxiv, no. 5865, 4 March 1953: 303.
24 *Parl. Deb.*, 5th ser., vol. 535 (1954), col. 75.
25 Ibid., col. 76.
26 C. Knight, *The Making of Tory Education Policy in Post-War Britain 1950–1986*, London: Falmer Press, 1990, p. 5.
27 Ibid., p. 11.
28 Ibid., pp. 12–13.
29 Chall, *Learning to Read: The Great Debate*, p. 3.
30 Ibid., p. 4.
31 Ibid.
32 J.C. Daniels and Hunter Diack, *Progress in Reading*, Nottingham: University of Nottingham, Institute of Education, 1956.

33 See *Schoolmaster*, unsigned review, CLXX1, 8 February 1957; *Education Today*, unsigned review (Colleges of Preceptors) R.S., 7(1), 1957.
34 J.C. Daniels and Hunter Diack, *Progress in Reading in the Infant School*, Nottingham: University of Nottingham, Institute of Education, 1960.
35 Morris, *Reading in the Primary School*.
36 Ibid.
37 V. Southgate, 'Formulae for beginning reading tuition', *Educational Research*, xi (November 1968): 23.
38 A.E. Sanderson, 'The idea of reading readiness: a re-examination', *Educational Research*, vi, November 1963: 7.
39 Morris, *The First R. Yesterday, Today and Tomorrow*, pp. 14–15.
40 Ibid., p. 12.
41 Ministry of Education, *Standards of Reading 1948–1956*, Ministry of Education Pamphlet No. 32, London: HMSO, 1957, p. 7.
42 Ibid., p. 18.
43 Ibid., p. iii.
44 Morris, *The First R. Yesterday, Today and Tomorrow*, p. 12
45 E.M. Harper, 'Nursery and infant schools in England'. Report to Director of Education, 21 May 1950, pp. 2–3 (7pp., unpublished, handwritten). ABEP. W2462. Box 659. 16/1/5. Education System in Great Britain. Part 1. Archives New Zealand, Wellington.
46 Ibid., p. 3.
47 *Parl. Deb.*, 5th ser., vol. 537 (1955), cols 2239–2240.
48 *Parl. Deb.*, 5th ser., vol. 569 (1957), cols 1149–1150.
49 *Parl. Deb.*, 5th ser., vol. 585 (1958), col. 168.
50 Knight, *The Making of Tory Education Policy in Post-War Britain*, p. 15.
51 G. McCulloch, G. Helsby and P. Knight, *The Politics of Professionalism: Teachers and the Curriculum*, London and New York: Continuum, 2000, p. 11.

3 Reading debates and the *Bullock Report*, 1968–1975

1 The debate perceptibly slackened after Prime Minister Callaghan's Ruskin speech in 1976, subsiding rapidly after the election of the Conservative Government in 1979. The Index to the *TES* and *The Times* from 1977 until 1980 also revealed a marked decline in articles directly concerned with literacy standards after 1976, with a further fall-off, post-1979.
2 K. Jones, *Right Turn: The Conservative Revolution in Education*, London: Radius, 1989, p. 100.
3 Report entitled 'Concern over school English standards', *The Times*, 25 June 1963, p. 4. No author given.
4 See, for instance, *Hansard Parliamentary Debates*, 5th ser., vol. 654 (1962), col. 1508.
5 *Parl. Deb.*, 5th ser., vol. 662 (1962), col. 676.
6 *Parl. Deb.*, 5th ser., vol. 690 (1964), col. 60.
7 *Parl. Deb.*, 5th ser., vol. 695 (1964), cols 179–180.
8 *Parl. Deb.*, 5th ser., vol. 654 (1962), col. 63.
9 C. Jeffries, *Illiteracy: A World Problem*, London: Pall Mall Press, 1967, pp. 71–72.
10 Ibid., p. 77.
11 Ibid., p. 169.
12 Ibid., p. 6.
13 *Parl. Deb.*, 5th ser., vol. 654 (1962), cols 1518–1519.

14 *Parl Deb.*, 5th ser., vol. 745. (1967) col. 1053.

15 Ibid., col. 1057.

16 C. Knight, *The Making of Tory Education Policy in Post-War Britain 1950–1986*, London: Falmer Press, 1990, pp. 7, 48.

17 B. Simon, *Education and the Social Order 1940–1990*, London: Lawrence and Wishart, 1991, p. 365.

18 B. McArthur, 'Literacy survey in schools: complaints about "three Rs"', *The Times*, 10 May 1967, p. 2.

19 N. Smart (ed.), *Crisis in the Classroom*, London: Hamlyn, 1968. This book should not be confused with the slightly later but now better known book with a similar title by the American liberal educator, C.E. Silberman. See C.E. Silberman, *Crisis in the Classroom: the Remaking of American Education*, New York: Random House, 1970.

20 K. Gardner, 'State of reading', in Smart (ed.) *Crisis in the Classroom: An Enquiry into State Education Policy*, London: Hamlyn, 1968, pp. 18–30.

21 In 1965, Longden had been elected Honorary Secretary of the Conservative Teachers Association National Advisory Committee (CTANAC). He retained this position in the Conservative Party's National Advisory Committee on Education (NACE) that subsequently succeeded CTANAC.

22 *Parl. Deb.*, 5th ser., vol. 774 (1968), cols 1809–1910.

23 B. Cox and A. Dyson, *Fight For Education: A Black Paper*, London: Critical Quarterly Society, 1969. This is the first of five Black Papers produced between 1969 and 1977.

24 See 'Comment: Letter to Members of Parliament', in Cox and Dyson, *Fight for Education*, pp. 1–6.

25 Ibid., p. 1.

26 Ibid.

27 S.J. Ball, *Politics and Policymaking in Education: Explorations in Policy Sociology*, London and New York: Routledge, 1990, p. 24.

28 *Parl. Deb.*, 5th ser., vol. 787 (1969), col. 146.

29 *Parl. Deb.*, 5th ser., vol. 794 (1970), col. 176.

30 B. MacArthur, 'Standards of literacy', *The Times*, 6 September 1969, p. 8.

31 Staff reporter, 'Concern at pupil's poor reading', *The Times*, 18 November 1969, p. 2.

32 Simon, *Education and the Social Order*, p. 390.

33 See Cox and Dyson, *Fight for Education*, p. 3.

34 Knight, *The Making of Tory Education Policy in Post-War Britain*.

35 Ibid., p. 68.

36 *Parl. Deb.*, 5th ser., vol. 804 (1970), cols 161–162.

37 *Parl. Deb.*, 5th ser., vol. 806 (1970), col. 1413.

38 *Parl. Deb.*, 5th ser., vol. 806 (1970), cols 1413–1414.

39 *Parl. Deb.*, 5th ser. vol. 817 (1971), col. 217. Thatcher clearly meant here the Ministry of Education's pamphlet, *Standards of Reading 1948–1956*, so frequently cited by her Labour and Conservative predecessors in response to similar questions.

40 *Parl. Deb.*, 5th ser., vol. 806 (1970), cols 1410–1412.

41 *Parl. Deb.*, 5th ser., vol. 820 (1971), col. 173.

42 K.B. Start and B.K. Wells, *The Trend of Reading Standards*, Windsor: NFER, 1972, p. 9.

43 Ibid., p. 66.

44 Ibid., p. 67.

45 Ibid., p. 68.

46 Ibid., p. 72.
47 'The First of the three R's', *TES*, 5 April 1972, p. 13.
48 See for instance, *Parl. Deb.*, 5th ser., vol. 834 (1972), col. 208; *Parl. Deb.*, 5th ser., vol. 837 (1972), col. 161.
49 *Parl. Deb.*, 5th ser., vol. 837 (1972), col. 505.
50 Knight, *The Making of Tory Education Policy in Post-War Britain*, pp. 73, 85.
51 R. Dale, 'Thatcherism and education', in J. Ahier and M. Flude (eds), *Contemporary Education Policy*, London: Croom Helm, 1983, pp. 236–238.
52 Simon, *Education and the Social Order*, p. 414.
53 'ATCDE conference: new teachers must have jobs', *TES*, 20 December 1974, p. 5.
54 See 'Houghton blow for young teachers', *TES*, 20 December 1974, p. 3. See also Houghton Committee, *Houghton Report on Teachers' Salaries*, HMSO Command no. 5848, December 1974.
55 Simon, *Education and the Social Order*, pp. 444–445.
56 Knight, *The Making of Tory Education Policy in Post-War Britain*, pp. 58, 82.
57 T. Howath, 'A time to read', *TES*, 20 December 1974, p. 4.
58 Ibid., p. 4.
59 T. Devlin, 'Professions call for exam to test literacy of recruits', *TES*, 24 January 1975, p. 3.
60 Department of Education and Science, *A Language for Life*, Report of the Committee of Inquiry appointed by the Secretary of State for Education and Science under the Chairmanship of Sir Alan Bullock FBA, London: HMSO, 1975, p. 1. Henceforth cited as the *Bullock Report*.
61 *Bullock Report*, p. 78.
62 H. Rosen, 'Editorial', in H. Rosen (ed.), *Language and Literacy in Our Schools: Some Appraisals of the Bullock Report*, University of London: Institute of Education, 1975, p. 6.
63 *Bullock Report*, cited in A. Corbett, *Much To Do About Education: A Critical Survey of the Fate of the Major Educational Reports*, Council for Educational Advance: Macmillan Education for the Council for Educational Advance, 4th edition, 1978, p. 59.
64 'Literacy and liberty', *Guardian*, 19 February 1975, p. 12. Editorial.
65 Corbett, *Much To Do About Education*, p. 59.
66 M. Wilkinson, 'A school report to disturb every parent', *Daily Mail*, 19 February 1975, p. 10.
67 'The man who says modern stuff is rubbish', *Daily Mail*, 19 February 1975, p. 10.
68 M. Wilkinson, 'Now Oxford finds standards are slipping', *Daily Mail*, 20 February 1975, p. 10.
69 M. O'Connor, A. Spoule and M. Pollard, 'New readers start here', *Education Guardian*, 18 February 1975, p. 19.
70 Ibid., p. 19.
71 *Bullock Report*, pp. 517–518.
72 *Bullock Report*, p. 518. See also E. Hunter-Grundin, 'Introduction: The *Bullock Report*, and then...', in E. Hunter-Grundin and H.U. Grundin (eds), *Reading: Implementing the Bullock Report*, Proceedings of the fourteenth annual course and conference of the United Kingdom Reading Association, Avery Hill College, London, United Kingdom Reading Association, Ward Lock Educational: London, 1977, pp. 2–3.
73 Corbett, *Much To Do About Education*, 1978, p. 59.
74 In G. McCulloch, G. Helsby and P. Knight, *The Politics of Professionalism: Teachers and the Curriculum*, London and New York: Continuum, 2000, p. 11.

75 *Parl. Deb.*, 5th ser., vol. 837 (1972), col. 177.
76 *Parl. Deb.*, 5th ser., vol. 887 (1975), cols 1248–1250.

4 Post-Bullock reactions to a literary crises, 1975–1983

1 C. Knight, *The Making of Tory Education Policy in Post-War Britain 1950–1986*, London: Falmer Press, 1990, pp. 96–99; B. Simon, *Education and the Social Order 1940–1990*, London: Lawrence and Wishart, 1991, p. 442.
2 See, for example, *Daily Telegraph*, 'Schools urged to ignore "nonsensical" advice on reading', 3 January 1975, p. 2; *Daily Mail*, 'Parent power: the intriguing shop-around answer for everyone worried about their child's school', 18 January 1975, p. 6.
3 'Serving two Masters', *TES* features page, 26 June 1981, p. 21.
4 R. Boyson, *The Crisis in Education*, London: Woburn Press, 1975, p. 3.
5 Ibid., p. 10.
6 See *Who's Who: An Annual Biographical Dictionary*, London: A & C Black, 2005.
7 C.B. Cox, R. Boyson and Kingsley Amis, *Black Paper 1975: The Fight for Education*, London: Dent, 1975, p. 3.
8 Ibid.
9 Ibid.
10 *Hansard Parliamentary Debates*, 5th ser., vol. 981 (1975), cols 1189–1190.
11 *Parl. Deb.*, 5th ser., vol. 894 (1975), cols 335–336.
12 *Daily Telegraph*, '"Trendy" teaching on the way out says professor', 13 January 1975, p. 5.
13 Ibid.
14 See, for example, 'Lowering of School Standards' a letter to the Editor by I.F. Lowenstein, consultant educational psychologist, Winchester. *Daily Telegraph*, 18 January 1975, p. 16. See also *Daily Telegraph*, 'Schools urged to ignore "nonsensical" advice on reading', 3 January 1975, p. 2.
15 *TES*, 31 October 1975, p. 1.
16 Ibid.
17 'Call to action over reading', *TES*, 31 October 1975, p. 6.
18 See 'Mr Mulley speaks softly', *TES*, 28 November 1975, p. 6; 'Help proposed for unqualified 300,000', *TES*, 28 November 1975, p. 6.
19 'Secondary school comes to rescue of poor readers', *TES*, 7 November 1975, p. 3.
20 G.E. Bookbinder, 'Test or teachers? One is wrong about reading', *TES*, 21 November 1975, p. 19. It should be noted that Bookbinder had been a strong critic of variations in reading tests on previous occasions in academic and professional journals. See, for instance, G.E. Bookbinder, 'Variations in reading test norms', *Educational Research*, 12(2), 1970: 99–105.
21 'Reading levels "Not good enough"', *TES*, 21 November 1975, p. 4.
22 'Reading standards in London: genuine progress has been made', *TES*, 12 December 1975, p. 14.
23 *TES*, 12 December 1975, p. 6.
24 Ibid., p. 446.
25 *Parl. Deb.*, 5th ser., vol. 912 (1976), col. 1171.
26 *Parl. Deb.*, 5th ser., vol. 912 (1976), col. 648.
27 *Parl. Deb.*, 5th ser., vol. 912 (1976), col. 649.
28 Simon, *Education and the Social Order*, p. 446. See also J. Gretton and M. Jackson, *William Tyndale: Collapse of a School or a System?* London: Allen and Unwin, 1976; Knight, *The Making of Tory Education Policy in Post-War Britain*, pp. 94–95.

29 Simon, *Education and the Social Order*, pp. 445–446.
30 'Don't you wish your child went to a school like this?', *Daily Mail*, 28 June 1975, p. 6.
31 ' Exams – the crumbling standards', *Daily Mail*, 3 July 1975, p. 1.
32 ' Exams – the crumbling standards', *Daily Mail*, 19 July 1976, p. 2.
33 See references to the *Daily Mail* and *Daily Mirror* between 1975 and 1977 in 'Serving two Masters', *TES* features page, 26 June, 1981, p. 21.
34 See, for example, *Daily Mail*, 'Decline and fall of a trendy head's school', 17 July 1976, p. 9; *Daily Mail*, 'Class of '86', 19 July 1976, p. 6.
35 See C. Chitty, *Towards a New Education System: The Victory of the New Right?* London: Falmer, 1989, especially Chapter 3.
36 *TES*, 15 October 1976, p. 1.
37 'Edited extracts from the Yellow Book, the DES memorandum to the Prime Minister. Has something gone wrong? How is it to be put right'? *TES*, 15 October 1976, p. 2.
38 Ibid.
39 'What the PM said', *TES*, 22 October 1976, pp. 1, 72.
40 'Great Debate opens with an anticlimax', *TES*, 22 October 1976, p. 1.
41 *Daily Mail*, 19 October 1976, p. 9.
42 'Classroom warning by Callaghan', *Daily Telegraph*, 19 October 1976, p. 1.
43 *Parl. Deb.*, 5th ser., vol. 918 (1976), col. 107.
44 *Parl. Deb.*, 5th ser., vol. 918 (1976), col. 535.
45 See, for instance, *Parl. Deb.*, 5th ser., vol. 918 (1976), cols 1191–1192.
46 *Parl. Deb.*, 5th ser., vol. 918 (1976), col. 539.
47 'Brighter New Year for the 16–19s'? *TES*, 31 December 1976, p. 1.
48 *Education in Schools. A Consultative Document*. Cmnd 6869, London: HMSO.
49 See, for instance, the extensive debate following its release, *Parl. Deb.*, 5th ser., vol. 935–932 (1977), cols 1858–1879.
50 *Education in Schools*, p. 2.
51 Ibid., p. 8.
52 *Parl. Deb.*, 5th ser., vol. 955 (1978), col. 376.
53 *Parl. Deb.*, 5th ser., vol. 964 (1979), col. 260.
54 DES, *Progress in Education: A Report on Recent Initiatives*, London: HMSO, 1978.
55 Ibid., p. 6.
56 See, for instance, HMI, *Primary Education in England*, London: HMSO, 1978; DES, *Progress in Education*, p. 22.
57 Ibid.
58 *Parl. Deb.*, 5th ser., vol. 976–972 (1979), col. 108.
59 *Parl. Deb.*, 5th ser., vol. 978 (1980), col. 143. In 1991, APU was absorbed by the School Examinations and Assessment Council (SEAC), becoming, in effect, the Council's evaluation and monitoring unit.
60 'Falling standards evidence in doubt', *TES*, 23 May 1980, p. 1.
61 M. Galton and B. Simon, writing as educational researchers in the *TES* features page, 'Where the Wildman aren't', 4 April 1980, p. 18.
62 'Serving two Masters', *TES* features page, 26 June 1981, p. 21.
63 Ibid., pp. 21–23.
64 J. Kirkham, M. Morris and an LEA advisor writing in the *TES* features page, 'Documents, Documents', 8 February 1980, p. 21.
65 Ibid., p. 19.
66 'Reading test for all at 8 years considered', *TES*, 29 February 1980, p. 6.
67 Ibid.
68 'Extra £20m cuts to be made', *TES*, 4 April 1980, p. 1.

69 'Curriculum hit by cuts in part-time staff', *TES*, 23 May 1980, p. 3.
70 See, for example, *TES*, 25 May 1980, p. 6.
71 *Parl. Deb.*, 5th ser., vol. 980 (1980), cols 227–228.
72 *Parl. Deb.*, 5th ser., vol. 980 (1980), cols 516–517.
73 *Parl. Deb.*, 5th ser., vol. 981 (1980), cols 750–751.
74 *Parl. Deb.*, 5th ser., vol. 996 (1981), cols 847–848.
75 *Parl. Deb.*, 5th ser., vol. 1,000 (1981), col. 431.
76 *Parl. Deb.*, 5th ser., vol. 1,000 (1981), col. 260.
77 *Parl. Deb.*, 6th ser., vol. 8 (1981), col. 373.
78 'Another year of declining standards', *TES* Editorial, 9 April 1982, p. 2.
79 B. Passmore, 'Back to tradition, Boyson argues', *TES*, 14 May 1982, p. 8.
80 *Parl. Deb.*, 6th ser., vol. 24 (1982), cols 185–186.
81 *Parl. Deb.*, 6th ser., vol. 31 (1983), cols 411–412.
82 'Improving teacher quality', *TES*, 25 March 1983, p. 10.
83 'The hand the HMIs are playing', *TES*, 12 August 1983, p. 2.
84 See, for example, the HMI Reports published in the *TES*, 30 September 1983, p. 12.
85 'Sir Keith voices fears over standards', *TES*, 15 July 1983, p. 1.
86 'Study of London primaries to examine low achievement', *TES*, 23 July 1983, p. 3.
87 'Election manifesto may push to abolish shires and set up regions', *TES*, 18 February 1983, p. 4.
88 'HMI expansion given go-ahead', *TES*, 1 April 1983, p. 6.
89 'County ends secrecy over pupils' records', *TES*, 22 April 1983, p. 1.
90 Professor Denis Lawton, quoted from his William Walker lecture in 'Battleground DES where three ideologies wage ceaseless war', *TES*, 4 November 1983, p. 6.
91 M. Apple, 'Creating difference: neo-liberalism, neo-conservatism and the politics of educational reform', *Educational Policy*, 18(1), 2004: 14.
92 See D. Callaghan, '"The believers": politics and personalities in the making of the 1988 Education Act', *History of Education*, 24(4), 1995: 369–385.

5 The renewed reading standards debate of the early 1990s

1 Literacy Task Force, *A Reading Revolution: How We Can Teach Every Child to Read Well, The Preliminary Report of the Literacy Task Force*, London: Institute of Education, 1997, Preface.
2 S. Ball, *Politics and Policymaking in Education: Explorations in Policy Sociology*, London: Routledge and Kegan Paul, 1990.
3 Ibid., p. 171.
4 See Education, Science and Arts Committee, *Third Report: Standards of Reading in Primary Schools*, Vol. 1, 268–261, May 1991. See also *TES*, 29 June 1990; M. Turner, *Sponsored Reading Failure: An Object Lesson*, IPSRT Education Unit, 1990.
5 J. Clare, 'Tests reveal fall in standard of pupils' reading', *Daily Telegraph*, 29 June 1990, p. 1.
6 Ibid., p. 4.
7 *Guardian*, 'The right test for schools', leading article, 30 June 1990, p. 22.
8 Ibid.
9 M. Turner, *Sponsored Reading Failure: An Object Lesson*, Education Unit, Warlingham Park School: Warlingham, Surrey, 1990.
10 Ibid., pp. 4, 20–21.
11 Ibid., p. 7.
12 Ibid., pp. 11–12. See also J. Marks, 'Across the teaching divide', *The Times*,

3 September 1990. Online, available at: web.lexis.com/executive/ (accessed 3 January 2005).

13 *The Economist*, 'Britain's schools: trying harder', 28 July 1990, p. 49.

14 *Financial Times*, 'Reading probe', 26 July 1990, p. 10.

15 S. Bates, 'Claims on children's reading disowned: authority says psychologist not backed by evidence', *Guardian*, 3 July 1990, p. 3.

16 *Hansard Parliamentary Debates*, 6th ser., vol. 176 (1990), col. 150.

17 *Parl. Deb.*, 6th ser., vol. 176 (1990), col. 232.

18 *Standards of Reading in Primary Schools*, p. vii.

19 *Parl. Deb.*, 6th Ser., vol. 177 (1990), cols 286–287; *Standards of Reading in Primary Schools*, p. vii.

20 'Home news', *The Times*, 10 January 1991, p. 3.

21 M. Phillips, 'Commentary: educashun still isn't working', *Guardian*, 28 September 1990, p. 23.

22 'Home News', *The Times*, p. 3.

23 HMI, *The Teaching and Learning of Reading in Primary Schools*, London: DES, 1991, ref. 10/91/NS; V. Cato and C. Whetton, *An Enquiry into LEA Evidence on Standards of Reading of Seven Year Old Children*, a report prepared for the SEAC by NFER, London, 1991.

24 *Standards of Reading in Primary Schools*, p. vii.

25 P. Marston, 'Reading: the secret is out. Brought to book', *Daily Telegraph*, 18 July 1991, p. 2.

26 L. Lightfoot, 'Losing the battle at Culloden', *Mail on Sunday*, 3 March 1991, p. 5.

27 L. Lightfoot, 'Clarke orders probe at Culloden', *Mail on Sunday*, 10 March 1991, p. 5.

28 L. Lightfoot, 'Analysis: the battle of Culloden (continued)', *Mail on Sunday*, 21 April 1991, pp. 8–9.

29 J. O'Leary, 'Reading guru wins real notoriety', *The Times*, 22 April 1991, p. 1.

30 J. Clare, 'Who was he talking about? Prince Charles has warned against "fashionable trends" in our classrooms', *Daily Telegraph*, 24 April 1991, p. 17.

31 *Parl. Deb.*, 6th ser., vol. 189 (1991), cols 891–892.

32 *Parl. Deb.*, 6th ser., vol. 189 (1991), col. 892.

33 *Parl. Deb.*, 6th ser., vol. 189 (1991), col. 892.

34 *Standards of Reading in Primary Schools*, p. vii.

35 Ibid., p. viii.

36 Ibid., pp. ix–x.

37 Ibid., p. xii.

38 Ibid., p. xiii.

39 D. MacLeod, 'MPs dismiss claims of reading crisis in primary schools', *Independent*, 17 May 1991, p. 10.

40 J. Judd, 'Revision expected as teachers slate school tests', *Independent*, 5 May 1991, p. 6.

41 *Guardian*, 'The right test for schools', p. 22.

42 Marston, 'Reading: the secret is out. Brought to book', p. 10.

43 S. Bates, 'Leeds' £14 m project fails to improve teaching', *Guardian*, 3 August 1991, p. 3.

44 J. Judd, 'Major settles old score: Tories want a return to traditional', *Independent*, 20 October 1991, p. 19.

45 Ibid.

46 *Parl. Deb.*, 6th ser., vol. 193 (1991), cols 851–852.

47 *Parl. Deb.*, 6th ser., vol. 195 (1991), col. 683.

48 *Parl. Deb.*, 6th ser., vol. 195 (1991), cols 684–685.
49 R. Beard, 'Letter: balance required in the reading debate', *Independent*, 30 November 1991, p. 17.
50 *Daily Telegraph*, Leading Article, 'Facing primary facts', 7 November 1991, p. 20.
51 *Parl. Deb.*, 6th ser., vol. 198 (1991), col. 58. The results from the first round of reading tests for seven-year-olds was announced in late December 1991, and the percentage of LEA returns was revealed in response to a parliamentary question in February 1992. See *Parl. Deb.*, 6th ser., vol. 203 (1992), cols 375–376.
52 *Standards of Reading in Primary Schools*, Appendix, p. iv.
53 Ibid., Appendix, p. v.
54 Ibid., Appendix, p. vii.
55 *Guardian*, 'Testing, testing', leading article, 20 December 1991, p. 18.
56 J. Judd, 'Major settles an old score: Tories want a return to traditional', *Independent*, 20 October 1991, p. 19.
57 J. Judd and P. Wilby, 'Major rings the bell on playtime: the Prime Minister wants more sitting on the old school bench', *Independent*, 8 December 1991, p. 4.
58 F. Abrams, 'Pupils face testing tomes in "slimline" seven-plus', *Sunday Telegraph*, 1 December 1991, p. 2.
59 Judd and Wilby, 'Major rings the bell on playtime', p. 4.
60 D. Tytler, 'Let common sense take over', The Features Section, *The Times*, 27 January 1992, p. 7; D. MacLeod, 'Straw criticises fall in reading standards', *Independent*, 24 January 1992, p. 4.
61 Tytler, 'Let common sense take over', p. 7.
62 A. O'Hear, 'Education: end of the 7-year war?', *Daily Telegraph*, 22 January 1992, p. 43.
63 Tytler, 'Let common sense take over', p. 7.
64 Ibid.
65 Ibid.
66 Ibid.
67 S. Bates, 'Teachers told to rethink methods', *Guardian*, 23 January 1992, p. 3.
68 Tytler, 'Let common sense take over', p. 7.
69 Bates, 'Teachers told to rethink methods', p. 3; Tytler, 'Let common sense take over', p. 7.
70 Bates, 'Teachers told to rethink methods', p. 3; Tytler, 'Let common sense take over', p. 7.
71 Bates, 'Teachers told to rethink methods', p. 3.
72 Ibid., p. 3.
73 B. Stierer, 'Simply doing their job? The politics of reading standards and "real books"', in B. Stierer and J. Maybin (eds), *Language, Literacy and Learning in Educational Practice: A Reader*, Clevedon: Multilingual Matters, 1994, pp. 128–138.
74 M. Braid, 'Education experts doubt fall in literacy standard', *Independent*, 20 August 1990, p. 2.
75 J. Meikle, 'Reports fuel debate on poor reading', *Guardian*, 10 January 1991, p. 34
76 D. MacLeod, 'Clarke condemns reading levels in primary schools', *Independent*, 10 January 1991, p. 3.
77 J. Bald, 'Education: two lessons in learning to read; latest evidence confirms doubts about some teaching methods says John Bald', *Independent*, 10 January 1991, p. 19.

78 *Daily Telegraph*, 'Primary concerns', leading article, 24 January 1992, p. 16.
79 Plowden, para. 550, p. 10.

6 The advent of national literary strategies

1 J. Codd, 'Curriculum reform in New Zealand', *Journal of Curriculum Studies*, 23(2), 1991: 177–180.
2 R. Webb and G. Vulliamy, 'Managing curriculum policy changes: a comparative analysis of primary schools in England and Finland', *Journal of Education Policy*, 14(2), 1999: 117–137.
3 W. Roger, 'Phonic boom: adventures in the reading trade', *Metro*, 1995: 48–58.
4 J. Soler, 'Past and present technocratic solutions to teaching literacy: implications for New Zealand primary teachers and literacy programmes', *Pedagogy, Culture and Society: Journal of Educational Discussion and Debate*, 7(3), 1999: 521–538.
5 F. Rafferty, 'Labour gets back to basics', *Times Educational Supplement*, 31 May, 1996. Online, available at: web.lexis.com/executive/ (accessed 4 January 2005).
6 National Centre for Literacy and Numeracy, *The National Literacy Project*, London, 1997.
7 M.M. Clay, *The Early Detection of Reading Difficulties*, Auckland: Heinemann, 1985; M.M. Clay, 'The Reading Recovery Programme, 1984–1988: coverage, outcomes and education board district figures', *New Zealand Journal of Educational Studies*, 25(1), 1990: 61–70; M.M. Clay, *Reading Recovery: A Guidebook for Teachers in Training*, Portsmouth, NH: Heinemann, 1994.
8 National Centre for Literacy and Numeracy, 1997.
9 Editorial, 'No more quick fixes', *TES*, 28 February 1996. Online, available at: web.lexis.com/executive/ (accessed 4 January 2005).
10 Rafferty, 'Labour gets back to basics'.
11 Ibid.
12 F. Rafferty, 'The road to sanctuary buildings', *TES*, 12 July 1996. Online, available at: web.lexis.com/executive/ (accessed 4 January 2005).
13 G. Hackett, 'Map of influences redrawn', *TES*, 6 June 1997. Online, available at: web.lexis.com/executive/ (accessed 4 January 2005).
14 N. Ghouri, 'A good year for cynics and "normal" teachers', *TES*, 9 January 1998. Online, available at: web.lexis.com/executive/ (accessed 4 January 2005).
15 Editorial, 'The powers behind Blunkett's throne', *TES*, 3 October 1997. Online, available at: web.lexis.com/executive/ (accessed 4 January 2005).
16 S. Young, 'Reading standards static for 50 years', *TES*, 11 July 1997. Online, available at: web.lexis.com/executive/ (accessed 4 January 2005).
17 R. Rafferty, 'Barber rounds on political playground', *TES*, 13 December 1996. Online, available at: web.lexis.com/executive/ (accessed 4 January 2005).
18 M. Barber, 'Platform: how to achieve the impossible', *TES*, 13 December 1996. Online, available at: web.lexis.com/executive/ (accessed 4 January 2005).
19 Editorial, 'Ease sacking plea', *TES*, 5 July 1996. Online, available at: web.lexis.com/executive/ (accessed 4 January 2005); Rafferty, 'The road to sanctuary buildings'; G. Hackett, 'Blunkett revises with help of professors', *TES*, 4 February 1996. Online, available at: web.lexis.com/executive/ (accessed 4 January 2005); J. Sutcliffe, 'Trial by peers proposed to weed out bad staff', *TES*, 16 August 1996. Online, available at: web.lexis.com/executive/ (accessed 4 January 2005).
20 Hackett, 'Blunket revises with help of professors'.
21 Ibid.

22 D. Rosenthal, 'An effective, if Blunt, instrument', *TES*, 7 June 1996. Online, available at: web.lexis.com/executive/ (accessed 4 January 2005).

23 N. Pyke, 'Politicians join whole-class army', *TES*, 7 June 1996. Online, available at: web.lexis.com/executive/ (accessed 4 January 2005).

24 D. Hofkins, 'Literacy blueprint unveiled', *TES*, 6 December 1996. Online, available at: web.lexis.com/executive/ (accessed 4 January 2005).

25 See, for example: *The Dominion* 14 September 1990, p. 2; 15 February 1993, p. 1, and 12 June 1993, p. 2. See also *Computerworld New Zealand*, 30 November 1992, p. 7.

26 Articles appeared in the following: *The Press (Christchurch)* 7 June 1990, p. 3; *The Dominion*, 14 September 1990, p. 2, and 16 April 1991, p. 7; *The New Zealand Herald*, 16 April 1991, p. 20; 12 July 1993, p. 2; 16 August 1993, p. 9; *National Business Review*, 30 October 1992, p. 34; *New Zealand Listener*, 29 May 1993, p. 34.

27 See, for instance, Chapter 7.

28 J. Chamberlain, 'Our illiteracy: reading the writing on the wall', *North and South*, 1993, pp. 66–76.

29 *New Zealand Herald*, 24 June 1996, p. 2.

30 W.E. Tunmer and J.W. Chapman, 'Beginning reader's self-reports on strategies used for identifying unfamiliar words in text', a paper presented at the annual meeting of the New Zealand Association for Educational Research in Education, Nelson, New Zealand, December 1996, pp. 1–2. See also, W.E. Tunmer and J.W. Chapman, 'Language prediction skill phonological recoding ability, and beginning reading', in C. Hulme and R.M. Joshi (eds), *Reading and Spelling: Development and Disorder*, Hillsdale, NJ: Lawrence Erlbaum Associates, 1998, pp. 33–67; W.E. Tunmer and J.W. Chapman, 'Teaching strategies for word identification', in G. Thompson and T. Nicholson (eds), *Learning to Read: Beyond Phonics and Whole Language*, Newark: IRA, 1999, pp. 74–102.

31 N. O'Hare, 'What's wrong with reading?', *New Zealand Listener*, 1995: 18–22.

32 Ibid.

33 Ibid., p. 20.

34 Ibid., p. 22.

35 *Developmental Network Newsletter*, 'The O'Hare article, *Listener*, July 15, 1995: a new low in education reporting and academic behaviour', pp. 2–3.

36 Ibid.

37 W. Roger, 'Phonics boom: adventures in the reading trade', *Metro*, 1995, pp. 48–58.

38 For an example of US press coverage of the 'whole language method' versus 'phonics', see 'How Johnny should read', *Time Magazine*, South Pacific Edition, 27 October 1998. Online, available at: cgi.pathfinder.com/magazine/1997/dom/971027/box3.html (accessed 3 October 2003).

39 International Reading Association, 'IRA takes a stand on phonics', *Reading Today*, 14(5), 1997: 1.

40 *New Zealand Herald*, 19 July 1997, p. 20.

41 See Chapter 7 for further discussion of this report in the context of the controversy over RR in New Zealand.

42 ERO is the New Zealand equivalent of OFSTED.

43 *New Zealand Education Review*, 23 July 1997, p. 1. News items also appeared in the following newspapers: *New Zealand Herald*, 19 July 1997, p. 20; 13 August 1997, p. 1; 1 September 1997, p. 4; 11 September, 1997; p. 13; *The Otago Daily Times*, 14 August 1997, p. 5; *The Dominion*, 14 August 1997, p. 14.

44 *Otago Daily Times*, 1 September 1997. Online, available at: www1.odt.co.nz/01Sept97/startup-800.html (accessed 3 October 2003).

45 *New Zealand Herald*, 19 July 1997, p. 1.

46 *The Dominion*, 14 August 1997, p. 14.

47 *The Dominion*, 1 September 1997, p. 5.

48 *Time Magazine*, 'An Australian survey stirs debate over the best way to teach children the first two Rs', 29 September 1997. Online, available at: cgi.pathfinder.com/time/magazine/1997/int/970929/spacific.can_dick_and_htm l (accessed 3 October 2003).

49 *Independent*, 26 September 1997, p. 9.

50 *Otago Daily Times*, 1 October 1997. Online, available at: www1.odt.co.nz/cgi-bin/getitem?date=15Oct97&object=RAFA42F195OGH&type_html (accessed 3 October 2003).

51 *National Business Review*, 1 May 1998, p. 28.

52 Ibid.

53 New Zealand Government, Green Paper: *Assessment for Success in Primary Schools*, Wellington: Ministry of Education, 1998.

54 *Independent*, 7 November 1998, p. 11.

55 See, for example, the *New Zealand Herald*, 17 November 1998, p. 5; 21 November 1998, p. 3.

56 *The National Business Review*, 30 November 1998, p. 42.

57 See Literacy Experts Group, *Literacy Experts Group Report to the Secretary for Education*, Wellington, Ministry of Education, 1999.

58 T. Nicholson, 'The social and political contexts of reading: contemporary literacy policy', in P. Adams and H. Ryan (eds), *Learning to Read in Aotearoa New Zealand*, Palmerston North: Dunmore Press, 2002, pp. 36–45.

59 Ibid., p. 46.

60 Ibid.

61 Literacy Experts Group, *Literacy Experts Group Report to the Secretary for Education*.

62 See Literacy Task Force, *A Reading Revolution: How We Can Teach Every Child to Read Well*, London, University of London: Institute of Education, 1997.

63 R. Beard, 'Influences on the Literacy Hour', *Reading: A Journal about Literacy and Language in Education*, 33(1), 1999: 6–12; R. Beard, *National Literacy Strategy: Review of Research and Other Evidence*, Leeds: School of Education University of Leeds, 1999.

64 Literacy Task Force, 1997: 2.

65 Literacy Task Force, 1997: 3.

66 Literacy Taskforce, 1999: 2.

67 Literacy Taskforce, 1999: 4.

68 Literacy Task Force, 1997: paragraph 36.

69 Literacy Task Force, 1997: paragraph 39.

70 Literacy Task Force, 1997: paragraph 35.

71 Literacy Taskforce, 1999: 7–8.

7 Reading Recovery: a comparative study

1 See, for example, J. Clare, 'Home page news', *Independent*, 9 January 1992.

2 J. Soler, 'Past and present technocratic solutions to teaching literacy: implications for New Zealand primary teachers and literacy programmes', *Pedagogy, Culture and Society: Journal of Educational Discussion and Debate*, 7(3), 1999: 521–538.

3 R. Openshaw and J. Cullen, 'Teachers and the reading curriculum: lessons from the phonics debate', *New Zealand Journal of Educational Studies*, 36(1), 2001: 41–55.

4 Ibid. See also R. Openshaw, 'The social and political contexts of early intervention programmes: a case study of reading recovery', in P. Adams and H. Ryan (eds), *Learning to Read in Aotearoa New Zealand*, Palmerston North: Dunmore Press, 2002; pp. 82–93.

5 M.M. Simpson, *Suggestions for Teaching Reading in Infant Classes*, Wellington: Department of Education, 1962.

6 T. Nicholson, 'From ABC to Ready to Read', *Language and Literacy: Set Special*, 1997: 1–7.

7 M.M. Clay, 'The reading behaviour of five year old children: a research report', *New Zealand Journal of Educational Studies*, 2, 1967: 11–31.

8 Nicholson, 'From ABC to Ready to Read'.

9 J. Slane, 'Eric: a new concept for in-service education of teachers', *Education*, 27(2), 1978: 7–11.

10 Ibid., p. 8.

11 B. Randell, 'Matching books and beginners', International Reading Association. Wellington Council. *Reading is Everybody's Business*. Fourth New Zealand Conference. August, 1973, pp. 39–53.

12 New Zealand Department of Education, Reading Recovery in-service course 1980. Memo to Principals of all Auckland Metropolitan Schools, ABEP, W4262, Box 1715, 30/2/10/5; Reading Recovery, Part 1, 1979, Archives New Zealand, Wellington. All subsequent New Zealand archival material with an ABEP, W4262 prefix cited in this chapter is held at the Wellington branch of Archives New Zealand unless otherwise stated.

13 M.M. Clay, 'Comments relating to the Picot Report', Letter to the Prime Minister, the Rt Hon. D. Lange, 20 July 1988, ABEP, W4262, Box 3783, NS55/1/32 – MISC, Reading Recovery.

14 Openshaw, 'The social and political contexts of early intervention programmes', p. 86.

15 J.N. Cox, *Report on Reading Recovery*, undated but *c.* 2 March 1981, APEP, W4262, Box 1715, 30/2/10.5, Reading Recovery, Part 1. See also Openshaw, 'The social and political contexts of early intervention programmes', p. 86.

16 New Zealand Department of Education, Letter from T.F. Walbran, Deputy District Senior Inspector of Primary Schools to A. Gilchrist, Director of Schools Supervision, Wellington, 2 February 1981. ABEP, W4262, Box 1715, 30/2/10/5, Reading Recovery, Part 1.

17 Openshaw, 'The social and political contexts of early intervention programmes', p. 86.

18 A. Gilchrist, Memorandum to District Senior Inspectors of Primary Schools, 21 July 1981, ABEP, W4262, Box 1715, 30/2/10/5 Reading Recovery, Part 1.

19 Notes for Minister entitled 'Reading Recovery', December 1982, ABEP, W4262, Box 1715, 30/2/10/5, Reading Recovery, Part 2.

20 Monaghan, E.J., 'Phonics and whole word/whole language controversies, 1948–1998: an introductory history', 1998. Online, available at: www.american readingforum.org/98_yearbook/html/01_monaghan_98.htm (accessed 4 April 2005).

21 A. McGregor, Memorandum from A. McGregor, Inspector of Primary Schools to Auckland Education Board, 16 June 1989, ABEP, W4262, Box 3783, NS55/1/32-RR, Reading Recovery Policy.

22 B. Watson, *National Implementation of Reading Recovery*. Submission to the Minis-

ter of Education from Barbara Watson, Director Reading Recovery, 20 June 1988, ABEP, W4262, Box 3783, NS55/1/32 – MISC Reading Recovery.

23 Cited in *The Times*, 6 January 1992, p. 1.

24 See Chapter 6.

25 Preston, Press Association News file, 9 January 1992.

26 Her Majesty's Inspectorate, *The Teaching and Learning of Reading in Primary Schools*, London: Department for Education, 1991.

27 J. Willman and A. Smith, 'Political battle over education intensifies', *Financial Times*, 4 January 1992, p. 1.

28 Ibid.

29 S. Strickland, 'Parties clash over credit for schools reading idea', *Independent*, 4 January 1992, p. 1.

30 N. Crequer, 'Intensive help is central to better reading: Ngaio Crequer looks at how some New Zealand teachers are helping the poorest readers to catch up with their classmates', *Independent*, 4 January 1992, p. 2.

31 F. Beckett, 'Feat of Clay lies in avoiding politics', *Guardian*, 4 January 1992, p. 2.

32 Willman and Smith, 'Political battle over education intensifies'.

33 Beckett, 'Feat of Clay lies in avoiding politics'.

34 Ibid.

35 Ibid.

36 J. O'Leary, 'On the road to recovery', *The Times*, 6 January 1992, Features, p. 1.

37 Ibid.

38 J. Clare, 'Rush to adopt plan to cut illiteracy', *Daily Telegraph*, 4 January 1992, p. 1.

39 J. Clare, *Independent*, 9 January 1992, p. 5, see Preston, Press Association Newsfile, 29 January 1993.

40 M. Whittle, 'Education inner reading scheme "will be best in world"', Press Association Newsfile, Home News, 9 January 1992.

41 J. Bald, 'Reading between the lines', *The Times*, 17 January 1994, Features.

42 See Letters to the Editor, *Guardian* 14 January 1992, p. 23.

43 O'Leary, *Independent*, 16 January 1992, p. 17.

44 *Hansard Parliamentary Debates*, 6th ser., vol. 204 (1992), col. 464.

45 Ofsted (Office for Standards in Education), *Reading Recovery in New Zealand. A report from the Office of Her Majesty's Chief Inspector of Schools*, London: HMSO, 1993, preface, p. v.

46 Ibid., p. 1.

47 Ibid., p. v.

48 Ibid., p. 12.

49 Ibid., p. 20.

50 Ibid., p. 20.

51 Ibid., p. 21.

52 Ibid., p. 22.

53 Ibid., p. 23.

54 B. Preston, 'More cash for inner city schools', Press Association Newsfile, 29 January 1993, Home News.

55 Wearmouth, unpublished, personal interview with New Zealand-based RR tutor.

56 Ibid.

57 S. Bates, 'School reading aid "No Quick Fix"', *Guardian*, 3 February 1992, London, p. 3.

58 Wearmouth, unpublished, personal interview with RR trainer in the UK.

59 Ibid.
60 Preston, 'More cash for inner city schools'.
61 Department for Education and Employment, *The National Literacy Strategy: Framework for Teaching*, London: DfEE, 1998.
62 R. Openshaw, J. Soler, J. Wearmouth and A. Paige-Smith, 'The socio-political context of the development of Reading Recovery in New Zealand and England', *The Curriculum Journal*, 13(1), 2002: 53–69.
63 R. Beard, 'Research and the National Literacy Strategy', *Oxford Review of Education*, 26(3&4), 2000: 421–436.
64 Openshaw *et al.*, 'The socio-political context of the development of Reading Recovery in New Zealand and England'.
65 See, for example, M.M. Clay, *The Early Detection of Reading Difficulties*, Auckland: Heinemann, 1985; M.M. Clay, 'The Reading Recovery Programme, 1984–1988: coverage, outcomes and education board district figures', *New Zealand Journal of Educational Studies*, 25(1): 61–70; M.M. Clay, *Reading Recovery: A Guidebook for Teachers in Training*, Portsmouth, NH: Heinemann, 1994.
66 Beard, 'Research and the National Literacy Strategy', p. 427.
67 Rafferty, F., 'Labour gets back to basics', *Times Educational Supplement*, 31 May 1996. Online, available at: web.lexis.com/executive/ (accessed 4 January, 2005).
68 Rafferty, 'Labour gets back to basics'.
69 See Literacy Task Force, *A Reading Revolution: How We Can Teach Every Child to Read Well*, London, University of London: Institute of Education, 1997, especially paragraphs 105–106.
70 DfEE, *The National Literacy Strategy: Framework for Teaching*.
71 Ibid., p. 8.
72 M. Mroz, F. Smith, and F. Hardman, 'The discourse of the Literacy Hour', *Cambridge Journal of Education*, 30(3), 2000: 379–390.
73 See, for example, R. Byers, 'The National Literacy Strategy and pupils with special educational needs', *British Journal of Special Education*, 26(1), 1999: 8–12.

8 Conclusion

1 S. de Castell and A. Luke, 'Models of literacy in North American schools: social and historical conditions and consequences', in S. de Castell, A. Luke and K. Egan (eds), *Literacy, Society and Schooling: A Reader*, Cambridge: Cambridge University Press, 1986, pp. 87–109.
2 See, for example: S. Ball, *Politics and Policy making in Education: Explorations in Policy Sociology*, London: Routledge and Kegan Paul, 1990; R. Dale, *The State and Educational Policy*, Milton Keynes: Open University Press, 1989; K. Jones, *Education in Britain, 1944 to the Present*, Cambridge: Polity Press, 2003; K. Jones, *Right Turn: The Conservative Revolution in Education*, London: Radius, 1989; C. Knight, *The Making of Tory Education Policy in Post-War Britain, 1950–1986*, New York: Falmer Press, 1990; B. Simon, *Education and the Social Order 1940–1990*, London: Lawrence and Wishart, 1991.
3 J. Coldron and R. Smith, 'The construction of reflective practice in key policy documents in England, pedagogy, culture and society', *Journal of Educational Discussion and Debate*, 7(2), 1999: 305–320.
4 R. Fisher, 'Developmentally appropriate practice and a National Literacy Strategy', *British Journal of Educational Studies*, 48(1), 2000: 58–69.
5 M. Hilton, 'Raising literacy standards: the true story', *English in Education*, 32(3), 1998: 4.
6 See, for example, P.D.K. Ramsay, 'The dynamics of curriculum change', in

W.J.D. Minogue (ed.), *Adventures in Curriculum*, Sydney: Allen and Unwin, 1983, pp. 1–9. See also J. Nisbet, 'Curriculum process: international perspectives', in P.D.K. Ramsay (ed.), *Curriculum Issues in New Zealand*, Wellington: NZEI, 1979, pp. 51–64.

7 See, for example, R.L. Allington and H. Woodside-Jiron, 'The politics of literacy teaching: how "research" shaped educational policy', *Educational Researcher*, 28(8), 1999: 4–12.

8 T. Loveless, 'The use and misuse of research in educational reform', in D. Ravitch (ed.), *Brookings Papers on Educational Policy*, Washington, DC: Brookings Institute, 1998, pp. 279–303.

9 R.L. Allington, and H. Woodside-Jiron, 'The politics of literacy teaching: How "research" shaped "Educational policy"', *Educational Researcher*, 28(8), 1999: 8.

10 T. Nicholson, 'The social and political contexts of reading: contemporary literacy policy in Aotearoa, New Zealand', in P. Adams and H. Ryan (eds), *Learning to Read in Aotearoa, New Zealand*, Palmerston North, New Zealand: Dunmore Press, 2002, pp. 22–50.

11 C. Lankshear and M. Knobel, 'New times! Old ways? Contextualising difficulties in literacy development', in J. Soler, J. Wearmouth and G. Reid (eds) *Contextualising Difficulties in Literacy Development: Exploring Politics, Culture, Ethnicity and Ethics*, London and New York: Open University, Routledge Falmer, 2002, p. 273.

12 G. McCulloch and W. Richardson, *Historical Research in Educational Settings*, Buckingham: Open University, 2000, pp. 97–113.

Bibliography

Abrams, F., 'Pupils face testing tomes in "slimline" seven-plus', *Sunday Telegraph*, 1 December 1991, p. 2.

Aldrich, R., 'Educational standards in historical perspective', in Harvey Goldstein and Anthony Heath (eds), *Educational Standards*, Oxford: Oxford University Press, 2000.

Allington, R.L. and Woodside-Jiron, H., 'The politics of literacy teaching: how "research" shaped educational policy', *Educational Researcher*, 28(8), 1999: 4–12.

Apple, M., 'Creating difference: neo-liberalism, neo-conservatism and the politics of educational reform', *Educational Policy*, 18(1), 2004: 12–44.

Arnowitz, S. and Giroux, H.A., *Education Still Under Siege* (second edn), London: Bergin and Gavey, 1993.

Bald, J., 'Education: two lessons in learning to read; latest evidence confirms doubts about some teaching methods says John Bald', *Independent*, 10 January 1991, p. 19.

Bald, J., 'Total revision based on practice, not theory', *Independent*, 16 January 1992, p. 17.

Bald, J., 'Reading between the lines', *The Times*, features, 17 January 1994.

Ball, S.J., *Politics and Policymaking in Education: Explorations in Policy Sociology*, London and New York: Routledge, 1990.

Ball, S.J., *Educational Reform: A Critical and Post-Structural Approach*, Buckingham: Open University Press, 1994.

Ball, S.J., 'You've been NEFRed! Dumbing down the Academy: National Educational Research Forum: a National strategy-consultation paper: a brief and bilious response', *Journal of Education Policy*, 16(3), 2001: 265–268.

Barber, M., 'Platform: how to achieve the impossible', *Times Educational Supplement*, 13 December 1996. Online, available at: www.tes.co.uk/search/story (accessed 10 August 2005).

Bates, S., 'Claims on children's reading disowned: authority says psychologist not backed by evidence', *Guardian*, 3 July 1990, p. 3.

Bates, S. 'Leeds' £14 m project fails to improve teaching', *Guardian*, 3 August 1991, p. 3.

Bates, S., 'Teachers told to rethink methods', *Guardian*, 23 January 1992, p. 3.

Bates, S., 'School reading aid "no quick fix"', *Guardian*, 3 February 1992, p. 3.

Beard, R., 'Letter: balance required in the reading debate', *Independent*, 30 November 1991, p. 17.

Beard, R., 'Influences on the Literacy Hour', *Reading: A Journal about Literacy and Language in Education*, 33(1), 1999: 6–12.

Beard, R., *National Literacy Strategy: Review of Research and Other Evidence*, Leeds, School of Education: University of Leeds, 1999.

Beard, R., 'Research and the National Literacy Strategy', *Oxford Review of Education*, 26(3&4), 2000: 421–436.

Beckett, F., 'Feat of Clay lies in avoiding politics', *Guardian*, 4 January 1992, p. 2.

Bookbinder, G.E., 'Variations in reading test norms', *Educational Research*, 12(2), 1970: 99–105.

Bookbinder, G.E., 'Test or teachers? One is wrong about reading', *Times Educational Supplement*, 21 November 1975, p. 19.

Boyson, R., *The Crisis in Education*, London: Woburn Press, 1975.

Braid, M., 'Education experts doubt fall in literacy standard', *Independent*, 20 August 1990, p. 2.

Brooks, G., 'Trends in standards of literacy in the United Kingdom, 1948–1996', paper presented at UK Reading Association conference, University of Manchester, July 1997, and at the British Educational Research Association conference, University of York, September 1997.

Burt, C., 'The education of illiterate adults', *British Journal of Educational Studies*, xv, February 1945, part 1: 20–27.

Byers, R., 'The National Literacy Strategy and pupils with special educational needs', *British Journal of Special Education*, 26(1), 1999: 8–11.

Callaghan, D., ' "The believers": politics and personalities in the making of the 1988 Education Act', *History of Education*, 24(4), 1995: 369–385.

Carter, B. and Burgess, H., 'Testing, regulation and control: shifting education narratives', *Journal of Education Policy*, 1(2), 1993: 233–245.

Cato, V. and Whetton, C., *An Enquiry into LEA Evidence on Standards of Reading of Seven Year Old Children*, a report prepared for the SEAC by NFER, London, 1991.

Chall, J., *Learning to Read: The Great Debate*, New York: McGraw-Hill, 1967.

Chamberlain, J., 'Our illiteracy: reading the writing on the wall', *North and South*, 1993, 66–76.

Chitty, C. *Towards a New Education System: The Victory of the New Right?* London: Falmer, 1989.

Clare, J., 'Tests reveal fall in standard of pupils' reading', *Daily Telegraph,* 29 June 1990, p. 1.

Clare, J., 'Who was he talking about? Prince Charles has warned against "fashionable trends" in our classrooms', *Daily Telegraph*, 24 April 1991, p. 17.

Clare, J., 'Rush to adopt plan to cut illiteracy', *Daily Telegraph*, 4 January 1992, p. 1.

Clare, J., *Independent*, 9 January 1992, Home page news, p. 5.

Clay, M.M., 'The reading behaviour of five year old children: a research report', *New Zealand Journal of Educational Studies*, 2, 1967: 9–31.

Clay, M.M., *The Early Detection of Reading Difficulties*, Auckland: Heinemann, 1985.

Clay, M.M., 'Comments relating to the Picot Report', Letter to the Prime Minister, the Rt Hon. D. Lange, 20 July 1988, Archives New Zealand, Wellington ABEP, W4262, Box 3783, NS55/1/32 – MISC, Reading Recovery.

Clay, M.M., 'The Reading Recovery Programme, 1984–1988: coverage, outcomes and Education Board District figures', *New Zealand Journal of Educational Studies*, 25(1), 1990: 61–70.

Clay, M.M., *Reading Recovery: A Guidebook for Teachers in Training*, Portsmouth, NH: Heinemann, 1994.

Codd, J., 'Curriculum reform in New Zealand', *Journal of Curriculum Studies*, 23(2), 1991: 177–180.

Coldron, J. and Smith, R., 'The construction of reflective practice in key policy documents in England, pedagogy, culture and society', *Journal of Educational Discussion and Debate*, 7(2), 1999: 305–320.

Collins, J., 'How Johnny should read', *Time Magazine*, South Pacific Edition, 27 October 1998. Online, available at: cgi.pathfinder.com/magazine/1997/dom/971027/box3.html (accessed 3 October 2003).

Corbett, A., *Much To Do About Education, A Critical Survey of the Fate of the Major Educational Reports*, Council for Educational Advance: Macmillan Education for the Council for Educational Advance, 4th edition, 1978.

Cox, B. and Dyson, A., *Fight For Education: A Black Paper*, London: Critical Quarterly Society, 1969.

Cox, C.B., Boyson, R. and Amis, Kingsley, *Black Paper 1975: The Fight for Education*, London: Dent, 1975.

Cox, J.N., *Report on Reading Recovery*, 2 March 1981, APEP, W4262, Box 1715, 30/2/10.5, Reading Recovery, Part 1.

Crequer, N., 'Intensive help is central to better reading: Ngaio Crequer looks at how some New Zealand teachers are helping the poorest readers to catch up with their classmates', *Independent*, 4 January 1992, p. 2.

Cunningham, P., *Curriculum Change in the Primary School since 1945: Dissemination of the Progressive Ideal*, London: Falmer Press, 1988.

Daily Mail, 'Parent power: the intriguing shop-around answer for everyone worried about their child's school', 18 January 1975, p. 6.

Daily Mail, 'The man who says modern stuff is rubbish', 19 February 1975, p. 10.

Daily Mail, 'Don't you wish your child went to a school like this?', 28 June 1975, p. 6.

Daily Mail, 'Exams – the crumbling standards', 3 July 1975, p. 1.

Daily Mail, 'Decline and fall of a trendy head's school', 17 July 1976, p. 9.

Daily Mail, 'Exams – the crumbling standards', 19 July 1976, p. 2.

Daily Mail, 'Class of '86', 19 July 1976, p. 6.

Daily Telegraph, 'Schools urged to ignore "nonsensical" advice on reading', 3 January 1975, p. 2.

Daily Telegraph, '"Trendy" teaching on the way out says professor', 13 January 1975, p. 5.

Daily Telegraph, 'Lowering of school standards', a letter to the Editor by I.F. Lowenstein, consultant educational psychologist, Winchester, 18 January 1975, p. 16.

Daily Telegraph, 'Classroom warning by Callaghan', 19 October 1976, p. 1.

Daily Telegraph, 'Facing primary facts', leading article, 7 November 1991, p. 20.

Daily Telegraph, 'Primary concerns', leading article, 24 January 1992, p. 16.

Dale, R., 'Thatcherism and Education', in J. Ahier and M. Flude (eds), *Contemporary Education Policy*, London: Croom Helm, 1983.

Dale, R., *The State and Educational Policy*, Milton Keynes: Open University Press, 1989.

Daniels, J.C. and Diack, Hunter, *Progress in Reading*, Nottingham: University of Nottingham, Institute of Education, 1956.

Daniels, J.C. and Diack, Hunter, *Progress in Reading in the Infant School*, Nottingham: University of Nottingham, Institute of Education, 1960.

de Castell, S. and Luke, A., 'Models of literacy in North American schools: social and historical conditions and consequences', in S. de Castell, A. Luke and K. Egan (eds), *Literacy, Society and Schooling: A Reader*, Cambridge: Cambridge University Press, 1986.

Department for Education and Employment (DfEE), Standards and Effectiveness Unit. *The National Literacy Strategy: Framework for Teaching*. London: DfEE, 1998.

Department of Education and Science, *A Language for life, Report of the Committee of Inquiry Appointed by the Secretary of State for Education and Science (Bullock Report)*, London: HMSO, 1975.

Department of Education and Science, *Primary Education in England: A Survey by HM Inspectors of Schools*, London: HMSO, 1978.

Department of Education and Science, *Progress in Education: A Report on Recent Initiatives*, London: HMSO, September 1978.

Developmental Network Newsletter, 'The O'Hare article, *Listener*, July 15, 1995: a new low in education reporting and academic behaviour', August 1995, 2–3.

Devlin, T., 'Professions call for exam to test literacy of recruits', *Times Educational Supplement*, 24 January 1975, p. 3.

Economist, The, 'Britain's schools: trying harder', 28 July 1990, p. 49.

Eden, G., 'Impressions of Parliament', *Punch*, vol. ccxxiv, no. 5865, 4 March 1953.

Editorial, 'Ease sacking plea', *Times Educational Supplement*, 5 July 1996. Online, available at: web.lexis.com/executive/ (accessed 4 January 2005).

Education Today, unsigned review (Colleges of Preceptors) R.S., 7(1), 1957.

Education, Science and Arts Committee, *Third Report: Standards of Reading in Primary Schools*, Vol. 1, 268–261, May 1991.

Educational Correspondent, 'Illiterates and backward readers: conditions in England since the War', *The Times*, 13 February 1953, p. 7.

Financial Times, UK News, 'Reading probe', 26 July 1990, p. 10.

Fisher, R., 'Developmentally appropriate practice and a National Literacy Strategy', *British Journal of Educational Studies*, 48(1), 2000: 58–69.

Foucault, M., 'The subject and power', in L. Dreyfus and P. Rainbow (eds), *Foucault: Beyond Structuralism and Hermeneutics*, Chicago: University of Chicago Press, 1983.

Galton, M. and Simon, B. 'Where the Wildman aren't', features page, *Times Educational Supplement*, 4 April 1980, p. 18.

Gardner, K., 'State of reading', in N. Smart (ed.), *Crisis in the Classroom: An Enquiry into State Education Policy*, London: Hamlyn, 1968.

Ghouri, N., 'A good year for cynics and "normal" teachers', *Times Educational Supplement*, 9 January 1998. Online, available at: web.lexis.com/executive/ (accessed 4 January 2005).

Gilchrist, A., Memorandum to District Senior Inspectors of Primary Schools, 21 July 1981, ABEP, W4262, Box 1715, 30/2/10/5 Reading Recovery, Part 1.

Goodman, K.S., *In Defense of Good Teaching: What Teachers Need to Know About the 'Reading Wars'*, New York: Me, Stenhouse Publications, 1998.

Gretton, J. and Jackson, M., *William Tyndale: Collapse of a School – or a System?*, London: Allen and Unwin, 1976.

Guardian, 'The right test for schools', leading article, 30 June 1990, p. 22.

Guardian, 'Literacy and liberty', Editorial, 19 February 1975, p. 12.

Guardian, 'Testing, testing', leading article, 20 December 1991, p. 18.
Guardian, Letters to the Editor, 14 January 1992, p. 23.
Hackett, G., 'Blunkett revises with help of professors', *Times Educational Supplement*, 4 February 1996. Online, available at: web.lexis.com/executive/ (accessed 4 January 2005).
Hackett, G., 'Map of influences redrawn', *Times Educational Supplement*, 6 June 1997. Online, available at: web.lexis.com/executive/ (accessed 4 January 2005).
Hansard Parliamentary Debates, 5th ser., vol. 511, 1953.
Hansard Parliamentary Debates, 5th ser., vol. 535, 1954.
Hansard Parliamentary Debates, 5th ser., vol. 537, 1955.
Hansard Parliamentary Debates, 5th ser., vol. 569, 1957.
Hansard Parliamentary Debates, 5th ser., vol. 585, 1958.
Hansard Parliamentary Debates, 5th ser., vol. 654, 1962.
Hansard Parliamentary Debates, 5th ser., vol. 662, 1962.
Hansard Parliamentary Debates, 5th ser., vol. 690, 1964.
Hansard Parliamentary Debates, 5th ser., vol. 695, 1964.
Hansard Parliamentary Debates, 5th ser., vol. 745, 1967.
Hansard Parliamentary Debates, 5th ser., vol. 774, 1968.
Hansard Parliamentary Debates, 5th ser., vol. 787, 1969.
Hansard Parliamentary Debates, 5th ser., vol. 794, 1970.
Hansard Parliamentary Debate, 5th ser., vol. 804, 1970.
Hansard Parliamentary Debates, 5th ser., vol. 806, 1970.
Hansard Parliamentary Debates, 5th ser., vol. 817, 1971.
Hansard Parliamentary Debates, 5th ser., vol. 820, 1971.
Hansard Parliamentary Debates, 5th ser., vol. 834, 1972.
Hansard Parliamentary Debates, 5th ser., vol. 837, 1972.
Hansard Parliamentary Debates, 5th ser., vol. 887, 1975.
Hansard Parliamentary Debates, 5th ser., vol. 894, 1975.
Hansard Parliamentary Debates, 5th ser., vol. 981, 1975.
Hansard Parliamentary Debates, 5th ser., vol. 912, 1976.
Hansard Parliamentary Debates, 5th ser., vol. 918, 1976.
Hansard Parliamentary Debates, 5th ser., vol. 935–932, 1977.
Hansard Parliamentary Debates, 5th ser., vol. 955, 1978.
Hansard Parliamentary Debates, 5th ser., vol. 964, 1979.
Hansard Parliamentary Debates, 5th ser., vol. 976–972, 1979.
Hansard Parliamentary Debates, 5th ser., vol. 978, 1980.
Hansard Parliamentary Debates, 5th ser., vol. 980, 1980.
Hansard Parliamentary Debates, 5th ser., vol. 981, 1980.
Hansard Parliamentary Debates, 5th ser., vol. 996, 1981.
Hansard Parliamentary Debates, 5th ser., vol. 1,000, 1981.
Hansard Parliamentary Debates, 6th ser., vol. 8, 1981.
Hansard Parliamentary Debates, 6th ser., vol. 24, 1982.
Hansard Parliamentary Debates, 6th ser., vol. 31, 1983.
Hansard Parliamentary Debates, 6th ser., vol. 176, 1990.
Hansard Parliamentary Debates, 6th ser., vol. 177, 1990.
Hansard Parliamentary Debates, 6th ser., vol. 189, 1991.
Hansard Parliamentary Debates, 6th ser., vol. 193, 1991.
Hansard Parliamentary Debates, 6th ser., vol. 195, 1991.

Hansard Parliamentary Debates, 6th ser., vol. 198, 1991.

Hansard Parliamentary Debates, 6th ser., vol. 203, 1992.

Hansard Parliamentary Debates, 6th ser., vol. 204, 1992.

Harper, E.M., *Nursery and Infant Schools in England*. Report to Director of Education, 21 May 1950, pp. 2–3 (7pp., unpublished, handwritten). ABEP, W2462, Box 659, 16/1/5. Education System in Great Britain, Part 1. Archives New Zealand, Wellington.

Her Majesty's Inspectorate, *The Teaching and Learning of Reading in Primary Schools*, London: Department for Education, 1991.

Hilton, M., 'Raising literacy standards: the true story', *English in Education*, 32(3), 1998: 4–21.

Hofkins, D., 'Literacy blueprint unveiled', *Times Educational Supplement*, 6 December 1996. Online, available at: web.lexis.com/executive/ (accessed 4 January 2005).

Houghton Committee, *Houghton Report on Teachers' Salaries*, HMSO Command no. 5848, December 1974.

Howath, T., 'A time to read', *Times Educational Supplement*, 20 December 1974, p. 4.

Hunter-Grundin, E. and Grundin, H.U. (eds), *Reading: Implementing the Bullock Report, Proceedings of the Fourteenth Annual Course and Conference of the United Kingdom Reading Association*, Avery Hill College, London, United Kingdom Reading Association, Ward Lock Educational: London, 1977.

International Reading Association, 'IRA takes a stand on phonics', *Reading Today*, 14(5), 1997: 1.

Jeffries, C., *Illiteracy: A World Problem*, London: Pall Mall Press, 1967.

Jones, K., *Right Turn: The Conservative Revolution in Education*, London: Radius, 1989.

Jones, K., *Education in Britain, 1944 to the Present*, Cambridge: Polity Press, 2003.

Journals to the House of Commons, vol. 208, 1952–1953.

Judd, J., 'Revision expected as teachers slate school tests', *Independent*, 5 May 1991, p. 6.

Judd, J., 'Major settles an old score: Tories want a return to traditional', *Independent*, 20 October 1991, p. 19.

Judd, J. and Wilby, P., 'Major rings the bell on playtime: the Prime Minister wants more sitting on the old school bench', *Independent*, 8 December 1991, p. 4.

Kirkham, J., Morris, M. and an LEA advisor, 'Documents, documents', *Times Educational Supplement*, 8 February 1980, p. 21.

Kliebard, H.M., *The Struggle for the American Curriculum 1893–1958* (second edn), New York: Routledge and Kegan Paul, 1995.

Knight, C., *The Making of Tory Education Policy in Post-War Britain 1950–1986*, London: Falmer Press, 1990.

Lankshear, C. and Knobel, M. 'New times! Old ways? Contextualising difficulties in literacy development', in J. Soler, J. Wearmouth and G. Reid (eds), *Contextualising Difficulties in Literacy Development: Exploring Politics, Culture, Ethnicity and Ethics*, London and New York: Open University, Routledge Falmer, 2002.

Lightfoot, L., 'Losing the battle at Culloden', *Mail on Sunday*, 3 March 1991, p. 5.

Lightfoot, L. 'Clarke orders probe at Culloden', *Mail on Sunday*, 10 March 1991, p. 5.

Lightfoot, L. 'Analysis: the battle of Culloden (continued)', *Mail on Sunday*, 21 April 1991, pp. 8–9.

Literacy Experts Group, *Literacy Experts Group Report to the Secretary for Education*, Wellington: Ministry of Education, 1999.

Literacy Task Force, *A Reading Revolution: How We Can Teach Every Child to Read Well, The Preliminary Report of the Literacy Task Force*, London: Institute of Education, 1997.

Literacy Taskforce, *Report of the Literacy Taskforce*, Wellington, Report prepared for the New Zealand Minister of Education, 1999.

Loveless, T., 'The use and misuse of research in educational reform', in D. Ravitch (ed.), *Brookings Papers on Educational Policy*, Washington, DC: Brookings Institute, 1998.

Luke, A. 'The social construction of literacy in the primary school', in U. Unsworth (ed.), *Literacy, Learning and Teaching: Language as Social Practice in the Primary School*, Melbourne: Macmillan Education, 1993.

Luke, A. and Baker, C.D., 'Towards a critical sociology of reading pedagogy: an introduction', in C.D. Baker and A. Luke (eds), *Towards a Critical Sociology of Reading Pedagogy*, Amsterdam and Philadelphia: John Benjamins, 1991.

Luke, A. and Freebody, P. (eds), *Constructing Critical Literacies: Teaching and Learning Textual Practice*, Cresskill, N.J.: Hampton Press, 1997.

Luke, A. and Freebody, P., 'Critical literacy and the question of normativity', in S. Muspratt, A. Luke and P. Freebody (eds), *Constructing Critical Literacies: Teaching and Learning Textual Practice*, Cresskill, N.J.: Hampton Press, 1997.

McArthur, B. 'Literacy survey in schools: complaints about 'three Rs'', *The Times*, 10 May 1967, p. 2.

MacArthur, B., 'Standards of literacy', *The Times*, 6 September 1969, p. 8.

McCulloch, G. and Richardson, W., *Historical Research in Educational Settings*, Buckingham: Open University Press, 2000.

McCulloch, G., Helsby, G. and Knight, P., *The Politics of Professionalism: Teachers and the Curriculum*, London and New York: Continuum, 2000.

McGregor, A., Memorandum from A. McGregor, Inspector of Primary Schools to Auckland Education Board, 16 June 1989, ABEP, W4262, Box 3783, NS55/1/32-RR, Reading Recovery Policy.

MacLeod, D., 'Clarke condemns reading levels in primary schools', *Independent*, 10 January 1991, p. 3.

MacLeod, D., 'MPs dismiss claims of reading crisis in primary schools', *Independent*, 17 May 1991, p. 10.

MacLeod, D., 'Straw criticises fall in reading standards', *Independent*, 24 January 1992, p. 4.

Marks, J., 'Across the teaching divide', *The Times*, 3 September 1990. Online, available at: web.lexis.com/executive/ (accessed 3 January 2005).

Marston, P., 'Reading: the secret is out. Brought to book', *Daily Telegraph*, 18 July 1991, p. 2.

Meikle, J., 'Reports fuel debate on poor reading', *Guardian*, 10 January 1991, p. 34.

Ministry of Education, *Reading Ability: Some Suggestions for Helping the Backward*, Pamphlet no. 18, London: HMSO, 1950.

Ministry of Education, *Standards of Reading 1948–1956*, Ministry of Education Pamphlet No. 32, London: HMSO, 1957.

Monaghan, E.J., 'Phonics and whole word/whole language controversies, 1948–1998: an introductory history', 1998. Online, available at: www.american-readingforum.org/98_yearbook/html/01_monaghan_98.htm (accessed 4 April 2005).

Morris, J.M., *Reading in the Primary School: An Investigation into Standards of Reading and their Association with the Primary School*, London: Newnes Educational Publishing for NFER, 1959.

Morris, J.M., 'Introduction', in J.M. Morris (ed.), *The First R. Yesterday, Today and Tomorrow: A Selection of Papers from Conferences of the United Kingdom Reading Association*, London: Ward Lock Educational, 1972.

Mroz, M., Smith, F. and Hardman, F., 'The discourse of the Literacy Hour', *Cambridge Journal of Education*, 30(3), 2000: 379–390.

Muspratt, A., Luke, A. and Freebody, P., *Constructing Critical Literacies: Teaching and Learning Textual Practice*, Cresskill, N.J.: Hampton Press, 1997.

National Centre for Literacy and Numeracy, *The National Literacy Project*, London Department for Education and Employment, 1997.

New Zealand Department of Education, Reading Recovery in-service course 1980. Memo to Principals of all Auckland Metropolitan Schools, ABEP, W4262, Box 1715, 30/2/10/5.

New Zealand Department of Education, Letter from T.F. Walbran, Deputy District Senior Inspector of Primary Schools to A. Gilchrist, Director of Schools Supervision, Wellington, 2 February 1981, ABEP, W4262, Box 1715, 30/2/10/5, Reading Recovery, Part 1.

New Zealand Government, Green Paper, 'Assessment for success in primary schools', Wellington: Ministry of Education, 1998.

Nicholson, T., 'From ABC to Ready to Read', *Language and Literacy: Set Special*, 1997: 1–7.

Nicholson, T., 'The social and political contexts of reading: contemporary literacy policy in Aotearoa, New Zealand', in P. Adams and H. Ryan (eds), *Learning to Read in Aotearoa, New Zealand*, Palmerston North, New Zealand: Dunmore Press, 2002.

Nisbet, J., 'Curriculum process: international perspectives', in P.D.K. Ramsay (ed.), *Curriculum Issues in New Zealand*, Wellington: NZEI, 1979.

Notes for Minister entitled 'Reading Recovery', December 1982, ABEP, W4262, Box 1715, 30/2/10/5, Reading Recovery, Part 2.

O'Connor, M., Spoule, A. and Pollard, M., 'New readers start here', *Education Guardian*, 18 February 1975, p. 19.

O'Hare, N., 'What's wrong with reading?' *New Zealand Listener*, 1995; 18–22.

O'Hear, A., 'Education: end of the 7-year war?', *Daily Telegraph*, 22 January 1992, p. 43.

O'Leary, J., 'Reading guru wins real notoriety', *The Times*, 22 April 1991, p. 1.

O'Leary, J., 'On the road to recovery', *The Times*, 6 January 1992, Features, p. 1.

Ofsted (Office for Standards in Education), *Reading Recovery in New Zealand*, A report from the Office of Her Majesty's Chief Inspector of Schools, London: HMSO, 1993.

Openshaw, R., 'The social and political contexts of early intervention programmes: a case study of reading recovery', in P. Adams and H. Ryan (eds), *Learning to Read in Aotearoa, New Zealand*, Palmerston North: Dunmore Press, 2002.

Openshaw, R. and Cullen, J., 'Teachers and the reading curriculum: lessons from the phonics debate', *New Zealand Journal of Educational Studies*, 36(1), 2001: 41–55.

Openshaw, R., Soler, J., Wearmouth, J. and Paige-Smith, A., 'The socio-political context of the development of Reading Recovery in New Zealand and England', *The Curriculum Journal*, 13(1), 2002: 53–69.

Otago Daily Times, 1 September 1997. Online, available at: www1.odt.co.nz/01Sept97/startup-800.html (accessed 3 October 2003).

Otago Daily Times, 1 October 1997. Online, available at: www1.odt.co.nz/cgi-bin/getitem?date=15Oct97&object=RAFA42F195OGH&type_html (accessed 3 October 2003).

Passmore, B., 'Back to tradition, Boyson argues', *Times Educational Supplement*, 14 May 1982, p. 8.

Phillips, M., 'Commentary: educashun still isn't working', *Guardian*, 28 September 1990, p. 23.

Preston, B., 'More cash for inner city schools', Press Association Newsfile, 29 January 1993, Home News.

Pyke, N., 'Politicians join whole-class army', *Times Educational Supplement*, 7 June 1996. Online, available at: web.lexis.com/executive/ (accessed 4 January 2005).

Rafferty, F., 'Labour gets back to basics', *Times Educational Supplement*, 31 May 1996. Online, available at: web.lexis.com/executive/ (accessed 4 January 2005).

Rafferty, F., 'The road to sanctuary buildings', *Times Educational Supplement*, 12 July 1996. Online, available at: web.lexis.com/executive/ (accessed 4 January 2005).

Rafferty, R., 'Barber rounds on political playground', *Times Educational Supplement*, 13 December 1996. Online, available at: web.lexis.com/executive/ (accessed 4 January 2005).

Ramsay, P.D.K., 'The dynamics of curriculum change', in W.J.D. Minogue (ed.), *Adventures in Curriculum*, Sydney: Allen and Unwin, 1983, pp. 1–9.

Randell, B., 'Matching books and beginners', Wellington, Reading is Everybody's Business, Fourth New Zealand Conference. August 1973, pp. 39–53.

Reading Recovery, Part 1, 1979, Archives New Zealand, Wellington, ABEP, W4262.

Report of the Central Advisory Council for Education, *Children and Their Primary Schools* (*The Plowden Report*), London: HMSO, 1967.

Roger, W., 'Phonics boom: adventures in the reading trade', *Metro*, 1995, 48–58.

Rosen, H., 'Editorial', in Rosen, H. (ed.), *Language and Literacy in our Schools: Some Appraisals of the Bullock Report*, University of London: Institute of Education, 1975.

Rosenthal, D., 'An effective, if Blunt, instrument', *Times Educational Supplement*, 7 June 1996. Online, available at: web.lexis.com/executive/ (accessed 4 January 2005).

Sanderson, A.E., 'The idea of reading readiness: a re-examination', *Educational Research*, vi, November 1963: 3–9.

Schonell, F.J., 'Problems of illiteracy: an examination of present needs', *Times Educational Supplement*, 23 February 1946, p. 87.

Schoolmaster, unsigned review, CLXX1, 8 February 1957.

Silberman, C.E., *Crisis in the Classroom: The Remaking of American Education*, New York: Random House, 1970.

Simon, B., *Education and the Social Order 1940–1990*, London: Lawrence and Wishart, 1991.

Simpson, M.M., *Suggestions for Teaching Reading in Infant Classes*, Wellington: Department of Education, 1962.

Slane, J., 'Eric: a new concept for in-service education of teachers', *Education*, 27(2), 1978: 7–11.

Smart, N. (ed.), *Crisis in the Classroom*, London: Hamlyn, 1968.

Soler, J., 'Past and present technocratic solutions to teaching literacy: implications for New Zealand primary teachers and literacy programmes', *Pedagogy, Culture and Society: Journal of Educational Discussion and Debate*, 7(3), 1999: 521–538.

Southgate, V., 'Formulae for beginning reading tuition', *Educational Research*, xi, November 1968: 23–30.

Staff reporter, 'Concern at pupil's poor reading', *The Times*, 18 November 1969, p. 2.

Start, K.B. and Wells, B.K., *The Trend of Reading Standards*, Windsor: NFER, 1972.

Stierer, B., 'Simply doing their job? The politics of reading standards and "real books"', in B. Stierer and J. Maybin (eds), *Language, Literacy and Learning in Educational Practice: A Reader*, Clevedon: Multilingual Matters: 1994.

Strickland, S., 'Parties clash over credit for schools reading idea', *Independent*, 4 January 1992, p. 1.

Sutcliffe, J., 'Trial by peers proposed to weed out bad staff', *Times Educational Supplement*, 16 August 1996. Online, available at: web.lexis.com/executive/ (accessed 4 January 2005).

Time Magazine, 'An Australian survey stirs debate over the best way to teach children the first two Rs', 29 September 1997. Online, available at: cgi.pathfinder.com/time/magazine/1997/int/970929/spacific.can_dick_and_html (accessed 3 October 2003).

Times, The, 'Concern over school English standards', 25 June 1963, p. 4.

Times, The, 'Home news', 10 January 1991, p. 3.

Times Educational Supplement, 'The first of the three R's', 5 April 1972, p. 13.

Times Educational Supplement, 'ATCDE conference: new teachers must have jobs', 20 December 1974, p. 5.

Times Educational Supplement, 'Houghton blow for young teachers', 20 December 1974, p. 3.

Times Educational Supplement, 'Call to action over reading', 31 October 1975, pp. 1 and 6.

Times Educational Supplement, 'Secondary school comes to rescue of poor readers', 7 November 1975, p. 3.

Times Educational Supplement, 'Reading levels "Not good enough"', 21 November 1975, p. 4.

Times Educational Supplement, 'Help proposed for unqualified 300,000', 28 November 1975, p. 6.

Times Educational Supplement, 'Mr Mulley speaks softly', 28 November 1975, p. 6.

Times Educational Supplement, 'Reading standards in London: genuine progress has been made', 12 December 1975, p. 14.

Times Educational Supplement, 'Edited extracts from the Yellow Book, the DES memorandum to the Prime Minister. Has something gone wrong? How is it to be put right?' 15 October 1976, p. 2.

Times Educational Supplement, 'Great Debate opens with an anticlimax', 22 October 1976, p. 1.

Times Educational Supplement, 'What the PM said', 22 October 1976, pp. 1, 72.

Times Educational Supplement, 'Brighter New Year for the 16–19s?', 31 December 1976, p. 1.

Times Educational Supplement, 'Reading test for all at 8 years considered', 29 February 1980, p. 6.

Times Educational Supplement, 'Extra £20m cuts to be made', 4 April 1980, p. 1.

Times Educational Supplement, 'Curriculum hit by cuts in part-time staff', 23 May 1980, p. 3.

Times Educational Supplement, 'Falling standards evidence in doubt', 23 May 1980, p. 1.

Times Educational Supplement, 'Serving two Masters', features page, 26 June 1981, p. 21.

Times Educational Supplement, 'Another year of declining standards', *Times Educational Supplement*, Editorial, 9 April 1982, p. 2.

Times Educational Supplement, ' Election manifesto may push to abolish shires and set up regions', 18 February 1983, p. 4.

Times Educational Supplement, 'Improving teacher quality', 25 March 1983, p. 10.

Times Educational Supplement, 'HMI expansion given go-ahead', 1 April 1983, p. 6.

Times Educational Supplement, 'County ends secrecy over pupils' records', 22 April 1983, p. 1.

Times Educational Supplement, 'Sir Keith voices fears over standards', 15 July 1983, p. 1.

Times Educational Supplement, 'Study of London primaries to examine low achievement', 23 July 1983, p. 3.

Times Educational Supplement, 'The hand the HMIs are playing', 12 August 1983, p. 2.

Times Educational Supplement, 'HMI Reports', 30 September 1983, p. 12.

Times Educational Supplement, 'Battleground DES where three ideologies wage ceaseless war', 4 November 1983, p. 6.

Times Educational Supplement, 29 June 1990.

Times Educational Supplement, Editorial, 'No more quick fixes', 28 February 1996 Online, available at: web.lexis.com/executive/ (accessed 4 January 2005).

Times Educational Supplement, 'The powers behind Blunkett's throne', Editorial, 3 October 1997. Online, available at: web.lexis.com/executive/ (accessed 4 January 2005).

Tunmer, W.E. and Chapman, J.W., 'Beginning reader's self-reports on strategies used for identifying unfamiliar words in text', a paper presented at the annual meeting of the New Zealand Association for Educational Research in Education, Nelson, New Zealand, December 1996.

Tunmer, W.E. and Chapman, J.W., 'Language prediction skill, phonological recoding ability, and beginning reading', in C. Hulme and R.M. Joshi (eds), *Reading and Spelling: Development and Disorder*, Hillsdale, NJ: Lawrence Erlbaum Associates, 1998.

Tunmer, W.E. and Chapman, J.W., 'Teaching strategies for word identification', in G. Thompson and T. Nicholson (eds), *Learning to Read: Beyond Phonics and Whole Language*, Newark: IRA, 1999.

Turner, M., *Sponsored Reading Failure: An Object Lesson*, Education Unit, Warlingham Park School: Warlingham, Surrey, 1990.

Tytler, D., 'Let common sense take over', Features section, *The Times*, 27 January 1992, p. 7.

Vacca, R.T., 'Who will be the winners? Who will be the losers?', *Reading Today*, 14(2), 1996: 3.

Wall, W.D., 'Reading backwardness among men in the Army', *British Journal of Educational Studies*, xv, 1945: 28–40.

Watson, B., *National Implementation of Reading Recovery*. Submission to the Minister of Education from Barbara Watson, Director Reading Recovery, 20 June 1988, ABEP, W4262, Box 3783, NS55/1/32 – MISC Reading Recovery.

Webb, R. and Vulliamy, G., 'Managing curriculum policy changes: a comparative analysis of primary schools in England and Finland', *Journal of Education Policy*, 14(2), 1999: 117–137.

Welch, A.R. and Freebody, P., 'Introduction: explanations of the current international "literacy crises"', in P. Freebody and A.R. Welch (eds), *Knowledge, Culture and Power: International Perspectives on Literacy as Policy and Practice*, London and Washington D.C.: Falmer Press, 1993.

Whittle, M., 'Education inner reading scheme "will be best in world"', Press Association Newsfile, Home News, 9 January 1992.

Who's Who: An Annual Biographical Dictionary, London: A & C Black, 2005.

Wilkinson, M., 'A school report to disturb every parent', *Daily Mail*, 19 February 1975, p. 10.

Wilkinson, M., 'Now Oxford finds standards are slipping', *Daily Mail*, 20 February 1975, p. 10.

Williams, S. and Morris, J., *Education in Schools: A Consultative Document*, Cmnd 6869, London: HMSO, 1977.

Willman, J. and Smith, A., 'Political battle over education intensifies', *Financial Times*, 4 January 1992, p. 1.

Young, S., 'Reading standards static for 50 years', *Times Educational Supplement*, 11 July 1997. Online, available at: web.lexis.com/executive/ (accessed 4 January 2005).

Index